THE WATER RESOURCES OF CHILE

An Economic Method for Analyzing a Key Resource
in a Nation's Development

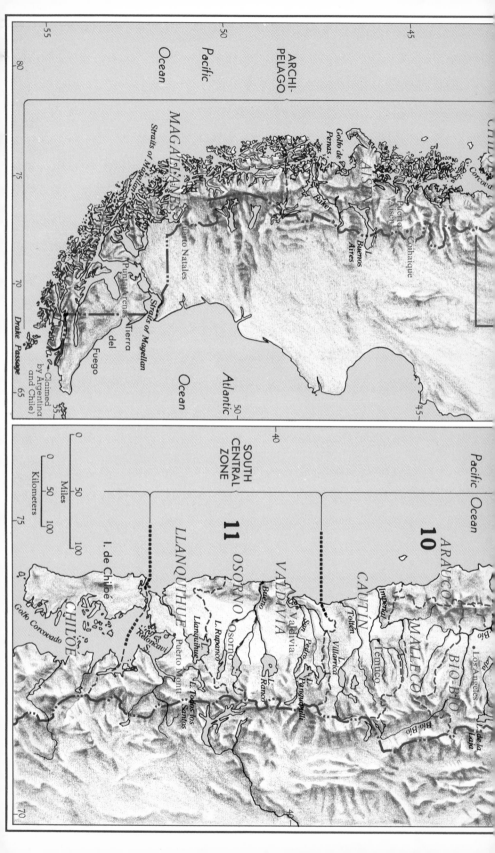

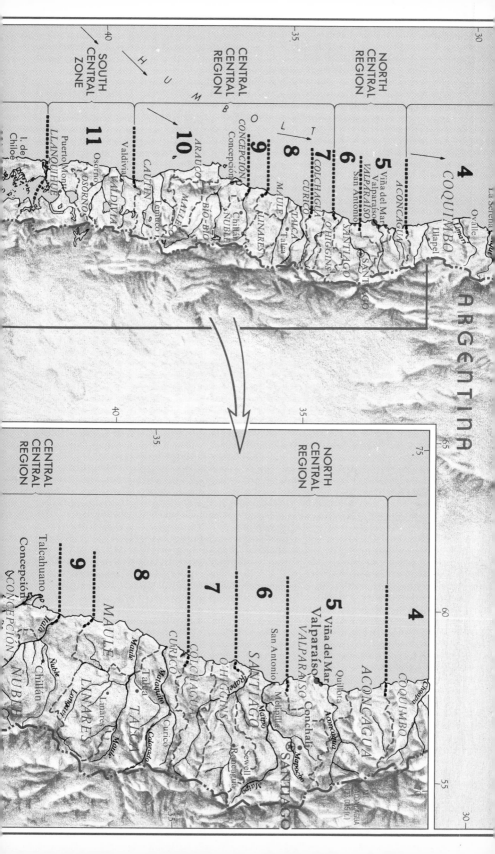

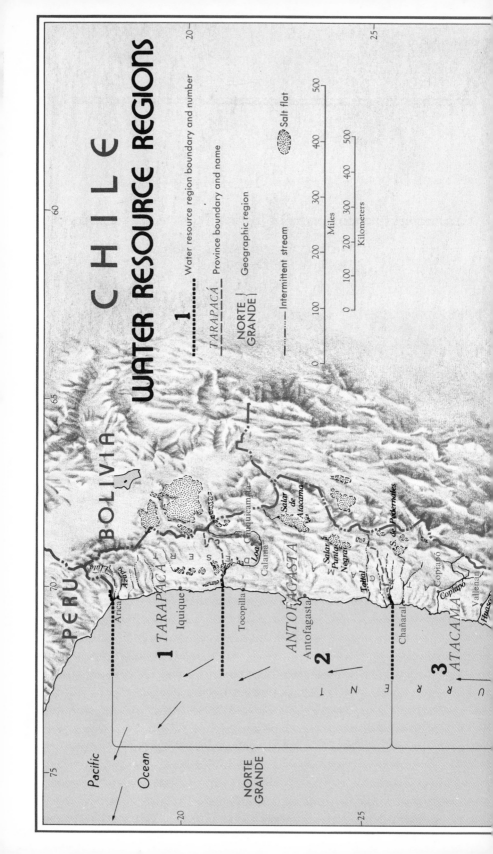

CHILE
WATER RESOURCE REGIONS

1 ······· Water resource region boundary and number

TARAPACÁ Province boundary and name

NORTE GRANDE } Geographic region

········· Intermittent stream

Salt flat

Miles
0   100   200   300   400   500

Kilometers
0   100   200   300   400   500

PERU

BOLIVIA

Arica

Azapa

Iquique

1 TARAPACÁ

Tocopilla

Loa

Calama

Chuquicamata

Salar de Atacama

ANTOFAGASTA

Antofagasta

Salar
Punta
Negra

2

Taltal

S. de Pedernales

Chañaral

3 ATACAMA

Copiapó

Copiapó

Vallenar

Huasco

NORTE GRANDE

Pacific

Ocean

NORTE
GRANDE

THE WATER RESOURCES
OF CHILE

An Economic Method for Analyzing a Key Resource
in a Nation's Development

by
Nathaniel Wollman

A study sponsored by the Latin American Institute
for Economic and Social Planning
and
Resources for the Future, Inc.

Published for
Resources for the Future, Inc.
by
The Johns Hopkins Press, Baltimore, Maryland

PREFACE

In all countries of the world the development and wise use of natural resources are of fundamental importance to economic growth and human welfare. Agriculture, forestry, mining, energy, and water resources remain the basic building blocks for economic advance. These, of course, cannot be separated from the skill, training, and enterprise of individual persons, nor can they be viewed in isolation from the industrial plant and equipment, the transportation network, and indeed the entire social infrastructure. But the fact remains that the careful planning and programming of natural resources development, within the framework of general economic and social planning, can contribute greatly to the achievement of national and regional goals.

Nathaniel Wollman's study is an example of an effort of this nature in the water resources field. A particular country, Chile, is examined here in order that Latin American technicians and administrators interested in water resource planning in particular, and economic development in general, may see in some detail a way by which some of the larger problems in formulating a water development program can be approached.

The main objective in preparing this study was to work out a methodology that could be adapted to a water development program in any country; Chile was chosen to serve as a case study solely for reasons of location and convenience. The significance of the work, therefore lies more in its methodological value than in its practical value for a specific country.

This project has been sponsored jointly by the Latin American Institute for Economic and Social Planning and Resources for the Future, Inc. It represents the first result of a co-operative program originated by Dr. Raúl Prebisch, Director-General of the Institute.

The Dirección de Riego of the Ministry of Public Works of Chile has made valuable comments on Professor Wollman's study, particularly with respect to the capacity of irrigation. We feel that the inclusion of a paper prepared by the Dirección de Riego ("Capacidad de Riego Actual de los Ríos de la Zona Central de Chile"), as an annex to Professor Wollman's study is useful not only from the academic point of view, as additional reference material, but also because the data it contains represent the accumulated knowledge of Chilean experts.

The Institute and Resources for the Future do not necessarily subscribe to all the findings of this study, the responsibility for the analysis and conclusions of which rests with the author. We believe, however, that the study deals with a subject of significance to resources and economic development in Latin America and that the analytical approach deserves attention.

CRISTÓBAL LARA BEAUTELL   JOSEPH L. FISHER

ACKNOWLEDGMENTS

The study of Chilean water resources was conducted under the auspices of the Instituto Latinoamericano de Planificación Económica y Social (an institution created by the member states of the United Nations Economic Commission for Latin America) and Resources for the Future, Inc. While responsibility for the conclusions reached and for the innumerable calculations that led to them is wholly mine, the study could not have been completed, or even begun, without the wholehearted co-operation of many people and many institutions in Chile.

I am especially indebted to Carlos Plaza V., of the Instituto, for assistance in formulating the project and for his critical review of the manuscript, and to Manuel Agosín, my research associate, for making all of the computations, interviewing government officials, conducting several investigations in connection with this study, and carefully checking the manuscript. I am indebted to Fernán Ibáñez, Ricardo Harboe, and Juan Poblete of the Centro de Planeamiento, Universidad de Chile, for their excellent report on Chilean water resources, and particularly to Mr. Harboe for the assistance he provided in the solution of problems as work on the study proceeded. I also wish to acknowledge the assistance of the Centro de Investigaciones Económicas, Universidad Católica, in making economic projections.

So many people in the Chilean government, international agencies, the U.S. AID Mission, and the Chile-California Program rendered generous assistance that any enumeration inevitably understates my obligation. The help provided by Michael Nelson and John Holsen, in particular, extends far beyond that which is acknowledged in the text. I am especially obligated to officials of the Chilean government that read and commented upon a preliminary draft.

I would like to thank Adolfo Dorfman, of ECLA, and Orris C. Herfindahl, of RFF, for the generosity with which they shared their time and thoughts and to thank Eduardo García of ECLA for his comments. I am indebted to Geraldine Jaimovich for supervising the preparation of the manuscript and for solving many administrative problems; and to Allen V. Kneese, Sterling Brubaker, Blair T. Bower, and Pierre R. Crosson, of RFF, for their suggestions after reading the first draft manuscript of this study. Lastly, I am indebted to Resources for the Future and the Instituto Latinoamericano de Planificación Económica y Social for making the investigation possible, and to the University of New Mexico for its administrative support.

A single eighteen-month sojourn in Chile provides a snapshot rather than a moving picture. For this reason I may have inadequately appreciated the changes that are taking place or the rate at which change is occurring. The period in question, July 1964–December 1965, was especially interesting since it was during this period that a new government, dedicated to social and economic reform, was elected. I have learned much from the economists, engineers, scientists, scholars, and administrators I met in Chile. What remains with me is admiration for a country of great beauty and a feeling of kinship for its people, since the 6,000 miles that separates Santiago from Albuquerque does not obliterate the fact that the Chilean world is also the world of New Mexico.

The opinions expressed in the ensuing chapters are mine, and in several instances they run counter to those held by people with whom I have been closely associated.

Albuquerque, New Mexico   NATHANIEL WOLLMAN
August 1967

CONTENTS

Preface   v
Acknowledgments   vii

I   SETTING OF THE STUDY   1
    Some geographic details   3

II   THE PROJECTION MODEL   9
    Projections of population and gross national product   18
    A preview of the results   21
    Unfinished business   26

III   AGRICULTURE: A GENERAL SURVEY   29
    Pattern of land use   32
    Land ownership: sizes of farms   37
    Output per hectare for the country   40

IV   THE USE OF WATER FOR IRRIGATION   43
    Measures of current water use   46

V   EXPERIENCE WITH GOVERNMENT IRRIGATION
    PROJECTS   52
    The costs of water   61
    Payments for water use: analysis of ten sample
    irrigation projects   66

VI   PROJECTION OF AGRICULTURAL WATER USE . .   73
    Production from dry and irrigated land   85

VII   MINING AND ELECTRIC POWER   93
    Mining   93

CONTENTS

Electric power 96
Multiple-purpose projects 102
Effect of hydroelectric requirements on economic models
  of water use 103

VIII   MANUFACTURING USES OF WATER 105
Manufacturing: projections of output 109
Food and beverages 111
Pulp and paper 111
Chemicals 112
Petroleum refining 112
Steel 113
All other manufacturing industries 113
Estimates of water use: revision of 1957 water use
  coefficients in manufacturing 114

IX   MUNICIPAL WATER USE 125
Organization of municipal supply 125
Projected municipal intake and loss 127

X   WASTE TREATMENT AND WASTE DILUTION . . . 130

XI   TOTAL WATER REQUIREMENTS 138
Intake 140
Losses 142
Water requirement as a combination of intake and loss . . . 145

XII   THE COST OF WATER 151
Storage requirements to meet seasonal variation in demand . . 155
Reservoir evaporation losses 157
The costs of regulating surface flow 158

XIII   THE EFFECTS OF WATER SHORTAGE 162
First estimate of the costs of storage 163
Marginal cost of water constraints 166

XIV   THE QUESTION OF WATER QUALITY 181

XV   VARIATIONS ON THE MAJOR THEME 190
Higher degrees of security 190

CONTENTS

Sequence and timing of additions to storage 192
Other projected rates of growth 200

XVI   CONCLUSIONS AND OBSERVATIONS 202
    Unfinished business 207

Appendix A—Supporting Tables—Projections, 1985 209
Appendix B—Productivity of Agriculture in Chile in Comparison
with Selected Countries 242
Appendix C—Current Irrigation Capacity of Rivers in the
Central Zone of Chile 249

Selected Bibliography 269
Index 272

LIST OF TABLES

1. Assumed distribution of manufacturing and urban population
between downstream and upstream points of water use 16
2. Percentage distribution of irrigated area between upstream and
downstream points 17
3. Gross national product and population, actual and projections for
1985 18
4. Projected population, medium growth rate, 1985 20
5. Comparison of alternative values for population, gross national
product, and selected industries in 1985 based on alternative
rates of growth 21
6. Selected economic indicators, Chile, 1950-62 30
7. Amount of irrigated land according to various sources 34
8. Distribution of arable land by type of crop, 1955 35
9. Distribution of irrigated land by major use, 1959-60 36
10. Size class of farms and land use 38
11. Central Chile: Comparative productivity by size of farm unit . 40
12. Irrigation rates currently experienced vs. optimum rates . . . 49
13. Experienced and optimum water requirements based on 1959-60
irrigated area 50
14. Average value of output per hectare, selected crops, 1959-60 . . 51
15. New and new-equivalent land placed under irrigation by Dirección de Riego, 1919-65 59
16. Construction and preliminary administration periods 68

CONTENTS

17. Costs and irrigator debts, selected irrigation projects 69
18. Costs and payments 70
19. Percentage distribution of land by size-class of holdings in selected government irrigation projects 71
20. Irrigable hectarage required on basis of projected demand, 1985 . 77
21. Irrigable land that requires irrigation 79
22. *Tasa de Riego* 80
23. Percentage distribution of irrigated land by major class of crop . 80
24. Computation of diversion and net losses from irrigation based on *Tasa de Riego* 81
25. Rates of water use per hectare per year 82
26. Agriculture (irrigation) diversion requirements and net loss for irrigable hectarage 83
27. Requirements for the watering of livestock, 1985 84
28. Monthly distribution of irrigation requirements 85
29. Estimated productivity of irrigated and dry land 87
30. Estimated production from irrigated land 88
31. Estimated production from dry land 90
32. Copper production and water requirements (intake) 95
33. Nitrate production and intake water requirements 96
34. Projected water use in thermal electric power 97
35. Manufacturing, percentage distribution of market value among industry classes, Chile, 1956 106
36. Percentage distribution of manufacturing output among provinces, based on market value, 1956 107
37. Percentage distribution of manufacturing output among provinces, 1985 110
38. Manufacturing, output projections, 1985 114
39. Manufacturing, total income and value added, Chile, 1957 . . 115
40. Manufacturing, water intake, 1957 120
41. Loss as per cent of intake 121
42. Manufacturing, rates of water use per unit of output, Chile . . 121
43. Manufacturing, intake and losses I and II, 1985, medium A and B 123
44. Municipal intake per capita per day 128
45. Municipal requirements, 1985, medium 129
46. Adaptation of Central Pacific coefficients to Chile 134
47. Waste dilution requirements, 1985, medium B, 4 mg/l D.O. . . 136
48. Intake (withdrawals), offstream uses, 1985, medium B 141
49. Losses, offstream uses, 1985, medium B 143

CONTENTS

50. Summary: Alternative ways for computing flow requirements, 1985, medium B 144
51. Losses plus waste dilution, 1985, medium B, 4 mg/1 149
52. Water resource regions 153
53. Flow-storage relationship, 85 per cent security 154
54. Coefficient to adjust storage from constant minimum flow to seasonally variable required flow 156
55. Assumed relationships between heights and volumes of reservoirs 157
56. Estimated average rate of evaporation 158
57. Unit cost schedule according to size-class 159
58. Assumed distribution of reservoir capacity by size-class 160
59. Case I: Costs of flow regulation (85 per cent security) 164
60. Average values for class IIIr land for tax assessment and adjustment for water use 167
61. Effect of constraint on marginal cost of water 168
62. Hectarage, irrigated and projected 174
63. Comparison of outputs and costs of water, alternative projections for agriculture, 1985 176
64. Costs of storage for alternative models, with storage coefficient . 178
65. Treatment costs per municipal and industrial population equivalent 183
66. Estimated costs of quality maintenance 184
67. Least cost combination of quality maintenance 185
68. Storage requirements for higher levels of security 191

SUPPORTING TABLES—PROJECTIONS, 1985

A-1. Manufacturing: Water intake 210
A-2. Food and beverages 212
A-3. Pulp and paper 213
A-4. Chemicals 214
A-5. Petroleum refining 215
A-6. Petrochemicals 216
A-7. Steel 217
A-8. All other industries 218
A-9. Manufacturing—Loss I 219
A-10. Manufacturing—Loss II 220
A-11. Industrial P.E.'s produced 221
A-12. P.E.'s discharged upstream and downstream 222

CONTENTS

A-13. Industrial waste dilution 223
A-14. Cases I, II, III, upstream losses 224
A-15. Case I, downstream requirements 225
A-16. Case III, downstream intakes 226
A-17. Upstream-downstream summary requirements 227
A-18. Costs of flow—Tarapacá 228
A-19. Costs of flow—Antofagasta 229
A-20. Costs of flow—Atacama 229
A-21. Costs of flow—Coquimbo 230
A-22. Costs of flow—Aconcagua-Valparaíso 231
A-23. Costs of flow—Santiago 232
A-24. Costs of flow—O'Higgins-Colchagua 233
A-25. Costs of flow—Curicó-Linares 233
A-26. Costs of flow—Ñuble 234
A-27. Costs of flow—Concepción-Cautín 235
A-28. Costs of flow—Valdivia-Llanquihue 236
A-29. Agricultural production: Case I, marginal constraint, agriculture residuary 237
A-30. Treatment costs of million population equivalents discharged into rivers, without collection costs 238
A-31. Treatment costs of million population equivalents discharged into rivers 239
A-32. Additional costs of storage for quality maintenance 240
A-33. Atacama: Smallest reservoirs first 241
A-34. Santiago: Smallest reservoirs first 241

CONVERSION FACTORS

$$
\begin{aligned}
1 \text{ hectare (ha.)} &= 2.471 \text{ acres} \\
1 \text{ meter (m.)} &= 3.28 \text{ feet} \\
1 \text{ kilometer (km.)} &= 0.62137 \text{ miles} \\
1 \text{ liter} &= 0.264 \text{ gallons (U.S.)} \\
1 \text{ cubic meter (m}^3) &= 8.1070 \times 10^{-4} \text{ acre-feet} \\
1 \text{ milliard cubic meters(milliard m}^3) &= 0.81071 \text{ million acre-feet} \\
1 \text{ metric quintal (Chile) (qqm)} &= 100 \text{ kilograms or } 220.46 \text{ lb.} \\
1 \text{ (1964) escudo (E}^o) &= \text{US\$0.3125} \\
1 \text{ escudo} &= 1,000 \text{ pesos}
\end{aligned}
$$

ABBREVIATIONS FOR NAMES OF ORGANIZATIONS

CAP   Compañía de Acero del Pacífico (Pacific steel company)

CELADE   Centro Latinoamericano de Demografía (Latin American center of demography)

CEPAL   Comisión Económica para América Latina, Naciones Unidas (United Nations Economic Commission for Latin America)

CIDA   Comité Interamericano de Desarrollo Agrícola (Interamerican Committee for Agricultural Development)

CORFO   Corporación de Fomento de la Producción (Production development corporation)

ENAP   Empresa Nacional de Petróleo (National petroleum authority)

ENDESA   Empresa Nacional de Electricidad, S.A. (National electric power authority)

IANSA   Industria Azucarera Nacional, S.A. (National sugar industry)

ODEPLAN   Oficina de Planificación Nacional (National planning office)

THE WATER RESOURCES OF CHILE

An Economic Method for Analyzing a Key Resource
in a Nation's Development

I

SETTING OF THE STUDY

The purposes of this study are, first, to ascertain what is the present state of water resource use, knowledge of water resources, and policies of water resource planning in Chile; and, second, to indicate how planning of water resource use can be related to national economic planning. As a by-product it is hoped that the project will serve as one of the needed bridges between engineers and physical scientists, on one side, and economists and economic policy makers, on the other, regarding the role of water in economic development.

Work undertaken by the United Nations Comisión Económica para América Latina (CEPAL) in connection with a series of national water resource studies has shown that investment in water resource projects—ranging from large multipurpose dams to wells drilled to meet the needs of a single user—has accounted for a substantial share of aggregate investment in most Latin American countries. Interest in water resource planning is high, since the payoff in possible economies, should such be revealed, might also be high. There is, in addition, a latent hope in many countries that an examination of water resources might reveal opportunities for economic development hitherto overlooked.

The choice of Chile as the focus for this water resource study was made for several reasons: Chile has a long tradition of irrigated agriculture and, with the possible exception of Mexico, it has better hydrologic data than can be found elsewhere in Latin America. In addition to the supply of raw data, several recent studies could be drawn upon. The first of CEPAL's national water resource studies[1] dealt with Chile. This, in turn, stimulated several investigations by the Dirección de Planeamiento in the Ministerio de Obras Públicas. In 1964, moreover, when preparations for the present study were being made by Resources for the Future, Inc. and the Instituto

---

[1] U.N., Comisión Económica para América Latina, *Los Recursos Hidráulicos de América Latina: I, Chile* (hereinafter referred to as CEPAL). (Mexico City: 1960.)

Latinoamericano de Planificación Económica y Social, there were rumblings of possible changes in Chile's administrative organization, legal basis of water rights, and extension of planning into regional questions, all of which encouraged the hope that a successful undertaking would find a receptive audience.

There is ample evidence that both national and international agencies are aware of the need for multiple-purpose river basin development and are in possession of the requisite skills to conduct whatever analysis might be necessary to accomplish the results. At the same time, the several studies made within CEPAL and the Chilean government approached but never fulfilled the requirements of a systematic "model," no matter how rudimentally defined such a model might be.[2]

Considering the fragmentary, uncertain, and often contradictory state of basic information concerning economic activity, techniques of water use, hydrologic measurements, and costs of developing water supplies, it is understandable that a comprehensive model of water resource use, no matter how primitive, might be considered beyond attainment. Such a view has, in fact, been expressed by some Chilean authorities in connection with the present study. I agree that all conclusions on matters of "fact" are, at present, scarcely better than tentative hypotheses subject to verification or disproof by better data. But I disagree strongly with the assertion that since high-quality data do not exist, what is available should not be used. If a model is useful for purposes of directing policy, it is equally useful as an indicator of the kinds of facts that are needed and the dangers of basing policies on poor data.

Some of the difficulties encountered in the course of analysis suggest several reasons why such a model hitherto has been lacking.

1) No optimizing or suboptimizing criteria had been formulated as the basis for a model.

2) Attention was normally concentrated on river *basin* development, whereby each basin is treated as a microeconomy.

3) The difficulty of making economic projections is increased by
   (a) a short historical record and one subject to discontinuous variations; and
   (b) the little attention given to disaggregation of the economy into regional components.

---

[2] To the best of my knowledge, no other Latin American country has gone farther than Chile in working toward the construction of a model; most have not gone as far.

4) There is a lack of governmental machinery to achieve the coordination needed for investigations of multiple uses served by a river system, and for the planning, financing, and administration of such a system. Collaboration among the various Chilean water resource agencies is informal rather than formal, and extends only as far as each agency sees fit.[3]

This study makes no claim to being comprehensive. It gives little attention to matters of law and water rights, benefit-cost analysis of river basin projects, and administrative organization; nor does it dwell on past successes or failures of particular water resource projects. These questions are not wholly ignored; but since they have been treated in other studies already completed or currently under way, they are given only a passing nod here except where my investigations have uncovered hitherto unpublished information.

While the study is wholly concerned with Chile, it is my hope and the expectation of members of the Institute and CEPAL staff, that the results will have a high transfer value. Chile has served as a laboratory specimen. However, since each Latin American country is a unique entity, it is only the method of analysis that can be transferred, and the extent to which even that is true remains uncertain until the findings of this study are tested out.

The succeeding chapters will deal, first, with a description of the economic model by which water requirements have been projected to the year 1985; second, with a discussion of the present state of water use and the state of information about water use from the point of view of what is required for the model; and third, with the results of the projections.

First, however, a brief word about the geography of Chile is necessary to provide background for the discussion of the country's water resources.

SOME GEOGRAPHIC DETAILS

Chile has an extraordinarily diversified terrain and climate. Rich in minerals, forests, and fisheries, its soil and climate reflect the extremes of altitude and relief which characterize the country. Because it is narrow, 221 miles at the widest stretch, Chile's twenty-five provinces are stacked

---

[3] Blair T. Bower, research associate with Resources for the Future, Inc., has suggested two additional factors to be considered: (1) failure to make explicit the problems of decision making under conditions of uncertainty—a subject which Estevam Straus, of the Instituto Latinoamericano de Planificación, has recently had under study—and (2) the difficulty of comparing the merits of investment in water resources with other forms of investment.

one on top of the other, so that the general configuration, complete with the political divisions as shown in the accompanying map, looks rather like a man's spinal column. The three northernmost provinces, Tarapacá, Antofagasta, and Atacama, and two southernmost, Aysén and Magallanes, are relatively large; the remainder are fairly small—on the order of a county in New Mexico or Arizona.

The climate of Chile ranges from very dry to very wet and from subtropical to polar. Climatic variation, going from east to west within continental Chile, is extreme enough for a *Santiaguino* to pick an orange off a tree while watching through binoculars a ski lift operating at Farellones 30 kilometers away.

In this study Chile has been divided into water resource regions so bounded that watershed and political boundaries are coterminous or approximately so. A number of regions contain several independent streams; some regions, only one. All rivers in Chile are relatively short; practically all of them flow from the Andes to the Pacific in a relatively straight line.[4]

Several dozen rivers flow through continental Chile. Thirty-six of these carry significant quantities of water and, with one exception, have a usable record of flows. It is clear that water supplies can impose no constraint on the economies of the three southern archipelagic provinces of Chiloé, Aysén, and Magallanes. Therefore they and their rivers for the most part are ignored here, although an occasional numerical value is assigned to them. Antarctic Chile and insular Chile to the west are ignored completely.

The eleven water resource regions are divided among the provinces as follows:

1) Tarapacá
2) Antofagasta
3) Atacama
4) Coquimbo
5) Aconcagua and Valparaíso
6) Santiago
7) O'Higgins and Colchagua
8) Curicó, Talca, Maule, and Linares
9) Ñuble
10) Concepción, Arauco, Bío-Bío, Malleco, and Cautín

[4] A few deviate from this pattern, but the deviation is inconsequential. For example, the Río Loa in Antofagasta forms a large "U" in the course of traversing the northern desert. In the south a river such as the Río Petrohue occasionally goes north and south.

11) Valdivia, Osorno, and Llanquihue.

These water resource regions can be grouped, in turn, into five larger geographic regions:

1. *Norte Grande* is the Chilean term applied to the two northern provinces, Tarapacá and Antofagasta (water resource regions 1 and 2) covering about 90,000 square kilometers,[5] much of which is one of the most arid desert areas in the world. According to local residents, it "never rains." According to official statistics, average annual rainfall at Tocopilla, for example, is 3 millimeters; and at Antofagasta, 11 millimeters. However, years intervene between rainfalls. In the desert are oases watered by streams that rise in the Andes. Occasionally the oases are man-made, being dependent upon aqueducts that carry water for a hundred or so kilometers. The aqueducts supply urban and mining communities, not irrigation. Farming takes place in the river valleys and at the very most accounts for about 1 per cent of the land area of the two provinces; irrigated land in 1959 was reported to be 11,000 hectares. The province of Tarapacá, which borders Peru, has two rivers, the Lluta and the Lauca, whose flows have been measured. No usable data are available for the Azapa.

The other province in the Norte Grande, Antofagasta, for many years has provided the bulk of the nitrate and copper on which Chile largely depends for its foreign exchange. The open-pit copper mine at Chuquicamata is one of the world's largest. Beneficiation and smelting of copper are carried on at several places within the province. Today, Antofagasta is still pre-eminent as a source of nitrate and copper, but it is challenged by O'Higgins Province, south of Santiago, which is also a major copper center; and, in the future, Atacama, to the south of the Norte Grande, may become important. Two manufacturing cities are located in the Norte Grande. Iquique and Arica, in Tarapacá, are centers of Chile's fish meal industry; Arica is the center of automobile and television assembly plants. The proximity of *anchoveta*, a kind of sardine, in the waters of the Humboldt current may have dictated the location of the fish meal industry in Iquique. Location of the automobile industry in Arica is harder to justify. "No assembler would have picked Arica of his own free will, but would obviously have picked a spot in or near Santiago. . . ."[6] Should the economic requirements of the industry override the desire to foster the econ-

[5] Metric units are used throughout this study. Conversions are listed on p. xv.

[6] Leland L. Johnson, *Problems of Industrialization in Chile: Some Preliminary Observations*, Memorandum RM-4794-AID (Santa Monica: The RAND Corporation, December 1965, p. 5).

omy of Arica, the industry would probably move south. Under these circumstances any projection of urban activity for Arica is subject to considerable uncertainty. Antofagasta has one measurable river, the Loa, which is also the longest river in Chile.

2. *Norte Chico,* immediately south of the Norte Grande, consists of two provinces, Atacama and Coquimbo, each of which constitutes a separate water resource region. In Atacama are the rivers Copiapó and Huasco. In Coquimbo are the rivers Elqui, Limarí, and Choapa. Both are transitional provinces between the desert of the north and the Mediterranean climate of the Central Valley. Both are primarily agricultural regions, although there is some mining and mineral processing, particularly in Atacama which is likely to become a major copper producing center in the future. The river valleys of the Elqui and Huasco are famous for the grapes that go into pisco, a clear-as-water distillation of grape juice. Fruits are grown. La Serena's chirimoyas command a premium price in Santiago.

3. *The North Central Region:* This geographic division contains two water resource regions—Aconcagua-Valparaíso and Santiago—that form the northern end of the Central Valley. The Río Aconcagua and two smaller independent rivers, the Petorca and the Ligua, flow through Aconcagua and Valparaíso. Santiago Province has approximately the same borders as the watershed of the Río Maipo. In these three provinces are the population center of Chile; the commercial, financial, and intellectual center; the seat of the national government; the site of the 1966 ski Olympics; and one of the most famous summer resorts and casinos of South America. In spite of the large urban concentrations around Santiago and Valparaíso-Viña del Mar, the two water resource regions are also major agricultural centers. The province of Santiago leads all provinces in hectarage under irrigation, a fact that explains as well as anything the reason for the Santiago City's dominance. Agriculture is diversified, ranging from fruits and vegetables to wheat, barley, corn, rice, feed crops, and pasture. Fruits include oranges, lemons, and tuna (prickly pear), chirimoyas, avocados, and olives, as well as grapes and other fruits common to the temperate zone.

Santiago is now a city of about two and a half million people. Its untreated waste is discharged into the Mapocho, a tributary of the Maipo; the Mapocho, carrying waste downstream from Santiago, is used for irrigation.

4. *The Central Central Region:* This geographic region contains the water resource region composed of O'Higgins and Colchagua provinces,

which together form the basin of the Río Rapel; the region composed of Curicó, Talca, Maule, and Linares, provinces containing the Mataquito and Maule rivers; the region of Ñuble Province, watered by the Itata; and the region of Concepción, Arauco, Bío-Bío, Malleco, and Cautín provinces, a region which has four rivers, the Bío-Bío, Paicaví, Imperial, and Toltén. Agriculture dominates. In addition, there is a major copper producing center at Sewell, in O'Higgins; light manufacturing (e.g., matches) in Talca and one or two other smaller communities; and a major industrial area (steel, textiles) around Concepción, where coal is mined.

Going from north to south, the Central Central zone is the first part of Chile in which the supply of water is great enough to warrant the removal of water scarcity from the list of obvious impediments to economic growth. We shall see that, viewed wholly in physical terms, projected requirements in this zone are only a small fraction of average annual runoff, but are great enough to create a need for some regulation. Water resources in the Concepción-Cautín region are largely unexploited, whether for agriculture, industry, or hydroelectric power. Irrigation is needed as far south as Cautín. Palm trees grow in Concepción (37 degrees south). It is the hope of the Chilean government that Concepción can become an important center of heavy industry. Paper mills have been established in this area and others are planned. The steel industry is growing.

5. *The South Central Zone:* This is the southern end of the central valley, a well-watered, green landscape, consisting of the provinces of Valdivia, Osorno, and Llanquihue, which together comprise the last of the eleven water resource regions around which this study is built. Quite clearly, water is no problem. Agriculture is unirrigated. The menace is too much, not too little, water. Present minimum flows are far in excess of foreseeable requirements unless dams are needed for hydroelectric power. Large power reserves remain untapped. Agricultural land is mostly in grains, forage, and pasture. Here are the lakes of Chile—Villarrica, Ranco, Llanquihue, and Todos los Santos, to name only a few. Here also are important timber reserves. Chileans frequently refer to South Central zone as "Sur Chico."

Puerto Montt, a seaport on Reloncavi Sound, in the province of Llanquihue, is the mainland contact with the island of Chiloé and the archipelagic mainland of Chiloé, Aysén, and Magallanes provinces. From Puerto Montt southward are the fjords and channels by which one can navigate to the Straits of Magellan almost without entering the open sea.

6. *The Archipelago:* The scenic grandeur of Chile's archipelago is unsurpassed. The growing desolation of the channel islands and the gleam of glaciers reaching down to the sea leave one unready for the view of

Punta Arenas and the forests and meadows that border the Straits of Magellan. Here is the gateway to a region of magnificent craggy mountains, deep lakes, and oak forests, and the only national park that Chile possesses. Within sight of Punta Arenas, lying low on the horizon, is Tierra del Fuego, the source of Chile's petroleum supply. The rivers of the Sur Grande, in the provinces of Aysén and Magallanes, may some day be used for hydroelectric power. At present, and for the foreseeable future, they flow undisturbed to the sea.

II

THE PROJECTION MODEL

For the purposes of our model, each water resource region in effect is assumed to be two points in space—one "upstream," the other "downstream"—between which all of the region's water supply and activity are assigned. The "water supply" is the quantity of surface water that is available, based upon the records of flow. In many instances—how much is not known—the movement of underground water becomes a part of the surface water record. A considerable quantity of ground water, however, never appears in records of surface flow.

"Normal" costs of water treatment and distribution will not be considered as part of the "costs of water," since such costs are incurred without reference to the quantity of water available, but rather in response to the number of consumers and quality of water that is delivered. Were there to be a significant deterioration in the quality of water or if, at the extreme, fresh water had to be manufactured out of ocean water, water treatment costs *would* be relevant. The possibility of a desalination plant for Antofagasta was being examined at the time this report was in preparation, but no desalination or especially high treatment costs will be incorporated in the analysis. Instead, I shall assume that industrial and municipal wastes are treated to remove biochemical-oxygen-demanding (BOD) substances, and that such treatment will enable subsequent users to avoid unusual treatment costs.

What then will costs of water include? They will consist of (1) the costs of regulating surface flow to achieve whatever pattern of flow is necessary to satisfy the water requirements of the region, including waste dilution flows to assure a designated amount of dissolved oxygen in the river after receiving discharged wastes, subject to the limit imposed by average annual flow as measured by the period of record, plus (2) the

9

costs of treating organic domestic and industrial wastes in order to reduce the quantity of biochemical substances discharged into a river.[1]

The costs of water, then, are a function of the underlying hydrology and the sum of all uses to which the water is put. This makes a "cost curve" for water different from a cost curve for, say, steel. The cost of an ingot of steel is a function of the metallurgical composition, production process, rate of production relative to capacity, and price per unit of inputs. The use to which the steel is put is not a relevant factor in fixing its cost. In the case of water, because of the possibility of reuse, costs for one user can be, but are not necessarily, a function of anterior uses to which the water has been put. Certain costs, such as those incurred to regulate virgin flow at a designated point on the river, can be ascertained independently of the uses to which water is put. A "cost-of-regulation" schedule (or curve) indicates the unit costs of successively higher degrees of regulation. One can estimate how many "units" of regulation will be "bought" by estimating the quantity of water that must flow by a particular point in space at a particular point in time. But even a cost-of-regulation schedule is not wholly determinate *ex ante*, since reservoirs of different sizes and different costs can be added in different sequences, so that only one arbitrarily selected sequence yields a cost curve for planning purposes.[2]

The cost of maintaining water quality is likewise a part of the cost of water with which we are concerned. In any market the "product" is defined to include specified quality characteristics; the same holds true for water. Quality can vary in a number of dimensions: chemical, physical, biological. These variations manifest themselves in the capacity of water to serve various duties. Unfortunately, all quality dimensions cannot be encompassed in the analysis, but the costs of treating wastes to remove decomposable organic substances will be estimated, as will the costs of assuring a flow of high-quality water to mix with the waste effluent after treatment. These estimates are subject to an unknown range of error for three reasons: (1) they are taken from computations made for the United States and reflect the waste-assimilating capacity of rivers in the Central Pacific region (mostly California); (2) they contain an unknown error factor for the United States; (3) finally, until we know more about quality problems, now and foreseeable, of Chilean rivers, it cannot be certain that dissolved oxygen and the assimilation of biodegradable substances are in fact the

---

[1] Costs of waste treatment, see below, are based upon estimates prepared for the United States and pertain to usual sewage treatment processes. It was assumed that comparable processes would be used in Chile.

[2] Subject to the statistical uncertainty of the underlying hydrology and the additional uncertainty of the costs of certain engineering features—e.g., outlets—until the use of a dam is established.

critical qualitative factors. Dissolved solids may turn out to be more important; but because the requisite data do not exist for Chile, and because they are not in such systematic form for the United States that a translation is possible, dissolved solids cannot be incorporated into the analysis.

When the costs of regulation and waste treatment have been estimated for a projected pattern of economic activity, one can ascertain three things: (1) whether projected water uses are compatible with physical supply, assuming "complete" regulation;[3] (2) the combination of waste treatment and dilution flow that minimizes costs of water; (3) whether marginal costs of water vary substantially among regions and, therefore, whether this suggests a different regional distribution of water use or different assortment of goods and services produced.

Economists object to a "requirements approach" to the study of any economic good or service because such approach typically fails to take into account the possibility that implicit technical coefficients are subject to change if economic conditions warrant. The model takes cognizance of the possibility of technological improvement by using rates of water use for irrigation that reflect more economical usage[4] than now prevails; but there is still a wide gap between theoretical plant requirements and the figures adopted for 1985. No special attempt has been made to project improved technology of water use for other activities. The projections indicate that certain adjustments will inevitably be made in either the rate of water use per unit of product, the geographic distribution of activity, or the composition of the national bill of goods, especially as it is divided between water-related and non-water-related goods. However, these are conclusions derived from the projections rather than assumptions adopted for the purpose of making the projections.

In order to ascertain the relationship between future demands for water and its availability, it is necessary to aggregate separate uses. The method of aggregation into what I call a "requirement" depends in part on assumed policies and objectives of the Chilean economy. For example, one must make an assumption regarding the standard of quality that will be adopted for instream water, since there is no statement of policy to which one can turn. The lack of information pertaining to routing water downstream from point to point (taking into account both quantity and quality requirements, the possibilities of instream and off-

[3] Because one can never be sure of the future variability of stream flow, it would be more accurate to speak of "very high regulation."
[4] Usage here refers to both gross and net measurements. See Chap. VI for more detailed discussion.

stream multiple use, the natural recuperative powers of the stream along with the benefits or damage of stream regulation, and the possibilities of treatment at points of intake and discharge) necessitates the substitution of looser, rule-of-thumb concepts of water requirements. The main task is to frame the concept of "requirement" in such a way that it is parallel to a concept of ability to meet the requirement and what it will cost.

A requirements approach does not ask whether the benefits of investment in water resources are equal to or more than the costs, even though the analysis may yield information that can intuitively be used toward that end. Generally speaking, a benefit-cost analysis is feasible for marginal decisions, where most of the elements related to the decision are given. Such, for example, would be the question of whether it is worth while to invest in an irrigation system in a particular valley, given the potential output and the expected market. The approach I have adopted starts with a national bill of goods and the quantity of fresh water available in the form of measured surface runoff, and concludes with a regional pattern of output that is consistent with specified outlays on water resources. By adopting a number of simplifying assumptions, tentative answers can be supplied, within the limits of the assumptions and the quality of the data, to the following questions:

1) What are the requirements for water if a reasonable extrapolation of presently observed trends or presently known plans are extended to 1985?

2) To what extent will shortages of water prevent the consummation of these plans?

3) What will be the critical costs of supplying the implied water requirements? By "critical costs" are meant those costs that can be readily avoided by transferring an activity from one region to another.

4) What modifications in projected activity are likely to have a significant effect on required outlays for water?

5) What modifications in projected activity are likely to be induced by rapidly rising marginal costs of water?

6) How will the physical and economic limits of supply affect the regional distribution of activity?

The simplifying assumptions that are to be adopted are the following:

1) Each water resource region is considered to be two points in space between which all of the region's activity is divided, an upstream point and a downstream point. The upstream point consists of all of the region that is so far from the ocean that water discharged from any industrial plant, mine, power plant, city, or irrigation

project can be used again. The downstream point is all of the region located so close to the sea that all fresh water discharged into a receiving body of water is considered to be irrecoverable as fresh water, and therefore to be lost just as though it were evapotranspired. In mining, thermal power, and manufacturing it is assumed that fresh water can be recirculated within the plant.

2) The water requirement for a region is considered to be equal to the largest of:

a) the sum of upstream losses (i.e., consumption by evaporation or transpiration) plus downstream intake; or

b) the sum of synchronous intakes at all points that are so separated from each other that the water discharged by a user at any of these points will not affect the supply available to a user at any of these points; or

c) the sum of losses plus waste dilution flows.

The amount of water "required" by any region depends not only upon the intake and losses of offstream activity but also upon the uses to which water in the stream is put, and, in a more complete model, on the balancing of intake costs against maintaining instream quality by waste treatment and dilution. Up to now the maintenance of instream quality, either to meet instream uses or to assure water of adequate quality to successive offstream users, has received little attention in Chile. Nor has much attention been directed to the quality of estuarine waters. The character of Chile's coastline is such that estuaries are small or nonexistent, or are fed by flows so great that there has been no concern over adverse effects of upstream uses. Chile's concern over pollution has been quite weak. Its capital city, Santiago, does not yet have a waste treatment plant, far less has there been any thought of providing waste dilution flows *after treatment*. Under these circumstances it is unlikely that waste dilution requirements will seriously compete with other demands for water within the next twenty years.

The Chilean government possesses authority to prevent an industrial plant from causing undue pollution, and presumably will use such authority to compel treatment when necessary. However, even high-level treatment of organic wastes will not remove dissolved solids from water. Information is lacking on the amount of dilution that would be necessary to prevent an undesirable buildup of salinity on the downstream side of a city of 5 million or so people. Consequently, a dissolved oxygen criterion of water quality has been used in this analysis, with levels of treatment ranging between zero and 90 per cent removal of BOD. One measure used for water requirement includes the flow needed, after mixing the *treated* discharged liquor, to maintain dissolved oxygen in the stream at 4 milligrams per liter, or approximately four parts of oxygen per million parts of water. Water meeting this standard normally requires no special treatment at points of intake and will support a relatively high level of aquatic life. By adding all losses to the dilution requirement we are saying that if requirements are met, the discharge of the river to the sea will be at least equal to the waste dilution flow.

The other two measurements of water requirement are designed to meet those circumstances where dilution flows are lower than the gross requirement at any single point or lower than the gross requirement at a group of independent points so situated that users at these points cannot utilize the water discharged by other users whose intake is being counted, or, in the limiting case, where no dilution flows are specified because no explicit account is taken of water quality.

In formulating these measures of requirement the following uses are taken into account: agriculture, manufacturing, mining, thermal power, and general municipal uses—domestic, commercial, civic, and light manufacturing. Possible instream uses, such as fishing, water-based recreation, navigation, and hydroelectric power, are ignored.

Where a waste dilution flow is retained in the requirement measure, this implicitly provides for some recreational (including fishing) uses and some power production. Hydroelectric power is ignored as a component of the requirement because, except for Rapel, the installations are upstream. Officials of Empresa Nacional de Electricidad, S.A. (ENDESA), the national electric power authority, believe that up to now hydroelectric installations have been administered in such a way as to conflict as little as possible with other uses. It is quite possible, however, that conflicts will increase, especially as relatively more power is produced from regulated flows and less from upstream run-of-the-river plants. The extent of these conflicts cannot be ascertained without information on the location of activities within a water resource region and information on the functioning of an electric grid system. In ignoring hydroelectric power we should recognize a failure to account for those possibilities in which revenues can be earned to offset in whole or in part the costs of regulation. We should also recognize the possibility of understating total expenditure on reservoir capacity.[5]

If all users of water, including municipal systems and irrigation projects, captured and reused all water that was not evaporated, transpired, or incorporated in the product, intake would be equal to what in this study

[5] See Chap. VII.

is termed "loss."[6] I have assumed that mines and thermal power plants recirculate all fresh water intake; whether these activities are located upstream or downstream, their requirement is considered to be measured by "loss." Manufacturing activities—steel mills, oil refineries, pulp and paper plants, and so forth, could, and in some cases do, recirculate their fresh water. In this event intake is equal to loss. Where no recirculation is practiced and the point of use is downstream, the required flow of the downstream point of use is equal to downstream intake plus upstream loss. Such a computation may be equal to, more than, or less than required flow as measured by losses plus waste dilution.

Another option in computing required flow based on a dilution requirement would be to assume that downstream losses could be met out of the dilution flow. In this case the flow requirement would be equal to upstream losses (not total losses) plus waste dilution flows, provided waste dilution flows exceeded downstream intake. In quantitative terms, a requirement stated in this way will not be greatly different in most regions from a requirement expressed as total losses plus waste dilution.

There is no need to know the intraregional location of activity in order to compute total losses, so long as "losses" are limited to evapotranspiration, incorporation in the product, and usual losses due to inefficiency, etc. in irrigation projects. However, when one distinguishes between "upstream" and "downstream" points of discharge, it is necessary to fix the geographical position of each activity to correspond to these points. In the case of municipal use, the division was made by extrapolating the trend of population. Manufacturing activities in the major water-using industries, other than food, are so easily located that a reasonably exact distribution could be made. For food, the distribution of activity was based on the distribution of population. (See Table 1.)

Mining and steam electric power were not intraregionally distributed because:

1) losses are relatively low;
2) recirculation is relatively easy if water supplies are scarce;
3) salt water can be used for cooling if recirculating equipment is too expensive.

Hence, requirements for these activities are measured by evapotranspiration losses, whether located upstream or downstream. Furthermore, they do not suffer pollution by organic, degradable substances for which

---

[6] Agricultural losses also include water that soaks into the ground and, for one reason or another, cannot be recovered. In another context, all waters discharged into salty or brackish bodies of water are classified as "loss."

Table 1
ASSUMED DISTRIBUTION OF MANUFACTURING
AND URBAN POPULATION BETWEEN DOWNSTREAM AND
UPSTREAM POINTS OF WATER USE

Province	All manufacturing except food and beverages		Percentage distribution of urban population and food and beverages	
	Coastal	Inland	Coastal	Inland
Tarapacá	x		88	12
Antofagasta	x		58	42
Atacama		x	14	86
Coquimbo	x		50	50
Aconcagua		x	3	97
Valparaíso	x		70	30
Santiago		x	2	98
O'Higgins		x	0	100
Colchagua		x	4	96
Curicó		x	1	99
Talca		x	0	100
Maule	x		30	70
Linares		x	0	100
Ñuble		x	1	99
Concepción	x		94	6
Arauco	x		39	61
Bío-Bío		x	0	100
Malleco		x	0	100
Cautín		x	2	98
Valdivia	x		58	42
Osorno		x	0	100
Llanquihue	x		70	30
Chiloé	x		85	15
Aysén	x		100	0
Magallanes	x		100	0

a dilution flow is specified. Where pollution is a problem, as in the disposition of acid wastes, the waste-carrying water is usually lagooned and the water requirement appears as evaporation loss (in which case intake is equal to loss).

To divide agricultural requirements between "upstream" and "downstream," no more practical way could be found than to use Chile's 1955 census of agriculture, which gave the irrigated area of local units of government known as *comunas*. *Comunas* were designated as upstream or

Table 2
PERCENTAGE DISTRIBUTION OF IRRIGATED AREA
BETWEEN UPSTREAM AND DOWNSTREAM POINTS

Province	Downstream	Upstream
Tarapacá	50	50
Antofagasta	0	100
Atacama	12	88
Coquimbo	19	81
Aconcagua	14	86
Valparaíso	10	90
Aconcagua-Valparaíso	12	88
Santiago	2	98
O'Higgins	0	100
Colchagua	1	99
O'Higgins-Colchagua	0.5	99.5
Curicó	3	97
Talca	1	99
Maule	100	0
Linares	0	100
Curicó-Linares	6	94
Ñuble	0	100
Concepción	3	97
Arauco	100	0
Bío-Bío	0	100
Malleco	0	100
Cautín	0	100
Concepción-Cautín	4	96

Source: Based on distribution of irrigated area by *comuna* according to the 1955 Censo Agropecuario.

downstream by the technique known as *al ojímetro* with the use of a map.[7] The 1955 distribution was assumed to persist to 1985. In the basic model agricultural requirements were considered to be equal to "net use" upstream plus "gross use" downstream. The distribution of irrigated area between upstream and downstream points is given in Table 2.

The need for defining "water requirements" in several alternative ways results from the absence of well-defined trends or policies, especially with respect to water quality and in-stream uses.[8] There is no information on the quality of estuarine and inland fisheries. Furthermore, it is impossible to ascertain whether the lack of data is a reflection of the fact that fisheries are in no danger, that deterioration in the foreseeable future has been

[7] Translated as "eyeballing."
[8] No account has been taken of possible increases in water losses attributable to soil conservation practices and reforestation.

brought to no one's attention, that deterioration is accepted with equanimity, or that it has been determined that the cost of preventing deterioration is greater than the benefits. There is some evidence that water supplies are being polluted by the discharge of untreated sewage. One is warned not to eat raw vegetables; the supermarkets feature strawberries with a cachet on the box indicating that they are grown where the irrigation water is safe. These comments do not apply, of course, to water distributed from water treatment plants. Such plants are planned for all communities of 1,000 population or more.[9]

PROJECTIONS OF POPULATION AND GROSS NATIONAL PRODUCT

Projected water use depends upon the output of water-related goods and services. Future outputs were estimated by assuming that production would be determined by the change in demand, modified by an assumed change in imports or exports, and that changes in demand would be determined by changes in the size and income of the population. Changes in income were assumed to be measured by changes in gross national product. (See Table 3.)

Table 3

GROSS NATIONAL PRODUCT AND POPULATION,
ACTUAL AND PROJECTIONS FOR 1985

Year	Gross National Product Mil. E° (1960)
1963	4,645
1965	4,998
1985 ("A" projection)[a]	10,326
1985 ("B" projection)[a]	14,579

Year	Population Total (000's)	Urban (000's)
1965	8,601	5,028
1985 (Low)[b]	13,289	10,365
1985 (Medium)[b]	13,902	10,844
1985 (High)[b]	14,372	11,210

a "A" projection based on rate of 3.75%; "B" projection based on rate of 5.5%.
b Low projection based on rate of 2.2%; medium projection based on rate of 2.43%; high projection based on rate of 2.6%.

[9] It has been alleged that infiltration of ground water pollutes water supply systems during periods of low pressure. I have been unable to verify or disprove the allegation.

Two rates of annual growth of gross national product were adopted. The lower rate, 3.75 per cent, is the average rate experienced during the period 1940-63. The higher rate, 5.5 per cent, is the rate around which current government planning is built. Projected demands for agriculture and manufacturing products were dependent upon the growth of GNP. Mining was projected at two levels, but independently of changes in population and income, since the output of most Chilean mineral products is not significantly affected by Chilean domestic demand. The effect of mineral production on GNP was not examined. Steam-electric power was projected on the basis of the plans of ENDESA. The projected main source of power is hydroelectricity; thermal plants are expected to meet a relatively small portion of future demand.

For population growth, the rate adopted for detailed elaboration of the models was 2.43 per cent.[10] This corresponds to a middle rate. (See Table 4.) Summary comparisons were made using a low rate of 2.2 per cent and a high of 2.6 per cent.

Urban population was estimated for 1985 by extending Sadie's percentages, on the assumption that the percentage decline in rural population would be the same for the decade 1975-85 as was projected for the five-year period 1970-75, namely 9 per cent. This gave an urban population for 1985 equal to 78 per cent of total. With the control totals of 13,902,400 for total and 10,843,900 for urban, total and urban population was distributed among the provinces on the basis of the historical percentage (1940, 1952, and 1960) each province's population bore to the national total. The general rule followed was to add to or subtract from the 1960 percentage one-half of the change that occurred in the province's percentage of total population between 1940 and 1960. In this way a trend, but one substantially dampened, was followed. In several instances where either the past figures seemed implausible or the results seemed unreasonable for the future, they were modified intuitively. The final results were reconciled to 100 per cent.[11]

While the medium rate of population growth, 2.43 per cent, and the high rate of GNP growth, 5.5 per cent, were the rates for which models were

[10] Estimated by Universidad Católica, Santiago. This figure coincides closely with an extension to 1985 of an estimate prepared by Professor Sadie, using cohort survival rates. Johannes L. Sadie, *Población y Mano de Obra de Chile, 1930-1975* (Santiago: Centro Latinoamericano de Demografía [CELADE], 1964).

[11] The estimates of municipal water use that were incorporated into the measure of requirements were based upon a slightly different distribution and larger size of urban population in comparison with the figures indicated in Table 4. The resulting overstatement is on the order of 10 per cent for the country as a whole and 20 per cent for the province of Santiago. A reduction of municipal loss by 20 per cent would reduce total losses in Santiago Province by eight-tenths of 1 per cent.

Table 4
PROJECTED POPULATION, MEDIUM GROWTH RATE, 1985
(*Thousands*)

Province	Total	Urban	Rural
Tarapacá	236.3	227.7	8.6
Antofagasta	458.8	444.6	14.2
Atacama	208.5	184.3	24.2
Coquimbo	542.2	347.0	195.2
Aconcagua	236.3	173.5	62.8
Valparaíso	1,167.8	1,051.9	115.9
Santiago	4,991.0	4,912.3	78.7
O'Higgins	458.8	292.8	166.0
Colchagua	278.0	108.4	169.6
Curicó	180.7	97.6	83.1
Talca	375.4	195.2	180.2
Maule	139.0	65.1	73.9
Linares	292.0	130.1	161.9
Ñuble	486.6	238.6	248.0
Concepción	1,070.5	976.0	94.5
Arauco	166.8	65.1	101.7
Bío-Bío	305.9	141.0	164.9
Malleco	292.0	151.8	140.2
Cautín	625.6	281.9	343.7
Valdivia	472.7	249.4	223.3
Osorno	278.0	141.0	137.0
Llanquihue	319.8	162.7	157.1
Chiloé	111.2	43.4	67.8
Aysén	83.4	43.2	40.2
Magallanes	125.1	119.3	5.8
Total	13,902.4	10,843.9	3,058.5

elaborated in greatest detail, less detailed projections were also made using the medium rate of population growth and lower rate of growth of GNP. Projections using the lower rate of GNP growth are labeled "A," and those using the higher rate, "B." "Medium A" refers to the combination of 2.43 per cent for population and 3.75 per cent for GNP. "Medium B" refers to the growth rates of 2.43 per cent and 5.5 per cent for population and GNP, respectively. The combination of a low population growth rate with each of the two GNP growth rates are designated "Low A" and "Low B," respectively. Similarly, we have "High A" and "High B."

The effects of the various combinations of population and GNP growth rates are summarized in Table 5 in the form of index numbers resting on

Table 5

COMPARISON OF ALTERNATIVE VALUES FOR POPULATION,
GROSS NATIONAL PRODUCT, AND SELECTED INDUSTRIES IN 1985
BASED ON ALTERNATIVE RATES OF GROWTH

Index numbers (Medium B = 100)

Economic indicator	"A"			"B"		
	Low	Med.	High	Low	Med.	High
Gross national product	72	72	72	100	100	100
Population	96	100	103	96	100	103
Manufacturing:						
Food	74	77	80	97	100	104
Pulp and paper	58	62	63	96	100	104
Petroleum refining	55	57	59	94	100	102
Steel	63	67	68	96	100	104
Agriculture	82	86	89	96	100	104

Medium B as equal to 100. Indexes of manufacturing and agricultural demand incorporate an income elasticity coefficient.

A PREVIEW OF THE RESULTS

If the water supplies of the country as a whole are compared with projected water requirements—both measured as a specified regulated flow—there is no foreseeable shortage. This is so even if one compares only the aggregate requirements and supplies of the provinces north of archipelagic Chile, where 1985 requirements amount to 99.7 per cent and supplies (average flow) to only 40 per cent of the national total. Projected requirements for 1985 (Medium B), for all provinces from Llanquihue to the northern boundary range between 31 and 34 billion cubic meters per year, depending upon the alternative used to measure requirements, whereas average flow for the same region is about 176 billion cubic meters annually. (Average flow of the three provinces south of Llanquihue amounts to about 269,000 million cubic meters while projected requirements for 1985 range between 46 and 103 million cubic meters.)

Evapotranspiration losses constitute Chile's main projected requirement; and of these 98.5 per cent consist of agricultural (irrigation) losses. Municipal losses account for 1 per cent, and mining, manufacturing, and steam-electric power together account for the remaining one-half of 1 per cent. Consequently, relatively large changes in non-agricultural uses of water will have relatively small effects on the total water picture, although local conditions, especially in the north, will be affected by changes in non-agricultural use.

Taking a rough two-thirds of the country, the province of Cautín north to the boundary, annual requirements for water differ only slightly when the several alternative measures are applied. The lowest amount, 30.4 billion cubic meters per year, covers evaporation-transpiration losses only. The highest, 34.1 billion cubic meters per year, covers evaporation and transpiration losses and also provides for waste dilution of effluent after treatment to remove 90 per cent of degradable organic material. Dilution is computed to yield 4 milligrams per liter of dissolved oxygen in the stream after the waste effluent mixes with the high-quality dilution water. These annual requirements are listed below:

	Billion m^3/yr
Evaporation-transpiration losses	30.4
Case I: Evaporation-transpiration losses plus downstream municipal and agricultural intake	31.3
Case II: Case I plus mining intake instead of evaporation loss	31.6
Case III: Evaporation-transpiration losses upstream; all intakes downstream	32.7
Evaporation-transpiration losses plus waste dilution to yield 4 mg/l dissolved oxygen in the stream after 90% removal of organic wastes[12]	34.1

If water quality should become a major consideration and if treatment should fall short of 90 per cent removal of biochemical-oxygen-demanding substances, water requirements for this same region (Cautín to the north) could rise substantially. At zero treatment, total required flows would be 61.7 billion cubic meters per year to assure 4 milligrams per liter of dissolved oxygen. With primary treatment (35 per cent removal of BOD), required flows would be 50.8 billion cubic meters per year. Estimated required flows, therefore, are apparently more responsive to decisions regarding water quality and waste treatment than to decisions regarding recirculation at the lower end of river basins.

When the focus of analysis is restricted to the northern half of the country (the province of Santiago and all others to the north), the picture changes from projected adequacy of supply with considerable room to spare, to one of serious shortage. Using Case I requirements (i.e., downstream municipal and agricultural intake plus evaporation-transpiration losses from all other uses), estimates indicate that an annual flow of 8.8 billion cubic meters is required as against an average available flow of

---

[12] Only wastes discharged upstream are assumed to require dilution.

6.2 billion cubic meters. This means that even if regulation were carried to the maximum possible degree, supply would fall 30 per cent short of requirements.

The disparity between required and available flows becomes greater when Cases II and III are considered, with all that they imply for less recirculation and for the need to maintain a flow of high-quality dilution water over and above projected evapotranspiration losses. If the costs of regulating flow are taken into account by fixing an upper limit on expenditure per unit of regulated flow, the disparity increases even more.

It is reasonable to assume that any restriction on water supply will be felt first in agriculture. As one of the bases for 1985 projections, application of water per hectare of land was assumed to reflect an improvement over present rates of water use to a degree that further economies in water use would be beyond normal expectation. For this reason, restrictions on water supply are likely to mean a roughly corresponding restriction on irrigated hectarage. Estimated irrigable land in the area we are discussing is about 566,000 hectares. If all available water, fully regulated, were used for irrigation, about 403,000 hectares could be cultivated. If non-agricultural uses were first met in full, this would shrink to 373,000 hectares. (Both estimates are based on Case I.) When one compares projected total agricultural output in this area (taking the restrictions imposed by water into account) with projected agricultural requirements (as based upon growth in population, dietary needs, and restriction of imports to a level in keeping with present experience) it is found that output per hectare must somewhat more than double. An improvement of this magnitude seems feasible. The question is whether the necessary steps will be taken to bring it about.

So far as projected non-agricultural water needs are concerned, it is unlikely that they cannot be met, provided steps are taken to regulate stream flow and recirculate water used for mining, power, and manufacturing purposes.

Stream regulation, based upon surface storage, involves a capital cost, but one which, according to the estimates made for this study, will not be unreasonably high unless regulation is carried to its theoretical physical limit. If the annual cost of flow assured 85 per cent of the year is equal to E⁰8,900 (1964 prices)[13] per million cubic meters, in the province of Santiago—and less elsewhere by varying amounts—and if all non-agricultural needs are met before allocating water to agriculture, irrigated hectarage in the northern provinces would amount to about 311,500 hectares.

---

[13] Equal to US $3.42 per acre-foot at 1964 official rate of exchange.

Total annual costs of regulation would be about E°37.5 million. If non-agricultural uses were met by regulation of flow *beyond* the constraint of E°8,900 per year per million cubic meters, but agriculture were to be bound by this limit, some 343,000 hectares would be under irrigation at a total annual cost of about E°47.2 million.

The expansion of irrigated hectarage from 311,500 to 343,000 in the northern provinces[14] would cost approximately E°10 million per year. Judging by 1964 prices of agricultural products as well as of water in Santiago, so large an extension of regulation seems unwarranted for 1985. Were it put into effect, the marginal cost of water would be about E°333 per hectare per year,[15] or almost E°14 per metric quintal of wheat (or wheat equivalent) for water alone, compared with a 1964 wholesale price of wheat of about E°21.

For Chile as a whole, cumulated capital costs of regulating stream flow up to the full capacity of the stream or the level of projected 1985 demand, whichever is lower, is estimated to be E°1 billion (1964 prices). The equivalent annual cost would be E°84 million. A marginal cost constraint, where agricultural needs are met only after non-agricultural, would reduce capital costs by about E°569 million, or 56 per cent. To state this in reverse, the cost of going to the full physical limit, and thus imposing the condition of agricultural expansion only, would represent a very high cost per additional unit of crop—about E°31 per metric quintal of wheat equivalent.

The investigation turned up several side issues, which were briefly explored. One dealt with the past experience of the Chilean government in financing irrigation projects. Whether Chile's experience with project selection is worse or better than the experience of other governments cannot be ascertained without extremely detailed comparisons. What is clear, however, is that the financial arrangements contemplated by law have been eroded by inflation. Another side issue, but central to the question of Chilean economic planning and progress, is the implied increase in productivity per hectare that is consistent with available land and water and Chilean agricultural output goals. Especially when seen in the light of the balance of payments difficulties experienced during the last few years, the conclusion that output per hectare will have to more than double between now and 1985 is the signal for a specific technological effort. What constitutes the optimum agricultural policy, expressed in terms of domestic production, exports, and imports, had not

---

[14] No problem is encountered in the provinces south of Santiago since all projected requirements there can be met at relatively low marginal costs of regulated flow.
[15] About $100 at 1964 exchange rate, or $45.45 per acre.

been formulated at the time of writing. An interregional agricultural model would constitute a major contribution to Chile's water resource planning tools.

Moving from the regulation of flow to meet evapotranspiration needs to the question of water quality, three considerations must be taken into account: (1) the quality standard, (2) the level of waste treatment, and (3) the quantity of high-quality water that is mixed with the effluent of waste treatment plants. These three factors must be appropriately related to each other. For example, a low level of treatment and a large dilution flow can serve to yield a designated in-stream quality equally with a higher level of treatment and smaller dilution flow. Given cost functions for regulation of flow and degrees of waste treatment, there is likely to be a combination of waste treatment and dilution flow that minimizes total cost in each basin for a designated quality standard. In a given basin, the range of possibilities may be limited by the available water supply; where supply is small the level of treatment may have to be high in order to achieve a designated quality with a designated output of waste-producing goods and services.

Although there is a deficiency of information regarding the incidence of pollution, the costs of its abatement, and the relationships between levels of treatment and required dilution flows, estimates were made with the assistance of U.S. coefficients. Annual costs of treatment were estimated at E°42.6 million. The additional flows needed for dilution were assumed to be used downstream for irrigation, in which case the dilution flows could irrigate about 25,000 additional hectares rather than go unused into the sea. The additional cost of stream regulation, beyond the costs of Case I—marginal cost constraint, agriculture in a residuary position— was estimated at E°15.5 million annually.[16] Total annual costs of quality maintenance, based on an in-stream quality standard of 4 milligrams per liter of dissolved oxygen was, therefore, about E°58.1 million. If collection costs of municipal systems are also taken into account, costs of treatment, collection, and additional flow amounted to E°74.5 million annually for the country as a whole. The estimated costs of maintaining quality— treatment, municipal collection, and additional flow to provide dilution— came to about twice the costs of flow regulation within the limits of a marginal cost constraint, agriculture residuary. Of the quality-maintenance outlays, the annual costs of collection, some E°16 million per year, cannot be sidestepped without serious health consequences. The remaining E°58.5 million can be avoided in whole or in part by accepting a lower

[16] See Chap. XI for definition of Cases I, II, and III. See Chaps. XIII and XIV for analysis of costs of regulation and waste treatment.

average in-stream quality standard, or by relocating people and activity from regions in which water supplies must be treated highly and regulated at high marginal cost to regions in which natural minimum flows are so great that quality can be maintained with low-level treatment and little or no additional flow regulation.

How do projected outlays compare with recent rates of investment for capital goods? In 1964, at 1961 prices, gross fixed investment at market prices was $E^{o}750$ million.[17] At 1964 prices this would be about $E^{o}1,785$ million. If streams were regulated in accordance with the marginal cost constraint, agriculture residuary, costs would be $E^{o}37.5$ million (1964 prices). If, in addition, stream quality of 4 milligrams per liter of dissolved oxygen were to be assured, total annual costs would be about $E^{o}112.0$ million, or about 6 per cent of the 1964 level of investment. However, since estimated annual costs are for the level of investment required for assumed conditions of 1985, the required outlays for water should be compared with expected 1985 investment. If gross investment grows at the same rate as Medium B projections of GNP—i.e., 5.5 per cent per year—by 1985 annual gross investment at constant prices should be three times the level obtained in 1964, or about $E^{o}5.4$ billion. Annual capital cost equivalents for water resource development would then amount to roughly 2 per cent of the gross investment budget. These costs exclude municipal treatment and delivery costs as well as long distance supply lines, manufacturing intake costs, to-the-farm and on-the-farm delivery costs, and the like, which would be incurred in any case. In the absence of an investment model, one cannot draw a firm conclusion regarding the over-all burden that investment in water resources would impose. There is no reason, however, for assuming that it would be intolerably high.

UNFINISHED BUSINESS[18]

The foregoing summary leaves untouched several important questions. The need for an interregional agricultural production model has already been mentioned. Among other topics inadequately treated in this study are the supply and disposition of ground water, storage requirements for hydroelectric power and additional evaporation losses, possible effects of

[17] *Boletín Estadístico de América Latina* (hereinafter referred to as *Boletín*), Vol. III, No. 1, February 1966 (Comisión Económica para América Latina, Naciones Unidas). Prices rose about 2.4 times between 1961 and the middle of 1964, based upon an unofficial consumer price index. The consumer price index and the wholesale price index tended to move together.

[18] This section is based largely on comments made by Adolfo Dorfman, Chief, Natural Resources and Energy Program, U.N. Economic Commission for Latin America, and Blair T. Bower, Research Associate, Resources for the Future, Inc.

nuclear power production, possible effects of desalination of sea water or inland brackish waters, legal-economic-institutional changes, urban capital costs for local treatment and distribution, costs of interbasin transfers of water, a host of financial questions such as the appropriate interest rate for the computation of costs and benefits, incidence of costs, benefit-cost comparisons, and the merits of expenditure on water resource projects compared with other activities.

Ground water cannot be systematically incorporated into a study of water resource development until more is known of its occurrence and behavior. I have assumed that surface-water measurements include the contribution made by ground water, an assumption that is reasonable for relatively large basins but not necessarily valid for small. By failing to go beyond this assumption I have neglected both the possibility of storing water in aquifers as an alternative to surface storage and the possibility of withdrawing ground water in excess of the rate of recharge. Should ground-water storage prove feasible, evaporation losses would be less than assumed. Should mining of ground water be a possibility in various basins of the north, the near-term disparity between projected requirements and supplies would be less. The use of ground storage in lieu of surface storage might affect estimated costs of regulating flow. Also ignored was the possibility of constructing artificial underground reservoirs by use of nuclear explosives.

Although the economic feasibility of large-scale interbasin transfers appears low at this time, there is little information on which to base a firm conclusion. There is also little information on other methods of augmenting supply. At the time of writing, the feasibility of using nuclear energy for production of power and desalination of sea water was under study by the Chilean government electric power corporation, ENDESA. When data have been acquired regarding (1) costs of desalted water (which at present are likely to be comparatively high), (2) the possibility of releasing water to agriculture from non-agricultural uses, and (3) the future place of agriculture for the northern provinces in the national picture, the role of desalination will be better understood. At the moment there is no reason to expect a substantial augmentation of supplies from this source, but since the state of technology may soon change materially, one can hardly reach a dogmatic conclusion. It is likely that ENDESA and other Chilean entities will continue their studies of possible applications of nuclear energy even if no power or desalination plants are constructed in the immediate future.

A number of interesting and broad topics related to national water resource planning demand the attention of experts in economic, legal, political, and social spheres. Chile's metamorphosis from a rural to urban economy will induce changes in land tenure, laws regarding water rights, and intensive competition for capital. Each of these changes will affect economic feasibility considerations, as well as the physical characteristics of the supply of and demand for water. To some extent these changes were taken into account in the assumptions used for making the projections of water demand and supply, but a number of things were left unsaid. For example, irrigation coefficients resting upon an implicitly assumed higher level of efficiency in water use may not materialize unless the conditions of ownership and use of water are changed, unless funds are available to landowners for necessary capital improvements, and unless alternative techniques for raising agricultural output are fully exploited within economic limits. Questions relating to the implicit or explicit pricing of water and the ease with which water can be transferred from one use or user to another will have to be settled. Furthermore, the benefits that flow from the marginal dollar spent on water resource projects relative to the benefits of the marginal dollar spent elsewhere cannot be ascertained by a study of water resources only. Nor is it enough, in view of the special problems of the Chilean capital market growing out of inflation, controlled interest rates, and the rationing of capital by the banking system, to study the flow of investment funds in response to market processes.

Chilean and United Nations experts are aware of these untouched topics and steps have been taken to fill some of the gaps. It would be presumptuous to second guess the outcome of investigations now under way or to anticipate what policy recommendations might emerge.

III

AGRICULTURE: A GENERAL SURVEY

In order to appreciate the most vexing aspects of Chile's water resource use we must understand the problems of Chilean agriculture. The "problems" stem from the fact that agricultural output has been stagnant over more than a decade. Total agricultural output, including forestry, amounted to E°450 million in 1950 at 1961 prices; output in 1962 was E°448 million.[1]

The failure of agricultural output to grow would not necessarily be evidence of economic distress were it not that Chile has had, and still has, an inadequate average diet, a high rate of population growth, a relatively high income elasticity of demand for food, and a serious balance of payments problem. The lag in productivity of the agricultural sector has probably contributed to Chile's inflation and the low growth rate of the economy as a whole.

Table 6 shows the disproportionate rates of change in gross product, agricultural output, and population. Even in 1959, when gross agricultural output amounted to E°536 million (1961 prices), output per capita was below the level of 1950. The growth in per capita gross product and, by implication, in per capita income, coupled with growth in population, has contributed to a rising demand for food and fibers that has been met by an increase in imports to a much greater degree than by more domestic production. The strain that this has imposed on the Chilean economy is indicated by Chile's balance of payments.

[1] *Boletín*, Vol. I, No. 1 (1964) p. 44.

Sr. Alvaro Marfan J., head of Chile's national planning office (Oficina de Planificación Nacional) has expressed doubt that the statistics indicate what they purport. He has stated (letter of January 30, 1967) that all studies of the planning office indicate an increase in physical output during the period 1951-62, although not enough to cover the increase in population and the increase in per capita demand.

29

Table 6

SELECTED ECONOMIC INDICATORS, CHILE, 1950-62

(*Money values in millions of 1961 escudos*)

Economic indicator	1950	1959	1962	Per cent change 1950-59	Per cent change 1950-62
Agriculture and forestry	450	536	448	+19.1	− 0.4
Gross domestic product	3,753	4,932	5,680	+31.4	+51.3
Population (1,000's)	6,073	7,465	7,987	+22.9	+31.5

Source: Boletín, Vol. I, No. 1 (1964), pp. 17, 44, 45.

Between 1950 and 1963, total exports grew by 16 per cent, but total imports grew by 219 per cent. Of imports, non-durable consumer goods constituted 10 per cent in 1950 and 16 per cent in 1963, rising, in real terms, by 245 per cent over the period 1950-63. In 1950, total exports exceeded imports by (1950) US$113.2 million; in 1963, imports exceeded exports by (1963) $95 million.[2]

There are differences in the rates of growth of subclasses of agricultural output. Production of livestock has lagged. During the period 1950-59, output of crops grew at an annual rate of 4.9 per cent, whereas output of livestock grew at an annual rate of 0.5 per cent.[3] In 1959-60, the output of meat, milk, and wool amounted to E°226 million out of total agricultural output of E°593 million.

Studies that have been made of Chilean agriculture attribute the low rate of growth to many different causes, some of which explain not only a low rate of growth but a low level of productivity per unit of input as well. The evidence that supports various explanations is likely to be somewhat impressionistic, since systematic measurements of land and water use, complementary inputs, and yields—all related to each other— have not yet been made. It is just as easy to demonstrate low outputs per unit of labor and per unit of capital as it is to show low outputs per hectare. Inadequate use of fertilizers, herbicides, insecticides, and high-quality seeds, and failure to employ proper genetic practices are deficiencies frequently cited. There is little doubt that unskilled labor is in oversupply and skilled labor capable of using, maintaining, and repairing farm machinery is in low supply.

[2] *Boletín*, Vol. II, No. 1, pp. 200, 202.
[3] Universidad de Chile, Instituto de Economía. *La Economía de Chile en el Período 1950-1963* (Santiago: 1963), p. 25.

Two commonly advanced explanations are contradictory. One is that discriminatory price controls keep prices of milk, meat, and wheat disproportionately low in the face of persistent and severe inflation, thereby discouraging investment. Another is that the high concentration of ownership of land is coupled with a relatively weak desire to maximize income. Lack of credit; lack of research and extension facilities; lack of personnel with adequate technical education; lack of marketing, transportation, and storage facilities help explain the backward state of agriculture. So far as water resources problems are concerned, these explanations ultimately focus on two parameters: the amount of land under irrigation and the amount of water required per unit of land.

A study of Chilean water resources planning could, perhaps, begin with the year 1952. In December of that year appeared the IBRD-FAO mission report.[4] The mission was asked to analyze agricultural problems and policies and "in consultation with the Government of Chile, to arrive at recommendations for a broad program of agricultural development . . . directed primarily at a program for the next five to seven years."

This statement meant that the mission's time horizon, from the point of view of water resource planning, would be brief indeed and would automatically exclude certain methods of analysis. The IBRD-FAO team concluded that agricultural output should increase and was capable of being increased by 3.12 per cent per year during the eight-year period of 1952-60. This rate of increase was designed to offset an estimated growth in population of 23 per cent during the corresponding period coupled with an increased per capita income of 18 per cent.

[4] Joint Mission of the International Bank for Reconstruction and Development and the Food and Agriculture Organization of the United Nations (hereinafter referred to as IBRD-FAO), *The Agricultural Economy of Chile* (Washington: 1952). The mission consisted of Egbert de Vries, Chief; Paul F. Craig-Martin, Agricultural Economist; Grace W. Finne, Transport Economist; Paul H. Hohl, Agricultural Engineer; and Norman McLeod, Civil Engineer. The mission acknowledged the assistance of E. I. Kotok and other FAO technicians, unnamed, and Paul T. Ellsworth. Although its cognizance of water was largely limited to assertions regarding the necessity of irrigation in semi-arid and arid regions, this report laid the foundation for other reports and plans more directly related to water resource planning. However, since the IBRD-FAO mission strongly influenced subsequent plans for agriculture and since the largest single use of Chile's water is in irrigation, the report's relevance goes far beyond the attention explicitly given to water resources.

The IBRD-FAO report made two notable contributions to water resource planning in Chile. First, the goals it set for Chilean agriculture have continued to influence plans made by the Chilean government up to the present; second, the way in which it approached irrigation plans and requirements was followed by all subsequent planning reports of the Chilean government and international agencies.

As events turned out, only the population increase was realized. The growth of national income was less than had been assumed; measured by per capita gross product it rose by only 7 per cent. And, as already shown, agricultural output in 1962 was no higher than the figure for 1950. Had the changes projected by the IBRD-FAO team been realized, imports of foodstuffs would have fallen to the level of the forties. As it was, annual agricultural imports in 1954 and 1955[5] were double the level of the annual average for the period 1940-44, measured in constant prices. In 1955, agricultural imports were $109 million; in 1960, $110 million.[6] A high rate of importation has persisted to the present. In July 1965, restrictions were imposed on the consumption of beef in order to reduce the drain on foreign exchange and stimulate the consumption of pork, poultry, and, especially, fish.

PATTERN OF LAND USE

Far more changeable than the agricultural economy is the state of information regarding agricultural resources. *La Agricultura Chilena* for the period 1951-55 shows the total of land in Classes I-IV (i.e., land fit for cultivation) in the province of Antofagasta as 1,000 hectares.[7] The same figure is repeated in the CEPAL report as the total amount of "irrigable land that requires irrigation."[8] In both documents the amount of land *actually irrigated* is also shown as 1,000 hectares. On the other hand, an FAO report[9] in a table listing projects under construction and projects under study, included projects designed to *improve* the irrigation of some 3,000 hectares and to provide for the *new* irrigation of some 2,100 hectares.

Of more importance than the quantity of land in Antofagasta is the amount of arable and irrigable land in the country as a whole. The first quinquennial report[10] indicated that land in Classes I-IV amounted to 11,079,000 hectares, almost double the estimate of 6.2 million hectares that had been made during the 1940's. CEPAL adopted the estimate of 11 million hectares in Classes I-IV and concluded that of this amount 7,163,000 hectares constituted "irrigable land that needs irrigation," i.e., all land in and to the north of the province of Cautín in Classes I-II and

[5] CEPAL, p. 69.
[6] *La Agricultura Chilena en el Quinquenio 1956-1960* (Santiago: Ministerio de Agricultura, 1963), Table 181, after p. 212. According to unofficial statements, food imports in 1965 were expected to reach $150 million.
[7] *La Agricultura Chilena en el Quinquenio 1951-1955* (1957), Cuadro Anexo No. 3, between pp. 24 and 25.
[8] CEPAL, *op. cit.*
[9] Jean Pourtauborde, *El Riego en Chile*, Report No. 1622 (Rome: Food and Agriculture Organization of the United Nations, November 1962), pp. 61-62.
[10] *La Agricultura Chilena . . . 1951-1955*, p. 24 and note to Graph 3.

II-III and 60 per cent of the land in Classes III-IV.[11] Pourtauborde's report, which was published by FAO about two years after the CEPAL study, stated that of the 30 million hectares that made up Chile's agricultural area 20 million hectares "ought to be irrigated."[12] Pourtauborde apparently reached the figure of 30 million hectares for Chile's "agricultural area" by adding 20 million hectares of land of Classes V and VI, temporary or permanent pasture, to the total of 11 million hectares in Classes I-IV.[13] How he reached the estimate of 20 million hectares that "ought to be irrigated" cannot be ascertained.

Between 1955 and 1960, the period covered by the second quinquennial report[14] land in Classes I-VI shrank from 30,888,000 hectares to 21,637,060 hectares.

Measurements of "arable land," apparently were as unsettled as the measurement of "agricultural land." In the first quinquennial report arable land—i.e., the sum of Classes I, II, and III—was given as 6,924,000 hectares, whereas the agricultural census showed only 5,514,000 hectares. Commenting on this difference, the report said:

"This area (i.e., arable area) is included in the soils classified in Classes I and II and III in the general scheme already seen, that is to say, those cultivable without or with light limitations and which amount to 6,924,000 hectares. Since the statistical sample of the Censo Agropecuario of 1955 indicates only 5,514,000 hectares as current arable area, one can say that there exists a margin of 1,410,000 hectares that can be immediately brought into cultivation within Class II and III whose only limitation consists of the need for a longer (period of) rotation with emphasis on artificial pasture. This margin of increase of arable area amounts to an increase of 25.6 per cent over the area now under cultivation."[15]

By the time of the second quinquennial report the census figure of 5.5 million hectares had won out and there was no further talk of 26 per cent margin for expansion.

None of the foregoing figures are confirmed by the Instituto de Investigaciones de Recursos Naturales, which has been tabulating data gathered by air photogrammetric survey.[16]

The photogrammetric survey indicates that the total amount of land in Classes I-IV, whether dry or irrigated, is no more than 4.6 million acres,

[11] CEPAL, p. 69.   [12] Pourtauborde, p. 3.
[13] See *La Agricultura Chilena . . . 1951-1955*, pp. 21-23, and CEPAL, p. 68, for definition of land classes.
[14] *La Agricultura Chilena . . . 1956-1960*, p. 26.
[15] *Ibid.*, p. 28 (my translation).
[16] Tables released in 1965. Unfortunately, the survey excludes the two northernmost and two southernmost provinces.

instead of the 11.1 million reported in the 1951-55 quinquennial report. Even if one adjusts for land that is in the two northernmost and two southernmost provinces, using the figures from the quinquennial report, no more than 230,000 hectares can be added.

Within the past decade irrigated land has been censused; estimates have been made by the Corporación de Fomento de la Producción (CORFO) and the Dirección de Riego; one independent investigator in the Ministerio de Obras Públicas has made his own estimate; and, most recently, the land has been mapped and photographed from the air. Between the highest and lowest quantity of "irrigated land" is a spread of 270,000 hectares. (See Table 7.) The same effect would be achieved by occasionally misplacing the province of Santiago.

Table 7

AMOUNT OF IRRIGATED LAND ACCORDING TO VARIOUS SOURCES

(*Hectares*)

First quinquennial report	1,362,800
CORFO (unpublished)	1,375,900
Second quinquennial report	
(1) according to Dirección de Riego and CORFO (1960)	1,366,100
(2) according to 1955 agricultural census	1,097,900
Basso [a]	1,260,000
Instituto de Investigaciones de Recursos Naturales [b]	
"irrigated"	1,212,601
"contingent irrigation"	700,594

[a] Eduardo Basso S., *Inventario de Recursos Hidrológicos Superficiales de Chile* (Santiago: Ministerio de Obras Públicas, May 1963), p. 34.
[b] Data from tables released by Instituto de Investigaciones de Recursos Naturales.

The probable explanation for the low figure revealed by the census is in underreporting by the farmers themselves; the high figures of CORFO and Riego are probably explained by their use of design area rather than area actually developed for irrigation. There is also the likelihood that one agency may include all area under a ditch as "irrigated land" whereas another may ignore land that is irrigated infrequently.

As already noted, the air photogrammetric survey throws into doubt previous estimates regarding total arable area and all estimates except Basso's regarding the area that can be described as "irrigated." Even more disconcerting than corrections being made in the global figures are changes in figures for particular provinces. According to the first and second quinquennial reports, the irrigated area of Maule is 40,000 hectares.

An unpublished table prepared by CORFO gives the figures as 4,000 hectares. The Institute's tables show 540 hectares "irrigated" and 3,116.3 hectares as capable of "contingent irrigation" (*riego eventual*).[17]

Another instance is the province of Cautín. The first and second quinquennial reports show 32,000 hectares irrigated. A special report on irrigation projects prepared by Jorge Chavez S., Ing. (chief of Studies Section, Departamento de Obras Públicas, CORFO),[18] lists three projects in Cautín Province that were completed between the years 1944 and 1959 with a design area of 35,700 hectares of which only 7,913 hectares were effectively irrigated. The photogrammetric survey shows 4,016 hectares now irrigated and 79,663 hectares as *riego eventual*. There is no way of reconciling the difference between the Chavez figure and the photogrammetric figure of land irrigated. Both presumably measure exactly the same thing—land under effective irrigation at present. If anything, the photogrammetric figure should be larger, since Sr. Chavez' figure of 7,913 hectares relates only to three Ministerio de Obras Públicas projects, ignoring all others.

Comparable uncertainty affects other characteristics of land use. Both quinquennial reports contain a table showing the distribution of arable

Table 8

DISTRIBUTION OF ARABLE LAND BY TYPE OF CROP, 1955

(*Hectares*)

Type of crop	First quin. report	Second quin. report
Annual crops (grains, beans, vegetables, potatoes, industrial crops)	1,326,800	1,300,700
Vineyards	108,100	96,800
Fruits	45,700	83,200
Cultivated pasture	454,000	487,400
Natural pasture	2,998,300	2,909,900
Fallow	590,000	665,400
Total	5,522,900	5,543,400

Source: *La Agricultura Chilena*, for 1951-55 and 1956-60.

[17] The definitions adopted by the air photogrammetric project are as follows: "Irrigated land" (Classes Ir-IVr, inclusive) consists of land in the descending order of quality from Class I through Class IV that is assured of water 85 per cent of the time and in the years of deficiency has at least 70 per cent of its supply. "Contingent irrigation" (*riego eventual*), shown as mixed classes, e.g. IIr-II, consists of two kinds of land: (1) land under a canal that because of unfavorable micro-relief is not irrigated; (2) land that lacks a security of water supply equal to that of "irrigated land."
[18] Chavez, *Informe Preliminar* (Santiago: CORFO, Oct. 7, 1963).

land by type of crop for the same year, 1955, but with different figures. (See Table 8.) The differences may reflect changes in classification more than in count. It is possible that part of the difficulty originates in self-censusing, and either because of unfamiliarity with the classification scheme or a desire to underreport certain types of land use, the census loses accuracy. A new agricultural census is under way.

Within the intercensal period of 1955-65, CORFO[19] made estimates of arable land among different crops. There presumably have been no significant changes since 1955, as is shown by the figures for 1962-63:

	(Hectares)
Annual crops	1,584,600
Vineyards and fruits	173,500
Cultivated and natural pasture and fallow	3,777,700
Total	5,535,800

Regardless of the uncertainty of the total amount of arable land and its pattern of use, one conclusion seems reasonably credible; a large fraction of arable land is used for pasture or is fallow and the area devoted to high-value crops—fruits, vegetables, and vineyards—is relatively small, amounting to about 250,000 hectares.

The low intensity of land use in Chile is even more striking when we consider land under irrigation (see Table 9).[20] More than half of all irrigated land is devoted to pasture; a significant amount is devoted to a use only slightly more rewarding, namely, wheat.[21]

Table 9

DISTRIBUTION OF IRRIGATED LAND BY MAJOR USE, 1959-60

(Hectares)

Annuals (except vegetables)		489,187
Vegetables		63,650
Vineyards		48,300
Fruits and olives		57,600
Pasture, total		730,847
Cultivated	328,210	
Natural	402,637	
Total		1,389,584

Source: CORFO, unpublished data.

[19] Unpublished.

[20] Total irrigated area given by CORFO implies that some of the land irrigated in 1959 came from the 700,000 hectares classified as "contingent irrigation" by the air photogrammetric project.

[21] See Chapter IV for discussion of water use.

LAND OWNERSHIP: SIZES OF FARMS

The relatively large amount of land used for natural pasture probably represents a dubious use of water as well as land. Apparently a combination of circumstances that include uncertainty of water supply; scarcity of skilled labor, capital, and marketing facilities; and conditions of land tenure keeps land out of cultivation. A study of land tenure reveals a direct correlation between the size of the farm unit and the percentage of its arable land devoted to natural pasture. According to the Comité Interamericano de Desarrollo Agrícola (CIDA), a combination of several international agencies, the "subfamiliar" (very small unit) allocated 29.2 per cent of its arable land to natural pasture, while the large multifamily unit allocated 46.8 per cent.[22]

The significance of CIDA's findings is somewhat obscured by the studies of the Ministerio de Agricultura which find the following percentages when farms are classified by size of total irrigated areas:

Size Class of Irrigated Area (*hectares*)[23]	Per Cent in Natural Pasture
1-5	29.3
5-9	28.0
10-15	19.7
15-30	19.0
30-50	19.0
50-100	20.0
100-200	17.5
200-500	22.5

Information on the distribution of farm land among units of various sizes is given in Table 10. Total irrigated land is underestimated and total arable land is overestimated in comparison with results of the air photogrammetric survey, but the relationships are not likely to be seriously in error.

The concentration of ownership of land under irrigation is somewhat less than the concentration of ownership of land in farms and somewhat more than the concentration of ownership of arable land. For example, 36 per cent of farm units have less than 100 hectares of total land area, and account for 7.4 per cent of total land in farms, 16.7 per cent of irrigated land, and 20.9 per cent of "arable" land. These figures do not reveal how ownership of unirrigated land in Classes I-IV is distributed, nor what

[22] CIDA, "Estudio Sobre la Tenencia de la Tierra en Chile" (Santiago; preliminary draft, 1964), p. 113.

[23] *La Agricultura Chilena . . . 1956-1960*, pp. 50-51.

Table 10

SIZE CLASS OF FARMS AND LAND USE

Size class of farm	Number of farms	Average area in farm	Average agricultural area in farm	Average arable area in farm	Average irrigated area in farm
		(———————————————— Hectares ————————————————)			
Less than 1 ha.	28,246	0.3	0.2	0.2	0.1
1- 9.9 ha.	47,381	4.4	3.9	3.0	0.9
10- 99.9 ha.	53,766	34.1	30.8	18.7	2.6
100- 499.9 ha.	15,240	214.2	195.8	101.7	21.8
500- 999.9 ha.	3,076	683.1	624.8	250.6	58.5
1,000-4,999.9 ha.	2,554	2,009.1	1,771.2	539.7	105.1
5,000 and up ha.	696	21,788.3	14,884.0	982.9	191.4
Country as a whole	150,959	183.6	143.2	36.7	7.3
Aggregates	150,959	27,712,308.9	21,637,060.8	5,543,380.7	1,097,984.9
		(———————————————— Per cent ————————————————)			
Per cent of total area in farms		100	78.1	20.0	4.0

Source: La Agricultura Chilena . . . 1956-1960, p. 27.

would be the distribution of ownership that would result from bringing new land under irrigation.

The amount of land under irrigation in the largest size class averages about 191 hectares in farms that average about 22,000 hectares in size. These are dimensions roughly equivalent to the large western United States cattle ranch owned by husband and wife, each of whom is entitled to irrigate 160 acres of land with water supplied by a federal irrigation project. As in the United States, the largest land holdings tend to be cattle or sheep ranches; and as indicated by the relationships between the amount of land in the farm (21,788 hectares) and arable land in the farm (983 hectares), the largest holdings are spread over land of low agricultural productivity.

Type of management and proportion of irrigated area devoted to crops are related to the distribution of land by size of unit. On farms operated by the owner, only 24 per cent of irrigated land is not in crops; where owner and operator share control, 30 per cent is not in crops; on absentee-owned farms managed by a salaried administrator, the percentage is 43.[24] CIDA also found an inverse correlation between size of farm unit and value of output per hectare and a direct correlation between size of farm unit and value of output per worker. The figures are given in Table 11. Insofar as there seems to be a relatively large amount of unemployed and underemployed labor in the country, so that labor is not a constraint, these figures indicate that total agricultural output would fall with consolidation and rise with diffusion of land holdings, other things being equal. The critical point, however, is under what circumstances the desired changes in "other things" can be most easily accomplished.

Sample studies of farm income indicate that net income per hectare from artificial pasture is equal to or more than income from crops, but substantially less than income per hectare from vineyards. (Income comparisons between crops and artificial pasture on the one hand and fruits on the other, yield somewhat ambiguous results.) The sample studies also suggest that farms that engage in milk production along with other activities earn a higher rate of income per hectare than farms that do not.[25] Unfortunately, the studies are fragmentary and do not fully isolate the various factors that bear upon productivity. Perhaps the most striking conclusion is that for a country that is almost as famous for its fruits and wines as for its copper and nitrate, the area devoted to orchards and

[24] From a CEPAL-FAO report, *Analysis of Some Factors Inhibiting the Growth of Livestock and Livestock Products*, 1953, pp. 44-45. (Obtainable from U.N. Publications Service, New York.)

[25] *La Agricultura Chilena . . . 1956-1960*, pp. 49–58.

Table 11

CENTRAL CHILE: COMPARATIVE PRODUCTIVITY BY
SIZE OF FARM UNIT

(*1960 escudos*)

	Value of output in 1955	
Size of unit	Per irrigated hectare	Per farm worker
Subfamily	904	322
Family	453	506
Medium	454	776
Large	243	1,150
Total	283	835

Source: CIDA, *op. cit.*, p. 116.

vineyards is small, amounting to about 175,000 hectares, or only 2 per cent of its arable land.

OUTPUT PER HECTARE FOR THE COUNTRY

There still remains the question of how output per hectare in Chile for any given crop compares with output in other countries. Comparisons of this sort are relatively complex and cannot be made without carefully framing all conditions within which the comparison is made. An attempt at constructing a summary comparison was made by M. I. Kendall[26] and adapted by Stamp for international use. The technique yields a ranking of countries according to yield per hectare. Out of the twenty countries studied by Stamp, Chile ranked as follows for the year 1946:

Wheat	11th
Rye	12th
Barley	8th
Oats	14th
Corn	11th
Potatoes	11th
Sugar beets	no data
Beans	11th
Peas	14th

For all nine crops taken together, using Kendall's ranking coefficient, Chile was in thirteenth place, followed by China, Argentina, Australia, and India, and preceded (from the top of the list downward) by Belgium,

[26] Quoted in L. Dudley Stamp, *Our Undeveloped World* (London: Faber & Faber, 1953), p. 92.

Denmark, Netherlands, Germany, Britain, Ireland, New Zealand, Egypt, Austria, France, Japan, Italy, United States, Canada, and Spain.

Stamp supplied production data for Chile that could be compared with other countries for only one specific crop: oats. In 1951 the yield in Chile was 0.87 metric tons per hectare. The world average was 1.39; the highest reported was 3.09 (Denmark) and the lowest was 0.43 (Roumania). Stamp's data reveal, moreover, that in 1951, for the twenty-two countries compared, Chile ranked next to last (Roumania being last) in productivity per hectare, whereas in 1945-47 there were six countries with lower productivity than Chile's, and in 1934-38 there were nine. Yield per hectare declined in Chile from 1.01 metric tons per hectare in 1934-48 to 0.87 metric tons per hectare in 1951, while the world average moved from 1.19 metric tons to 1.39 metric tons.

If we compare Chile's yields for the year 1950-51 in tons per hectare, as reported by the second quinquennial report, with world average yields as given by Stamp[27] we have the following:

Crop	Chile	World Average
	1950-51	1951
	(tons per hectare)	
Wheat	1.15	1.15
Corn	1.43	1.58
Rice	1.72	1.62
Barley	1.56	1.26
Oats	0.91	1.39
Rye	0.58	1.35
Sugar beets		
(1953-54)	15.26	24.8
(1959-60)	28.02	

These figures indicate that Chile's output per hectare, for 1950-51, exceeded the world average for rice and barley, equalled the world average for wheat, and fell below the world average, in some cases by substantial proportions, for corn, oats, rye, and sugar beets. The Chilean figures for sugar beets are for 1953-54, the first year of record. Since the crop was introduced only in that year perhaps a comparison is not meaningful. Yield in 1959-60 amounted to 28.02 tons, somewhat above the world average.

[27] Derived from FAO, *Yearbook of Food and Agricultural Statistics: Production*, Vol. VI, Part 1 (Rome, 1952).

The comparisons among yields conceal the varying proportions of total output, inside as well as outside Chile, that are produced on irrigated land and dry land, the relative productivity of which varies substantially.

What is the significance of knowing that in Chile the average output of wheat per hectare is about the same as that of the United States, when in Chile, according to one source,[28] about one-third of wheat land (1959-60) is irrigated, whereas in the United States very little is?

Statistics on productivity generally suffer from such deficiency of detail that most comparisons cannot readily be interpreted. For example, figures on comparative productivity per hectare (Table 11) fail to indicate that the large unit is usually a livestock enterprise, whereas the productivity of smaller units reflects another type of agriculture. Without additional information one cannot infer that the large unit is relatively "unproductive," since the "low" productivity per hectare probably reflects dedication of irrigated land to production of cattle feed—a use that if not supplied would make impossible the exploitation of large areas of unirrigated grazing land. Questions of "efficiency of land use," moreover, cannot be examined independently of "efficiency" in the use of labor and capital. The figures reveal that while the output per unit of land varies inversely with size of unit, the opposite is true per unit of labor. No information is supplied regarding output per unit of investment.

[28] CORFO, "Programa de Desarrollo Agrícola" (Santiago, processed).

IV

THE USE OF WATER FOR IRRIGATION

The main conclusions reached by investigators of Chilean irrigation are that water is used with a prodigality that can only mean great waste. Principal and secondary works are inadequate, antiquated, frequently in poor condition, easily damaged by moving water, clogged with weeds, and lined with thirsty trees. In many cases the land is not prepared for irrigation; the technique of irrigation commonly used—inundation—is extremely wasteful; and there is little knowledge of current rates of water use let alone optimum water requirements. The network of canals reflects haphazard development over decades, maybe centuries: long, parallel canals inhibit movement of men, animals, and machinery, as well as waste large quantities of water. Irrigating by turns, whereby ditches are alternately dried and wetted, and a "turn" may mean two hours every ten days, inhibits delivery of water rightfully claimed by the irrigator. Irrigating only during the day coupled with absence of nighttime storage allows water to run unused to the sea.

The degree to which the faults of Chilean land use—i.e., the extensive use of natural pasture and fallow fields rather than cultivation of crops, feeds, fruits, and vineyards—are a reflection of poor use of water, and the degree to which poor use of water reflects problems facing agriculture in general, are questions that demand investigation before a rational water resource policy can be developed. These questions, in turn, cannot be investigated without the acquisition of considerable information and analysis at both the technical and budgetary levels of farm operation. In the absence of such data, conclusions are largely inferential, based upon scattered bits of information.

The 1952 IBRD-FAO report, in passages that have lost none of their relevance, described Chilean irrigation as follows:

. . . Most of the water comes directly from the rivers, whose flow is not regulated in any way. Thus coarse silt, gravel and even small boulders cannot be

43

prevented from entering the canals. When floods occur, the head of the canal may be washed away and irrigation interrupted. Most canals are not protected against erosion and the water level decreases gradually; difficulties experienced in serving the fringes of the irrigated zone increase . . . many small canals of great length were built by individual owners or small groups with consequent unnecessary losses of water. Further lack of attention to irrigation during the night and weekends, except in the North where water is so precious that storage tanks are being built, causes additional losses. In the Central Valley fields with excessive applications of water (even to the point where crops suffer) alternate with others which get water only in a haphazard way.

. . . A conservative estimate puts the loss of water, i.e., the possibility of increasing the area under crops or artificial pasture, at 20 per cent. In some places qualified observers put the loss at 40 per cent. The main trouble is unequal application of the water over the fields due to failure to divide the fields into compartments; yields are depressed and where the flow of water is rapid, erosion threatens.

. . . Improved use of irrigation water is largely a matter of giving information to the farmers . . . in a number of cases, additional investments of a public character will be needed . . . underutilization (of land) is mainly a problem of the large farms and is found to a large degree on irrigated land. The mission found bad farm management by the owner, or more often by the mayordomo in his absence, among the reasons for the large percentage of irrigable land lying fallow in the Central Valley. . . . On the peasant holdings land use is already rather intensive.[1]

Somewhat surprisingly, in view of the poor state of many existing facilities and the low level of efficiency in the use of water, the mission recommended "early completion of the [irrigation] works under construction as the best available means to provide for the larger part of the desired new cultivable land and the construction of two additional schemes before 1960."[2] The total proposed irrigated acreage would provide 283,000 new irrigated hectares. In addition, the mission recommended drainage of about 300,000 hectares of non-irrigated land for pasture and truck farming. These recommendations, along with increased productivity of agriculture in general were intended to raise output by 38.5 per cent during the period 1952-60.

The mission dealt with many other aspects of farm management: fertilizers, equipment, credit, marketing, transportation, and so forth. In the mission's collective mind, ". . . the importance of irrigation in Chile has been stressed throughout this report."[3] In spite of such stress, however, the treatment of irrigation was somewhat casual. At no point did the report assess the relative merit of allocating available funds to the improvement of existing irrigation systems instead of building new ones, or to increasing the land under cultivation within a given system by in-

---

[1] *The Agricultural Economy of Chile*, pp. 176ff.   [2] *Ibid.*, p. 182.
[3] *Ibid.*, p. 278.

creasing the efficiency of water use. One cannot ascertain from the report the degree to which improper land use is a property of land *per se*, or a property of the availability of water, and if the latter, the ways in which its improvement would automatically be reflected in better land use.

A later study on irrigation by Bell[4] made the following recommendations:

1) Improved control and soil conservation practices, restriction of grazing accompanied by practices designed to encourage natural beneficial vegetation; forestation to protect the watersheds; river bank and canal erosion control.

2) Increased storage of surface flow for irrigation and other uses such as hydroelectric power, fishing and recreation; provision of storage tanks to capture nocturnal flows.

3) Surveys to determine optimum locations of principal irrigation intakes along the river; rearrangement of canals in order to maximize the number of hectares served per unit of length of canal—for both supply and drainage canals, taking into account the reuse of irrigation water.

4) Better supervision of distribution of water—inspectors, measurements, etc. to ensure delivery of water according to ownership of rights; domestic production of devices to measure, control, and distribute water; measurement of water use; instruction in amount and timing of irrigation.

5) Acquisition of more complete information regarding present use and available supply of ground water.

6) Study of soils and capacity of land under irrigation or planned for irrigation; determination of crops best suited for different soils.

7) Substitution of ditch and furrow irrigation for inundation; substitution of spray irrigation for gravity flows where soil erosion threatens; transfer of water from poor lands to better lands.

8) Development of programs to awaken the interest of farmers in progressive methods, use of equipment, improved techniques of irrigation and education of workers; more adequate treatment of irrigation problems and techniques in the university curriculum.

9) Expansion of the collection of basic hydrologic and meteorologic data, behavior of soils under irrigation, and duty of water.

The report pointed out that many of its proposals dealt with matters about which the Departamento de Conservación de Recursos Agrícolas y

[4] Ralph M. Bell, *Irrigation and Methods of Irrigation*, Report No. 879 to the Government of Chile (Rome: Food and Agriculture Organization of the United Nations, 1958), pp. 8 ff.

Forestales and the Departamento de Extensión Agrícola were cognizant and at work.

Unlike the IBRD-FAO report, Bell dealt with "reforms" of current irrigation practices and emphasized the need for changes in techniques, better knowledge of adaptability of soils and crops, and the need for more complete information regarding water use. Bell issued a mild reproof to the authors of the earlier report for not insisting "as they should have on the need for giving greater importance to what happened with the water once it reached the farm,"[5] and pointed out that improved use of water could yield results that "could be spectacular" and could avoid some construction projects. The author emphasized the need for twenty-four-hour irrigation seven days a week, which would be possible with improved land preparation and irrigation by furrow instead of inundation. Bell estimated that in addition to losses in canals leading to the farms, losses on the farm were probably about 60 per cent. If such losses could be reduced from 60 to 40 per cent, the total of irrigated acreage could be increased by about 280,000 hectares. Furthermore, improved application of water could raise yields about 10 per cent according to a "conservative calculation."[6] To achieve this would require an educational program, more and better machinery, credit facilities, and technical supervision. Bell concluded that the existing water supply with better management would supply an increased output of 30 per cent from irrigated land. Up to now neither Bell's nor the IBRD-FAO recommendation has been followed.

MEASURES OF CURRENT WATER USE

According to the CEPAL report on Chilean water resources, the irrigation input of water exceeds norms derived from applying coefficients for California to the Blaney-Criddle formula[7] by amounts that range between 20 per cent and 106 per cent. Norms based on Chilean investigations are not available. Rates of water use and requirements for irrigation were computed for four river basins; these are listed below.[8] Unfortunately

---

[5] *Ibid.*, p. 16.   [6] *Ibid.*, p. 18.

[7] The procedure with the Blaney-Criddle formula is to correlate existing consumptive-use data for different crops with monthly temperature, percentage of daytime hours, precipitation, frost-free (growing) period, or irrigation season. The coefficients so developed are used to transpose the consumptive-use data for a given area to other areas for which only climatological data are available.

[8] CEPAL, p. 68.

they provide no detail regarding crops, size of farm, or other characteristics:

Basin	Current rates	Needs according to Blaney-Criddle formula	Per cent of use over needs
(Cubic meters per hectare per year)			
Río Elqui	14,200	11,850	20
Río Maule	21,200	10,300	106
Río Maipo	14,800	10,230	45
Río Itata	15,100	11,660	30

The authors point out that part of the excess water returns to the river by infiltration. They also repeat Bell's recommendation to measure flows in the canals, accumulate data on water use by type of crop and by zone, and conduct studies designed to fix optimum water requirements based on Chilean conditions.

A study written by Eduardo Basso S.[9] examined several estimates of water use by crop and broad region within Chile and in comparable regions abroad (mainly California, it appears). Wide differences among estimates are not explained. It is possible that in some cases the figures are observed measures of actual inputs, whereas in other cases they refer to requirements determined experimentally under idealized conditions. In some cases they may represent water requirements on the field, and in other cases, deliveries to the farm. The lack of data based on Chilean experience —whether observed on operating farms or experimentally determined under carefully controlled conditions—led Basso to base his efficiency norms on results collected in California. Out of a mass of conflicting statistics, Basso constructed a table that represented current use of water by region and crop, excluding the highest reported rates, since some level of improvement could be anticipated "without a change in the idiosyncrasy of the Chilean farm worker." He then compared these figures with "optimum rates of irrigation, according to North American investigations (translated to Chilean conditions)." Basso indicated that the "optimum rates" would not be realized without a "gradual campaign of education" of the farmer.[10] Thus, the first set of figures represents, roughly, a picture of what all except the most prodigal farmers are already achieving, whereas

[9] Basso, *Inventario de Recursos Hidrológicos Superficiales de Chile.*
[10] *Ibid.*, pp. 40-41.

the second set presumably represents a higher order of efficiency, but one that is reasonably attainable. The differences between the two sets of figures reveal a minimum practicable quantity of saving.

We can get a better idea of estimated waste by translating the unit values of Table 12 into aggregates. This is done in Table 13, using the irrigated areas and cropping patterns estimated for the country by CORFO for the year 1959-60.[11] Gross irrigation inputs for the country as a whole were estimated to be about 9.2 billion cubic meters for the year 1959-60. Of this total, Zone II[12] accounted for 7.1 billion cubic meters and Zone III accounted for 1.6 billion cubic meters.

We can also estimate the amount of additional land that could be irrigated in each zone if water were used efficiently, assuming the same cropping pattern were retained:

> Zone   I—13 per cent or   1,456 hectares
> Zone   II—45 per cent or 476,119 hectares
> Zone III—45 per cent or 115,079 hectares
> Zone IV—44 per cent or   28,208 hectares
>
> Total, four zones   620,862 hectares[13]

The potential total increase would raise the 1959-60 estimated irrigated area by about 45 per cent. These estimates do not take into account the fact that water is recovered for further use in areas in which it has been applied to excess. Therefore, the potential total increase in irrigated area with the same water supply is overstated.

In all of these estimates there is a large uncertain factor represented by ignorance of the degree of security that can be assigned to the water supply of each hectare. All estimates of current water use contain an implicit assumption: that the water is there. There is no way of knowing how well each farm fared in a given year.

The estimates of Table 13 support the suspicion that a relatively large amount of water is used for low-yield production. About 70 per cent of estimated water use went into pasture and about 14 per cent went into

[11] There are slight differences between the provinces that comprise the four zones of Table 13 and the provinces that comprise the regions to which Basso's coefficients apply, but these are of little consequence.

[12] Zone II consists of Atacama and all provinces to the south as far as and including Linares. Zone III consists of Maule, Ñuble, Concepción. Bío-Bío. Zone IV consists of the provinces from Cautín to and including Llanquihue.

[13] Some readers of the preliminary version of this report interpreted this figure as land that could be irrigated without additional irrigation works. Such an implication was not intended since much of the waste may be the result of inadequate storage and distribution systems or poorly located lands.

Table 12

IRRIGATION RATES CURRENTLY EXPERIENCED VS. OPTIMUM RATES

(Cubic meters per hectare per year)

Crop	Tarapacá and Antofagasta			Atacama to Coquimbo			Aconcagua to Linares			Ñuble to Malleco			South of Cautín		
	E	O	O/E	E	O	O/E	E	O	O/E	E	O	O/E	E	O	O/E
Pasture	11,000	10,500	95.5	10,500	10,500	100.0	9,000	5,700	63.3	8,500	5,500	64.7	7,400	5,500	74.3
Vegetables	9,300	6,000	64.5	9,000	7,500	83.3	6,200	5,000	80.6	6,000	4,500	75.0	6,000	4,000	66.7
Fruits	10,500	6,600	62.9	10,000	8,100	81.0	9,700	6,000	61.9	8,900	4,200	47.2	7,300	4,000	54.8
Cereals	3,000	3,000	100.0	3,000	3,000	100.0	2,800	2,300	82.1	2,300	2,300	100.0	1,800	1,800	100.0
Vineyards	–	–	–	10,000	10,000	100.0	9,700	9,700	100.0	–	–	–	–	–	–

E = experienced; O = optimum.

Note: "Optimum" is not explicitly defined by Basso but presumably refers to a physical optimum on the assumption that water of satisfactory quality is available.

To illustrate the range of data yielded by Chilean sources, see below the estimates made by Fco. Javier Domínguez, Ing., as cited by Basso. Domínguez' estimates are ranges or averages for a region without distinction by type of crop:

Tarapacá-Antofagasta..........13,000-17,500 m³/hectare/year.
Atacama-Coquimbo ....13,000-17,500 m³/hectare/year.
Aconcagua-Linares ....10,000 m³/hectare/year.
Ñuble-Malleco .... 6,000 m³/hectare/year.
Cautín-Llanquihue .... 4,000 m³/hectare/year.

For the three regions between Tarapacá and Linares, the figures of Javier Domínguez are greater than any of those accepted by Basso as reflecting current experience. There is no way of knowing whose figures come closer to reality. In view of the prodigality of water use reported by Pourtauborde, Bell, and CEPAL, Domínguez' estimates might be the better, in which case the present report substantially underestimates the potential total savings of water.

Source: Basso, *Inventario de Recursos Hidrológicos Superficiales de Chile*, p. 41.

Table 13
EXPERIENCED AND OPTIMUM WATER REQUIREMENTS
BASED ON 1959-60 IRRIGATED AREA

Crop	Irrigated area [a] (has.)	Unit water use (gross)		Total water use		"Waste": current-optimum $m^3/10^6/yr.$
		Current [b] $m^3/ha/yr.$	Optimum [b] $m^3/ha/yr.$	Current $m^3/10^6/yr.$	Optimum $m^3/10^6/yr.$	
Zone I						
Annuals	–	3,000	3,000	–	–	–
Vegetables	1,910	9,300	6,000	18	11	7
Fruits and olives	576	10,500	6,600	6	4	2
Vineyards	–	–	–	–	–	–
Pasture	8,714	11,000	10,500	96	91	5
Total	11,200			120	106	14
Zone II						
Annuals	386,137	2,800	2,300	1,081	888	193
Vegetables	46,464	6,200	5,000	288	232	56
Fruits and olives	38,070	9,700	6,000	369	228	141
Vineyards	46,851	9,700	9,700	454	454	0
Pasture	540,521	9,000	5,700	4,865	3,081	1,784
Total	1,058,043			7,057	4,883	2,174
Zone III						
Annuals	88,668	2,300	2,300	204	204	0
Vegetables	5,092	6,000	4,500	31	23	8
Fruits and olives	3,888	8,900	4,200	35	16	19
Vineyards	1,449	–	–	–	–	–
Pasture	156,634	8,500	5,500	1,331	861	470
Total	255,731			1,601	1,104	497
Zone IV						
Annuals	14,382	1,800	1,800	26	26	0
Vegetables	10,184	6,000	4,000	61	41	20
Fruits and olives	15,066	7,300	4,000	110	60	50
Vineyards	–	–	–	–	–	–
Pasture	24,478	7,400	5,500	181	135	46
Total	64,110			378	262	116
Total						
Annuals	489,187	–	–	1,311	1,118	193
Vegetables	63,650	–	–	398	307	91
Fruits and olives	57,600	–	–	520	308	212
Vineyards	48,300	–	–	454	454	0
Pasture	730,347	–	–	6,473	4,168	2,305
Total	1,389,084			9,156	6,355	2,801

[a] CORFO, unpublished.
[b] Basso, *Inventario de Recursos Hidrológicos Superficiales de Chile*, p. 41.

annuals. Of the latter, a significant fraction went into wheat.[14] Unfortunately, there is no way of isolating the yield from irrigated land from all land devoted to a particular crop. Table 14 shows the value of output per hectare by crop. The fact that irrigated land cannot be separated from dry land is especially serious for pasture, since total area devoted to pasture is 3.2 million hectares, whereas only 731,000 hectares were irrigated and undoubtedly have a higher yield than is indicated.[15]

Table 14

AVERAGE VALUE OF OUTPUT PER HECTARE,
SELECTED CROPS, 1959-60

Crop	Cultivated (1,000 ha.)	Aggregate market value (E° 1,000)	Market value per ha. (E°)
Wheat	887.6	79,643.4	89.7
Corn	74.7	11,876.1	159.0
Rice	40.0	9,124.6	228.1
Beans	93.2	21,674.6	232.6
Potatoes	86.3	50,550.2	585.7
Sugar beets	18.6	8,311.1	446.8
Vegetables, incl. onions and garlic	63.7	36,881.6	579.0
Sunflower	51.1	5,398.3	105.6
Tobacco	3.1	1,599.9	516.1
Fruits	57.6	38,207.3	663.3
Vineyards	98.0	52,922.8	540.0
Pasture (total)[a]	3,217.8	245,153.4	76.2

[a] Aggregate market value includes all animal and poultry products. Includes natural and artifical pasture but fails to account for feed that might be supplied by crops.
Source: La Agricultura Chilena . . . 1956-1960, pp. 60-78. Hectares of vegetables, fruit, and pasture taken from unpublished CORFO sources.

[14] In Zone II, for example, of 386,137 irrigated hectares devoted to annuals, 131,000 hectares were in wheat.
[15] Cultivated pasture supports 1.5 to 2 animal units per hectare per year, whereas natural pasture maintains only 0.5 animal units. Of the 731,000 hectares of irrigated pasture, 328,000 were cultivated and the remainder natural.

V

EXPERIENCE WITH
GOVERNMENT IRRIGATION PROJECTS

Virtually all new irrigation in Chile developed during the last fifty years has been in the form of public projects. The present Dirección de Riego has its antecedents in an agency created in 1914. According to CEPAL,[1] by the beginning of the present century about one million hectares of land had been put under irrigation by privately financed works, mostly in the form of canals and ditches. Works constructed by the State during the last fifty years have added 362,751 hectares.[2]

In the context of the present study, little need be said about the economic merit of private irrigation projects. Presumably most of them were justified in the eyes of the farmers who singly or in groups supplied the money, labor, and materials for their construction. Private projects are usually administered by an association whose members are owners of the land under irrigation and who possess rights to the use of water. Water rights, rights of way, equitable relations among association members, and legal powers of the association were established by a series of laws culminating in a water code (1951) which has had subsequent amendments and is now in the process of being completely overhauled.[3] Separate laws cover the powers and responsibilities of the Dirección de Riego and the procedures whereby public irrigation projects are selected and financed.

The present deficiencies of irrigated agriculture in Chile are in the main a reflection of the private projects, since they account for most of the irrigated land. Most major private works are at least fifty years old;

---

[1] CEPAL, p. 66.

[2] René Villarroel B., and Heinrich Horn F., *Rentabilidad de las Obras de Regadío en Explotación Construidas por el Estado* (Santiago: Ministerio de Obras Públicas, Dirección de Planeamiento, June 1963), p. 25. The figure given by Villarroel and Horn is the design area of all projects for which data are available. The major exclusion is the Canal San Carlos, in the vicinity of Santiago, which was built by the government over a period of many years before Dirección de Riego was created.

[3] See CEPAL and Villarroel and Horn for summaries of the laws regarding water.

52

many go back to Chile's colonial period. Some, of course, are well designed and efficiently managed. In particular instances the distinction between "public" and "private" has been lost, since the purpose of a number of public projects was to improve or expand existing private systems.

Chilean officials make no claim that all is well regarding the level of agricultural efficiency; the use of water by irrigators; and the selection, construction, maintenance, and administration of all governmental irrigation projects. Critical studies of separate irrigation projects have been made by Chilean experts and by foreign authorities on invitation of the Chilean government.[4]

Pourtauborde's study identified and described ten projects in the four northern provinces—Tarapacá, Antofagasta, Atacama, and Coquimbo—that were already in operation, four projects under construction, and nine projects under study. The following brief summary of his comments[5] illustrates the problems that are encountered:

Many of these projects are small. The Caritaya Reservoir irrigates 500 hectares. The irrigable area could be extended to 1,000 hectares if there were a "well cared for" network of canals and a supply of underground water of better quality than the mineralized surface waters now being used. The Canales Catiña, Pocoma, y Pachica, taking water from the Tarapacá are in such mediocre state that irrigation is "uncertain."

Among the larger projects is Lautaro Reservoir constructed in 1938, with a capacity of 40 million cubic meters, designed to improve the irrigation of 7,800 hectares, add 2,100 hectares, and provide 85 per cent certainty of water supply. The reservoir has failed to function as expected because the flow of the Copiapó was overestimated. Design flow was based upon data covering a period of six years. In the one period that the reservoir was full (1940-42), leaks were observed through the alluvium on which the dam rested. Although the stability of the dam was not affected this has turned out to be an irrelevant virtue since the dam has been dry 90 per cent of the time since its construction. Today it is virtually abandoned.

By another project the meadows near the city of La Serena were drained and a network of irrigation canals fed by the Elqui River were built. The land was then divided into relatively small farm units (*parcelas*) and distributed to new settlers. The project has faced a continuous deficit of water owing to the older rights possessed by other landholders. The project was quite imprudent, especially in view of the water requirements that had been incorporated into the initial plans—16,000 to 22,000 cubic meters per hectare (5¼-7¼ acre-feet of water per acre). Those who hold prior rights

[4] Such studies are: (1) Bell, *Irrigation and Methods of Irrigation* (FAO Report No. 879); Pourtauborde, *El Riego en Chile* (FAO Report No. 1622); Villarroel and Horn, *Rentabilidad;* Chavez, *Informe Preliminar* (CORFO).
I am grateful to Eugenio Lobo, División de Estudios, Dirección de Riego, for the generosity with which he made his time available and shared his knowledge of the problems of irrigation in Chile.
[5] *El Riego en Chile.*

apparently lay claim to excessive quantities of water. (Pourtauborde mentioned the quantity of 32,000 cubic meters per hectare rather off-handedly —the equivalent of 10½ acre-feet per acre.) Apparently not all this water is used by the title holders; but those without legal rights cannot use it either. The project could be successful if (1) the flow of Elqui were regulated and (2) the water were distributed strictly on the basis of physical needs.

The "preliminary report" of Sr. Chavez[6] dealt with a different problem: the failure of a project to be completed after the principal works have been built. In their present unfinished state these presumably are projects that augment the supply of irrigable land at relatively low marginal costs. He examined twelve projects whose design area amounted to about 100,000 hectares, in order to ascertain why the secondary and on-the-farm elements had never been completed. The main works of nine had been finished at various dates extending back to 1944. Three were still under construction. Of the nine, 35 per cent of the design area was being irrigated, on the average. One project, for which the major works had been completed in 1944, had reached 31 per cent. Another, completed in 1959, had reached 6 per cent. One project had reached 72 per cent development, the highest of the twelve. Eleven were canals and one was a reservoir. The reservoir had been finished in 1953, but only 43 per cent of the planned area was under irrigation in 1963. In contrast with Pourtauborde's report, which dealt with the north, Chavez' report was limited to projects in the southern part of the Central Valley.

Among the three works still in progress, all were canals. One had been started ten years before the date of the study, and had reached 4 per cent of planned development. Another had been started three years before, but had not yet served new land. The third had been under way eight years and served 33 per cent of the planned area. CORFO tried to ascertain by questionnaire the reasons why complementary facilities had not been built along with the mother canals and why there had been such undue delay in completion of the three works still under way. Responses to the questionnaires yielded the following answers:

"economic" (farmers' lack of funds)	52%
lack of technical advice	48%
poor distribution of water	33%
lack of secondary canals	57%
inadequate rate (allowed?) of irrigation	3%
works are under construction	3%
poor quality of land	5%
lack of land preparation	16%

[6] *Informe Preliminar* (CORFO).

Since some of the categories are not mutually exclusive—e.g., lack of secondary canals and land preparation may be attributable to lack of economic resources—the responses yield a somewhat fuzzy picture. Nonetheless, the first four reasons are reasonably clear.

The responses from proprietors of farms dependent upon the three principal works still under construction were limited to two reasons:

"economic" (farmers' lack of funds) 59%
lack of technical assistance 65%

Chavez made the parenthetical observation that in addition to the data collected by the questionnaire, it was evident that appropriate techniques of irrigated agriculture either were little known or ignored in "almost all" of the works that were visited. This suggested to him the need for further investigation of the relationship between the small difference in yields between irrigated and dry land in the zones studied and the incentive to invest in irrigation works.

In commenting on various specific projects Sr. Chavez made the following additional observations:

1) Canal Allipén suffered from a poor distribution of water because the secondary and tertiary canals had been poorly placed when the land was still mostly forest. The more the land was cleared the more obvious it became that the canals were in the wrong places. Furthermore, for most of the project area the soils are thin.

2) Canal Duqueco Cuel is in the final stages of completion but delays in bringing the land under cultivation are already apparent. There are no plans for secondary canals, and future irrigators are largely ignorant of their respective areas and assigned shares of water. The Ministry of Public Works is constructing a new roll of irrigators since the one that exists was put together in a hurry and mingled the zone of Duqueco Cuel with that of Canal Laja.

3) Canal Bío-Bío Sur, second stage, Canal Quillaileo, and Canal Coreo, still under construction, all serve areas of poor soils.

4) Tutuvén Reservoir (43 per cent of design area is under irrigation) was completed in 1953. The project suffers from poor topography, making canals difficult and expensive to construct. Furthermore, the farmers of the zone, accustomed to sheep raising and vineyards, are apathetic to the advantages of irrigation. At least 25 per cent of the area is unirrigated solely because the farmers lack interest.

Chavez' "preliminary memorandum" of October 1963 had not, in 1965, been replaced by a definitive document. An official of Dirección de Riego indicated that when the final report appears it will be less critical and will show more land under irrigation. This opinion is not supported by the results of the air photogrammetric survey. I have already referred to the uncertainty over the extent of irrigated land in Maule Province. According to Chavez' report, Tutuvén now supplies water for the effective irrigation of 920 hectares out of a design area of 2,160 hectares. The air photogrammetric survey shows 540 hectares being irrigated in Maule Province, the region supplied by Tutuvén. In other words, less rather than more land is under irrigation than Sr. Chavez indicates. In Cautín Province the photogrammetric survey shows a total of 4,016 hectares as irrigated, whereas Sr. Chavez indicates a total of 7,913 hectares for three projects. If the air photogrammetric measurements are accurate, Sr. Chavez' preliminary evaluation has been too liberal rather than too restricted.

The severely critical study of Villarroel and Horn[7] is a disconcerting contribution to Chilean self-evaluation. The authors analyze forty-seven projects of Dirección de Riego that supply water to a new land equivalent of 362,751 hectares and account for more than 95 per cent of the area served by all projects built by the agency. All types of works are included: canals, reservoirs, drainage systems, and pumping facilities.

Each project was appraised on the basis of a comparison between the added output resulting from irrigation and the added costs of production —on-the-farm and project costs. Of a total of forty-seven projects, nineteen showed losses. Another seventeen experienced net yields on capital invested of less than 8 per cent. Since CORFO loans, on constant values, were considered by the authors to be at 8 per cent, earnings below this level were described as yielding less than the expected marginal yield on capital. Therefore, by varying degrees, thirty-six out of forty-seven projects failed to meet a test of economic efficiency.[8]

Projects that performed poorly were those for which yields were low rather than costs high. The authors concluded that poor performance was the result of a poor choice of crops, inept use of water, lack of technical assistance, and lack of necessary agricultural credit facilities.

The main criticism directed toward the Villarroel and Horn analysis by Dirección de Riego officials is that it underestimates additional productivity attributable to government projects. Since Villarroel and Horn did not have "before" and "after" data on production from land specifically a part of governmental projects, they estimated the effect of a project as equal to the output of an average irrigated hectare in the area minus the

---

[7] *Rentabilidad.*

[8] Allen V. Kneese of Resources for the Future, Inc., has commented that, "It might be a comfort to Chilean readers to know that most federal U.S. projects will not stand the test of a realistic rate of interest either."

output of an average dry hectare, based on the census of agriculture in each *comuna*. The effect of this measurement was twofold: (1) it overestimated output on unirrigated land because the authors' sample included land more favorably situated than the land that was put under irrigation; (2) it underestimated output on irrigated land because, by using the communal average, it failed to reflect the fact that irrigators on land served by government projects had a higher degree of security of water supply, and therefore a crop mix of higher value, than irrigators on non-project land. In other instances, the authors overestimated productivity by ignoring the fact that some projects were only modifications of existing irrigation systems and brought little if any new land under irrigation; yet the authors assigned to such projects the difference in output between irrigated and non-irrigated land.

It is difficult to evaluate the Villarroel and Horn study, in spite of the obvious weakness in the authors' method of analysis, because its results are partly corroborated by the investigation of Jorge Chavez and because there are no official (or unofficial) studies that make it possible to dispute the authors' conclusions.

If subsequent investigation should support the Villarroel and Horn conclusions, it is apparent that of the 362,751 hectares (new equivalent) served by public irrigation projects, about half, or 178,772 hectares, are within projects that cannot be justified by economic criteria. Total investment, i.e., capital costs plus the costs incurred by the State during the trial period of operation (*costos de explotación*), for all projects amounted to E°116 million (in 1962 escudos, which at the 1962 rate of exchange approximated $116 million), of which projects that could not be justified in economic terms amounted to E°70 million, or 60 per cent.

Because Villarroel and Horn computed investment costs per hectare on the basis of project design area, they underestimated costs by the ratio of design area to area actually under irrigation. On the basis of the Pourtauborde report on projects in the four northern provinces and of the Chavez report on projects in the southern part of the Central Valley, one can estimate that of a design area of 78,082 hectares only 35,403 hectares[9] are effectively irrigated. For these projects, therefore, the Villarroel and Horn costs per unit of land are approximately half the amount that they "actually" are. A modification of their computations, however, converts only two projects from "economic" to "uneconomic." All others whose costs would be raised were already classified as uneconomic.[10]

[9] A figure that is still too high, according to the air photogrammetric survey.

[10] According to Villarroel and Horn, an "economic" project is one for which the net increase in production (i.e., after netting out on-the-farm costs and current project costs) is equal to or more than 8 per cent of project investment.

It is possible that detailed studies of other regions would reveal additional differences between design area and area actually irrigated. The difference of about 200,000 hectares between the air photogrammetric survey's total of effectively irrigated land and the CORFO-Riego estimate based on design area of public projects plus land irrigated by private works suggests such a likelihood.

One scarcely knows what credibility can be attached to the conclusions of Villarroel and Horn regarding economic merit. So long as the best we can achieve is an opaque view of reality, there is a strong temptation to seize upon any "fact" and make the most of it. One should be reluctant in the present case to do so. On the other hand, past procedures in the selection of projects support their conclusions. First of all, then, one might question the criteria for project selection that are employed by Dirección de Riego. Second, one might question whether the criteria and priorities established by Riego are in fact followed.

Among the criteria used for the selection of projects has been the objective of stimulating the production of wheat and meat.[11] This meant emphasis on projects in the southern part of the Central Valley, the area with which Sr. Chavez was concerned. Furthermore, wheat and livestock production are relatively low-yield crops per hectare, even if reasonable levels of efficiency are attained in land and water use. In addition, the ranking of projects in order of desirability by Riego usually included engineering characteristics such as the quality of foundations and the ratio of earth moved to water impounded. There was no ranking on the basis of comprehensive benefit-cost ratios.[12]

The record shows that projects are usually under construction for many years, occasionally decades. We can infer that this reflects an obligation to distribute a relatively small budget among many claims for attention. On occasion procedures apparently are followed in letting contracts that result in an increase in costs beyond those originally contemplated. Special problems created by prolonged inflation, delay in payments to contractors, and delays in securing authorization of needed imports have raised costs. The professional staff of Dirección de Riego is far too small for the responsibilities thrust upon them, and there is a deficiency of basic data

[11] The next few paragraphs are based upon conversations with various people within the Chilean government and foreign technical aid missions.

[12] One should bear in mind, also, the possibility that decisions at higher levels than Riego may be subject to much the same political pressures in Chile as they are in the United States. Such considerations as benefits to special interest groups, the need to cope with local pockets of unemployment, and the need to distribute governmental largesse among many competing political units are not likely to be absent from the decision-making process in any government.

regarding hydrology, geology, soils, and other technical matters bearing upon the physical productivity of a project.

Table 15 indicates the rate at which new land has been brought under irrigation during the past four decades. The most productive period, if we exclude Embalse Laguna del Maule, was the decade ending in 1934, during which approximately 100,000 hectares (new equivalent) were added. In the thirty years that followed, another 116,000 hectares were added (about 3,000 hectares per year), plus controlling the flow out of Laguna del Maule, which added an approximately equal amount.

Table 15

NEW AND NEW-EQUIVALENT LAND PLACED UNDER
IRRIGATION BY DIRECCIÓN DE RIEGO, 1919-65

Year	Hectares	Year	Hectares
1919.......... 4,000		1950.......... 8,280	
1924.......... 500		51.......... 12,420	
25.......... –		52.......... –	
26.......... –		53.......... 17,745	
27.......... –		54.......... –	
28.......... –		55.......... 300	
29.......... –		56.......... 2,980	
1930..........63,600		57.......... –	
31..........22,250		58..........111,137	
32.......... 6,500		59.......... 2,400	
33.......... 400		1960.......... 1,909	
34.......... 5,500		61.......... 743	
35.......... 9,750		62.......... 2,600	
36.......... 0		63.......... 1,500	
37.......... 1,450		64.......... 18,000	
38.......... 0		65.......... 10,600	
39.......... 5,800			
1940.......... –			
41.......... –			
42.......... –			
43.......... –			
44.......... –			
45.......... –			
46..........10,862			
47..........10,560			
48.......... 160			
49.......... 8,500			

Sources: Villarroel and Horn, for years 1919-61. Hectarage is overstated for various years because (1) design area is used, (2) some projects modify existing projects. Michael Nelson, Chile-California Program, for 1962-65.

Plans of Dirección de Riego for the period 1965-73 call for putting about 425,000 hectares of new land under irrigation plus improving the water supply for 700,000 hectares. Should the Chile-California Program[13] proceed with full development of the Maule River basin, these figures would be augmented by 120,000 hectares of new land plus 150,000 with improved water supply. The consummation of such a program would not only mean that the average annual increase in irrigated land would surpass anything experienced in the past, but that by 1973 Chile would be irrigating all land in Classes I, II, III from Cautín to the north, plus all land now under irrigation. This reaches the limit of irrigation without terracing the mountains as the Incas once did.[14]

In view of the recent record, one cannot help but wonder how realistic are plans for putting some 90,000 hectares under irrigation each year[15] Even without the Chile-California project, the planned rate at which irrigated land would be augmented each year is 70,000 hectares. The government's basis for optimism rests on the expectation of finishing a number of projects that have been under construction or study for many years—amounting to some 1.2 million hectares,[16] exclusive of the Chile-California Program. In addition to questioning the capacity of the government to accomplish its projected rate of construction, one might question its wisdom in view of the uncertain state of information regarding land resources (a deficiency that the air photogrammetric project is intended to remedy) and water resources, including ground water. It seems hardly likely that this latter deficiency can be corrected between now and 1973 when one considers the short period of record for most rivers in Chile. According to the hydrologic report prepared by the Centro de Planeamiento of the University of Chile,[17] of the eighteen major rivers between the province of Cautín (the southern limit of irrigation) and the northern boundary of the country, twelve had a period of record that was thirteen years or less. The longest period of record, that of the Elqui River, was thirty-four years. The next longest, twenty-five years, was for the Rapel. Six rivers had a period of record less than ten years. If we assume that all rivers will be carefully gauged from now on, by 1973 thirteen will still have

[13] Program supported jointly by the state government of California and the U.S. AID Mission.
[14] Data on future plans taken from material prepared for the Chile-California Program by Michael Nelson, Economic Adviser in Regional Planning for the Program.
[15] 546,000 new hectares plus the "new equivalent" of the improved water supply to 850,000 hectares, counting 3 hectares improved as equal to one new, or, rounding, 840,000 new equivalent in nine years.
[16] CEPAL, p. 72.
[17] Fernán Ibáñez, Ricardo Harboe, and Juan Antonio Poblete, *Estudio de la Disponibilidad de Recursos Hidráulicos en Chile*, Publication No. 65-5/B (Santiago: Universidad de Chile, Centro de Planeamiento, 1965).

a period of record less than twenty-five years, and the average for all rivers of the country will rise from twelve to twenty-one years. Furthermore, existing measurements contain an unknown error by virtue of the fact that knowledge of ground water is severely limited, no record is kept of diversions into irrigation canals, and there are no measurements of return flow from irrigation diversions. There is also the pressure that is likely to develop against available water resources in the foreseeable future.[18]

A Note on the Significance of the State of Data

A lament over the state of data in Latin America is a stale recital of the commonplace. Why then be preoccupied with the obvious? The answer lies in the fact that what may be obvious to an insider appears inexplicable to an outsider. Chile's own experts are fully aware of the need for better information. Moreover, the Chilean engineer and scientist are not newcomers to the scene. They have themselves repeatedly pointed out the need for appropriate data collection and the uncertainties and risks that must be borne in the absence of reliable information.[19] Why, then, is it that a serious attack on the data problem has been begun only recently? A reasonable inference to be drawn from these conditions is that those responsible for making decisions have felt that the quality of decisions would not be materially enhanced if better information were available. This, in turn, implies that decisions have been based on criteria other than those that the economist and engineer consider relevant. If this inference is justified, another may follow hard upon its heels: namely, that economic and engineering studies serve to stimulate a dialogue among economists and engineers but have little connection with decisions made by those in authority. Recent interest in better data may signal a change.[20]

THE COSTS OF WATER

From the study *Rentabilidad*[21] we can extract an unexpected by-product. On the assumption of a fifty-year life (residual value zero), and an interest rate of 8 per cent, we can assume that the annual cost of water is approximately equal to 8.17 per cent of the capital cost of public works plus the charges for current operation and maintenance. (This assumes that all

[18] See Chaps. VI-IX.
[19] See Chapter VII for a discussion of paper presented by Raúl Saez to the Latin American Seminar on Electric Energy, 1962.
[20] The strength of the current movement toward more and better information will depend upon the insistence of the scientists and engineers themselves that data collection agencies are adequately staffed and follow appropriate procedures. For this to happen, at least according to one Chilean scientist, there will have to be a departure from the prevalent point of view that scientists do not occupy themselves with problems of census taking and other routine measurements.
[21] Villarroel and Horn.

costs are incurred in the first year, that depreciation is charged on a straight line basis, and interest is charged only on the unpaid balance. The appropriate life span of a structure such as a canal, when properly maintained, might be indefinite, but there is always a possibility of a shift in land use; hence, a fifty-year economic life is reasonable for both reservoirs and canals. There is also the question of whether additional capital on-the-farm costs should not be construed as a part of the "cost of water." These will be excluded, however, in order to compute the "cost of water delivered to the farm.")

For the current input of water per hectare, as already noted, there are conflicting estimates. For example, water requirements for vegetables (less than for pasture, fruits, and vineyards, but more than for cereals) given by Basso,[22] in cubic meters per hectare per year, are as follows:

Zone	m³/ha/yr
Tarapacá and Antofagasta	9,300
Atacama and Coquimbo	9,000
Aconcagua to Linares	6,200
Ñuble to Malleco	6,000
Cautín to Aysén	6,000

CEPAL[23] computed water needs by river basin, according to the Blaney-Criddle formula, weighted by crop, as follows:

Loa	7,500 m³/ha,
Elqui	11,850 m³/ha, including 35% loss in canals
Aconcagua	9,564 m³/ha, including 25% loss
Maipo and Mapocho	9,902 m³/ha, including 25% loss
Rapel	10,156 m³/ha, including 25% loss
Maule	10,230 m³/ha, including 25% loss
Itata	12,320 m³/ha, including 25% loss
Bío-Bío	10,438 m³/ha, including 25% loss

CEPAL also estimated current water use, apparently at the intake of the canal rather than at the point of delivery to the farm, for four basins, as follows:

Río Elqui	14,200 m³/ha
Maipo	21,200 m³/ha
Maule	14,800 m³/ha
Itata	15,100 m³/ha

[22] See Table 12. Since Basso's estimates of current use are conservative relative to other estimates such as Domínguez', the "true" cost of water might be lower.
[23] CEPAL, p. 68 for Elqui, Anexo III for the others.

These represent quantities that range between 20 and 106 per cent of required amounts, but include inevitable canal losses estimated at 25 per cent of farm requirements. In view of the frequently expressed opinion that water is used excessively by the average irrigator who possesses superior rights and has the water, we might assume that current use is 20 per cent above requirements as computed by formula. The estimated current rates of use on the farm (rounded) for the eight basins studied by CEPAL would therefore be:

Loa	9,000 m³/ha
Elqui	14,400 m³/ha
Aconcagua	12,000 m³/ha
Maipo-Mapocho	12,000 m³/ha
Rapel	12,000 m³/ha
Maule	12,000 m³/ha
Itata	14,400 m³/ha
Bío-Bío	12,000 m³/ha

Because of differences in elevation of irrigated lands and variations in microclimates of various stations, these figures do not correspond to what one would normally expect in going from north to south. We might just as well adopt a uniform value for all basins—say 12,000 cubic meters per hectare. This figure should err, if at all, on the low side of consumption. Conversion of annual 1962 escudo costs per hectare into 1962 U.S. dollars per acre-foot of annual supply (85 per cent security) yields the following:[24]

Reservoirs, weighted average, excluding Laguna del Maule (a natural lake requiring only regulation of the outlet) $5.93
Canals $4.30

If we assume that both reservoir and canals had to be built for a single project, the averages indicate that the annual equivalent capital cost of irrigation water has been on the order of $10.00 per acre-foot—a figure not unreasonably high in view of the fact that virtually all costs have been assigned to irrigation. The charges levied against farmers, however, have fallen far short of the costs.

Villarroel and Horn estimate that on-the-farm capital costs of water-distributing structures and land preparation fall between E°500 per hectare (at 1962 prices) in Tarapacá and Antofagasta (where all costs of land

[24] Conversions based on assumptions that 1 hectare used 12,000 m³ of water per year, or 4.4 acre-feet per acre, and that E°1.1 = $1.00. Annual costs were assumed to be equal to 8.17 per cent of capital costs. Projects consist of forty-seven projects, less Embalse del Maule, studied by Villarroel and Horn, *Rentabilidad* (see Table 3.2-2).

preparation must be incurred by new irrigated land, since in the absence of irrigation the land has virtually no use), and E°100 per hectare in the South, where only the water distributing facilities have to be added. The added cost in dollars per acre-foot range from $5.00 in the North to $1.00 in the South (at 1962 rates of exchange).

As has been indicated, Villarroel and Horn estimate capital costs per hectare on the basis of design area of the project, rather than actual area under irrigation. They therefore understate cost per hectare where less than the design area is actually under irrigation. Projects that have fallen short of design size in the four northern provinces have generally done so because of inadequate water supply and poor quality of soil. Caritaya Reservoir, designed to hold 42 million cubic meters, has never had more than 10 million.[25] Embalse Lautaro has been empty 90 per cent of the time. Recoleta Reservoir was built, only to find that the basin failed to supply enough water. A feeder canal was then constructed to supplement the water supply.[26] Cogotí Reservoir was designed for 12,000 hectares but has never had enough water for more than 4,650 hectares.[27] The water supply for Culimo Reservoir is 30 per cent less than anticipated.[28] Water yield was overestimated for the Casablanca Reservoir, as a consequence of which, the authors say, "utilization of the reservoir is low"[29]—but how low and by how many hectares the irrigated area falls below design area they do not say.

Since these projects in the North are unsatisfactory because of deficient water supply, it is reasonable to correct the cost per hectare by the factor: (design hectares)/(hectares actually irrigated). We can make this correction for five reservoirs. Costs rise from 50 to 150 per cent.

Cost of Water

Reservoir	Design cost	Cost based on estimated irrigated area
	(1962 US dollars per acre-foot)	
Caritaya	8	20
Lautaro	11	([30])
La Laguna	4	6
Recoleta	7	11
Cogotí	7	18

[25] Villarroel and Horn, p. 15.
[26] *Ibid.*, p. 16.
[27] Pourtauborde, p. 22.
[28] Villarroel and Horn, p. 16.
[29] *Ibid.*, p. 17.
[30] Lautaro has been dry most of the time.

The unsatisfactory projects in the South have their fault not in the deficiency of water supplied by the main structures, but by inadequate development of on-the-farm or other secondary structures. It does not seem reasonable, therefore, to adjust the "cost of water" to agree with the area actually under irrigation except, perhaps, for the Tutuvén Reservoir. Sr. Chavez points out that one reason for the failure of the Tutuvén to reach design size is the high cost of derived canals. It is of this area that he adds, however, that "25 per cent of the total area is not irrigated only because the farmers lack interest."[31] On the basis of design size, the cost of water would be about $7.50 per acre-foot. If we use the photogrammetric survey area, the cost would be five times greater.

It should also be noted that reservoirs built up to now are comparatively small. The largest—Cogotí—was designed to hold 150 million cubic meters, or about 120,000 acre-feet. Recoleta was designed for 100 million cubic meters, or about 80,000 acre-feet. Bullileo was designed for 50,000 acre-feet. The remaining seven are smaller.

There are, apparently, a number of reservoir sites that can retain much larger bodies of water. The dam now being built on the Rapel, for example, will provide a reservoir of 680 million cubic meters, and Paloma, designed to supplement Recoleta and Cogotí, was designed to hold 740 million cubic meters.

A possibility explored under the aegis of the Chile-California Program is a dam on the Maule River just before it spills into the Central Valley. Should the project be undertaken it will be the first truly multipurpose undertaking of the country as well as Chile's largest water resource project. According to a preliminary reconnaissance, the reservoir would hold 1,500 million cubic meters (twice the size of the largest now under construction) and have an installed capacity of 500,000 Kilowatts (100,000 Kilowatts more than the largest plant now under consideration). Should it be built with all costs of the dam assigned to power—which would, on the basis of very preliminary estimates, still make it a feasible power project—capital costs of the canals would be about E°500 per hectare (based on very rough estimates), or in the neighborhood of $1.25 per acre-foot of water per year (assuming 4 acre-feet of water per year per acre and the 1965 official exchange rate of E°4 = $1). Marginal costs of water for one of the major agricultural areas of the country are, therefore, estimated at still a relatively low level when financed on a multipurpose basis. The water resources of the Maule have received more attention recently than other basins because of the Chile-California Program. Whether other basins would reveal equal or better opportunities of water resource development if subjected to the same scrutiny is an interesting speculation.

[31] Chavez, p. 7.

PAYMENTS FOR WATER USE: ANALYSIS OF TEN SAMPLE IRRIGATION PROJECTS[32]

Three laws have controlled the construction and repayment of virtually all governmental irrigation projects: Law No. 4445 of 1928, Law No. 9662 of 1950, and Law No. 14536 of 1960.

Law No. 4445 of 1928: Salient provisions are as follows. The project must have the approval of 33 per cent of the irrigators potentially affected. After a trial period known as *explotación provisional* the works are turned over to an association of irrigators who begin repayment. Total debt charged irrigators cannot exceed 120 per cent of the original planned cost. Although the period of *explotación provisional* is supposed to be no more than three years, it can be extended; for most projects the period has been extended. During the first three years of the trial period the irrigators are assessed progressively larger amounts in order to cover administration costs. These assessments are $\frac{1}{2}$ per cent, 1 per cent, and $1\frac{1}{2}$ per cent, respectively, of the value of each irrigator's share, which is related to the cost of the project. (A share is a pro rata quantity of water based upon the amount of land to be irrigated.) After the third year the assessment remains at $1\frac{1}{2}$ per cent. Assessments are usually less than the costs of administration, the deficit being a subsidy by the government to the irrigators. Repayment is by level payments over thirty-six and a half years including a 5 per cent interest charge on the unpaid balance.

Law No. 9662 of 1950. Under Law No. 9662, irrigators are supposed to pay full monetary costs of the works and engineering studies as fixed when construction is completed. The period of preliminary administration is extended to four years; irrigators pay 1 per cent the first year, 2 per

---

[32] This section is a slightly condensed version of a report written by Manuel Agosín on the basis of a study of official records of the Dirección de Riego. The sample was intended to include all projects whose costs were E°3 million or more (1962 prices). For one—Chacabuco Canal—there were no data; for two others there was no repayment record because they had not yet been completed. The remaining eight projects were then supplemented by two others which, although not of large size, were the only ones completed under later legislation. The eight projects were Lautaro, Bullileo, Recoleta, and Cogotí reservoirs and Maule, Laja, Melado, and Recoleta canals. The two more recent projects are Quillón Canal and El Noviciado mechanical irrigation system. Cost data were taken from Villarroel and Horn. Repayment data came from records of Dirección de Riego. The information is, more accurately, not a record of repayment but of amounts charged the irrigators. Actual payments are about 75 per cent of amounts billed. (Interview with Luis Larroucau V., Ing., Head, Departamento de Explotación, Dirección de Riego.) All payments and costs were converted to 1962 escudos, a year in which the estimated parity rate was approximately E°1 = US$1.

cent the second year, and 3 per cent the third and fourth years. If there is any difference between payments and costs of administration, it is paid by irrigators together with and under the same conditions as the principal. The debt is repaid starting from the fifth year after the beginning of the preliminary administration period. The interest rate on the unpaid balance is 1 per cent the fifth year, 3 per cent the sixth year, and 5 per cent the seventh year and after. The amortization period is thirty years.

Law No. 14536 of 1960. This law introduced substantial changes. Investments and payments are to be readjusted annually by the wholesale price index published by Dirección de Estadística y Censos. It restored the limit of 120 per cent of the budgeted cost for the debt. The interest rate on the unpaid balance is 5 per cent and the amortization period is thirty years. Other conditions were not modified.

Most works, because of their long construction period, are affected by more than one law. There is no single criterion to follow in determining what law applies to a project whose construction period extends over two laws, but usually—especially when the work has been constructed under Laws No. 9662 and No. 14536—the investment is divided and each portion is reimbursed according to the law under which the investments were made. Sometimes a project is recontracted with the irrigators. In some cases when a unit was begun under Law No. 4445 and finished under Law No. 9662, so that parts could not be prorated to each law, applicable features were taken from both laws and fitted to meet the interest of the irrigators. Most of the works in the sample projects analyzed below are of this type.

Under Law No. 4445, the debt to be reimbursed was settled before the works were built, and repayment began after preliminary administration. Under Law No. 9662, the debt was set at the completion of the work and irrigators had to pay full money costs. In both cases, especially under the earlier law, inflation lightened substantially the weight of the fixed money debt. If the costs had been paid in full the year that irrigators began repayment, the state would have already lost a large amount. Table 16 shows the periods of construction and preliminary administration, and Table 17 compares costs incurred by the government and value of debts assumed by irrigators *the year reimbursement began,* in escudos of December 1962.[33]

[33] Cost figures present some irregularities: (1) for Recoleta Dam and Canal it was not possible to distinguish between construction and preliminary administration costs; (2) in many cases, preliminary administration costs include costs of complementary works, which should more accurately be considered as construction costs; (3) costs of project studies are not available.

Table 16
CONSTRUCTION AND PRELIMINARY ADMINISTRATION PERIODS

Project	Construction	Preliminary administration
Lautaro Reservoir	1929-46	1946-50
Bullileo Reservoir	1929-49	1949-53
Cogotí Reservoir	1928-46	1947-50
Laja Canal	1916-30	–
Maule Canal	1916-30	1931-50
Melado Canal	1916-32	1933-53
Recoleta Reservoir	1929-40	1940-50
Recoleta Feeding Canal	1942-49	1949-53
El Noviciado Mechanical Irrigation System	1953-55	1956-59
Quillón Canal	1951-59	1960-63

Charges to irrigators of works completed under Law No. 4445 covered only 36 per cent of their money costs. If these debts had been paid in full during the first year of repayment, because of inflation between the beginning of construction and the end of "preliminary administration," only 6 per cent of real costs would have been covered. As to the two newer works (affected by Law No. 9662), the law provides for a debt equal to money costs. But if the debt had been paid when repayment began, the State would have recovered only 13 per cent of the real costs of resources invested in these works. The long period of repayment further reduces its real value. Sometimes the materials used to prepare the invoices are more expensive than the amounts paid. The Departamento de Explotación of Dirección de Riego has estimated the cost of these materials as one-half escudo per invoice, without considering the labor costs involved, while in many instances the yearly payment of irrigators is considerably lower than this amount.[34]

Table 18 compares what the State has charged irrigators with what should have been paid to offset the decline in value of the escudo. "Service of Debt A" is included in order to complement Table 17; it indicates what irrigators would have paid in escudos of constant value (E° of December 1962) in order to meet the contractual obligation fixed by the State, even though this amount was less than full real costs. "Service of Debt B" shows the quantities the irrigators would have paid up to 1964, in escudos of December 1962, if they had been paying full costs. It has been assumed that preliminary administration costs were repaid the same

[34] Information furnished by Sr. Larroucau.

Table 17

COSTS AND IRRIGATOR DEBTS, SELECTED IRRIGATION PROJECTS

Project	Construction costs (in E° of each year)	Debt for construction costs (in E° of each year)	Construction costs (in E° of Dec. 1962)	Year in which debt reimbursement began	Debt for construction (in E° of Dec. 1962)[a]
Works under Law 4445:					
Lautaro Reservoir	17,655	4,000	3,550,807	1950	114,000
Bullileo Reservoir	80,463	30,125	8,408,211	1953	430,486
Cogotí Reservoir[b]		29,443		1951	641,563
New Shares[b]	105,347	8,226	10,699,025	1954	74,939
Huana Canal[b]		771		1954	7,024
Laja Canal	10,210	6,013	3,908,054	1935	1,018,602
Maule Canal	20,639	14,763	8,270,551	1949	493,084
Melado Canal	31,320	11,027	11,113,081	1949	368,636
Recoleta Reservoir	30,229	14,617	6,643,687	1951	318,504
Recoleta Feeding Canal	94,388 [c]	22,544 [d]	4,751,438	1953	322,154
Subtotal	390,251	141,529	57,344,854		3,788,992
Works under Law 9662:					
El Noviciado Mechanical Irrigation System	40,116	42,772	293,846	1960	55,176
Quillón Canal	278,540	292,533	1,260,538	1964	149,484
Subtotal	318,656	335,305	1,554,384		204,660
Total	708,907	476,834	58,899,238		3,993,652

[a] Amount that would have been reimbursed in escudos as of 1962 if irrigators had paid the full debt the year repayment began.

[b] Cogotí Reservoir, New Shares, and Huana Canal are subdivisions of the same project; costs should be interpreted as applying to a single project.

[c] Includes preliminary administration costs of the reservoir and the canal.

[d] Includes debt for difference between payments and preliminary administration costs.

year the government spent the money, since if there had been no preliminary administration period the irrigators would have had to assume responsibility.

The situation is not too dissimilar if we consider separately the works constructed before and after 1950. The strikingly different ratios of "Service of Debt A" to "Service of Debt B" can be explained by the fact that the debts on works finished after 1950 are fairly recent.

Table 18

COSTS AND PAYMENTS

Project	Costs (in E° of each year)		Costs (in E° of Dec. 1962)		Amounts charged up to 1964 (in E° of each year)		Amounts charged up to 1964 (in E° of Dec. 1962)		Payments that should have been made up to 1964 (in E° of Dec. 1962)		
	Preliminary administration	Construction	Preliminary administration	Construction	Preliminary administration	Construction	Preliminary administration	Construction	Preliminary administration	Service of Debt A [a]	Service of Debt B [b]
Lautaro Reservoir	818	17,655	31,289	3,550,807	120	3,098	4,404	25,608	31,289	102,600	3,195,720
Bullileo Reservoir	3,810	80,463	99,768	8,408,211	2,877	19,185	44,444	51,752	99,768	284,121	5,549,418
Cogotí Reservoir	2,722	105,347	106,863	10,699,025	838	22,958	26,576	116,406	106,863	567,581	8,345,246
Laja Canal	—	10,210	—	3,908,054	—	10,477	—	463,848	—	1,833,480	7,034,490
Melado Canal	33,099	31,320	1,682,861	11,113,081	18,066	9,702	233,736	59,278	1,682,861	342,829	10,335,167
Maule Canal	10,269	20,639	1,364,438	8,270,551	3,390	13,730	358,887	112,172	1,364,438	458,568	7,691,612
Recoleta Reservoir and Feeding Canal [c]		124,617		11,395,125		22,317		233,439		461,049	8,318,020
Subtotal	50,718	390,251	3,285,219	57,344,854	25,291	101,467	668,047	1,062,503	3,285,219	4,050,228	50,469,673
El Noviciado Mechanical Irrigation System	104,515	40,116	182,631	293,846	25,069	11,292	27,104	10,571	182,631	14,568	77,576
Quillón Canal	499,460	278,540	559,523	1,260,538	57,555	19,307	44,334	9,866	559,523	9,866	83,196
Subtotal	603,975	318,656	742,154	1,554,384	82,624	30,599	71,438	20,437	742,154	24,434	160,772
Total	654,693	708,907	4,027,373	58,899,238	107,915	132,066	739,485	1,082,940	4,027,373	4,074,662	50,630,445

[a] "Service of Debt A": Amounts irrigators would have paid to meet the real value of the debt fixed by the State the year reinbursement began.
[b] "Service of Debt B": Amounts irrigators would have paid if they had paid full real costs.
[c] Information on preliminary administration and construction costs is not available separately. Construction costs include preliminary administration costs, and service of the debt includes payments made for preliminary administration.

Table 19

PERCENTAGE DISTRIBUTION OF LAND BY SIZE-CLASS OF HOLDINGS IN SELECTED
GOVERNMENT IRRIGATION PROJECTS

(Per cent)

Project	Size-class							
	0.1-50 ha.		50.1-200 ha.		200.1-1,000 ha.		Over 1,000 ha.	
	Irrigators	Irrigated land	Irrigators	Irrigated land	Irrigators	Irrigated land	Irrigators	Irrigated land
Recoleta Reservoir and Feeding Canal [a]	86.0	22.3	4.5	7.5	8.7	55.1	0.8	15.1
Bullileo Reservoir [b]	32.0	3.3	25.4	9.9	33.3	42.8	9.3	44.0
Lautaro Reservoir	82.4	25.1	12.2	27.5	4.8	33.8	0.6	13.6
Melado Canal [c]	70.9	14.6	23.7	31.9	4.5	31.4	0.9	22.1
Cogotí Reservoir	81.0	27.0	15.7	32.9	2.9	30.8	0.4	9.3
El Noviciado Mechanical Irrigation System	100.0	100.0	–	–	–	–	–	–
Quillón Canal	94.8	48.3	4.0	28.3	1.2	23.4	–	–

[a] Intervals for Recoleta Dam are: 1. 0.1-66 2. 66.1-200 3. 200.1-1,050 4. Over 1,050

[b] Intervals for Bullileo Dam are: 1. 0.1-75 2. 75.1-225 3. 225.1-1,050 4. Over 1,050

[c] Intervals for Melado Canal are: 1. 0.1-45 2. 45.1-225 3. 225.1-1,050 4. Over 1,050

The joint effects of inflation and rules fixing the liability of irrigators meant that irrigators paid 3 per cent of total real costs under laws that ostensibly call for full reimbursement. The estimated subsidy for the sample group of projects is about E°53 million as of December 1962 (about US $53 million). Most of the subsidy has gone to a relatively small number of large landowners.[35]

Information on distribution of shares by size of holdings was available for seven projects. (See Table 19.) El Noviciado appears to be the only project to benefit mostly the small farmer. In the remaining projects the small irrigators in the aggregate constitute a minority interest of shares, and sometimes a very small minority, although accounting for the largest number of holdings.

There is no reason to suspect that the characteristics of this sample of irrigation projects are in any way unusual. A comparable study should be made of all projects, supplemented by information and analysis of payments actually made by irrigators. It would be interesting to know whether those who fail to pay are among the large landowners or the small.

[35] Analysis based upon distribution of shares to water taken from 1965 payment records. Each share is a unit related to a unit of land into which total irrigable land of the project is divided. Usually the unit of land is one hectare, and the share is its pro rata allotment of water.

VI

PROJECTION OF
AGRICULTURAL WATER USE

The dominant use of water in Chile is for irrigated agriculture. A clear understanding of the agricultural economy—prospective demands and prices of outputs, production functions, and prices of inputs used by the agricultural industry—are essential for rational planning of water resources. Very little information is available. Therefore, this study's estimates of agricultural water use are based on the following assumptions:

1) Agricultural output will respond to changes in domestic demand with an additional response to changes in import policy.
2) Irrigated and dry land production will share proportionately in any projected change in production, subject to land and water limitations.
3) Increases in demand will be met first by bringing available new land into use; if land and water resources are limited, projected deficits in new production will be met by increases in output per hectare.

Two methods of projecting demand were tested and it was found that they yielded approximately the same results. By one method, per capita consumption of agricultural products was projected on the basis of an average coefficient of income elasticity of demand equal to .45, and the results adjusted to take population change up to 1985 into account.[1] The other method consisted of establishing a relationship between aggregate consumption of agricultural products and per capita gross national product from historical data, excluding products not producible in Chile, and projecting the relationship to 1985, coupled with projected population change.[2]

[1] Based upon income elasticity coefficients for separate products supplied by the Centro de Investigaciones Económicas, Universidad Católica.
[2] This model was constructed by John Holsen, Economic Adviser, U.S. AID Mission in Chile.

In the second model the implicit elasticity of demand for agricultural products as a whole coincided exactly with the weighted average elasticity of demand used in the first method.[3]

The over-all demand for agricultural products, assuming an average income elasticity of demand of .45 and an average annual increase in population of 2.43 per cent, would grow by 86 per cent by 1985 if GNP grows at the rate of 3.75 per cent per year (the growth rate experienced in recent decades), or by 118 per cent if GNP grows at 5.5 per cent per year, which is the goal of the Chilean government.

Mr. Holsen's estimates, based on the relationship between changes in per capita consumption of agricultural products and per capita GNP as observed between the period 1941-58, and based upon a population growth rate of 2.5 per cent and a per capita GNP growth rate of 2 per cent, yielded a total increase in consumption amounting to 157 per cent over the 1958 level, or an annual rate of increase slightly less than is implied by a growth of 118 per cent in twenty-one years.

Thus, so far as demand for agricultural products is concerned, there is reason to believe that the next two decades should see an approximate doubling of total demand—a little less if GNP grows at the historical rate, a little more if it grows in accordance with present plans.[4] If the path of growth moves at the lower rate there will still be a dietary deficiency in terms of FAO standards unless imports per capita rise. One objective of present government planning, however, is to eliminate the need for importing the foods and fibers that Chile can produce: wheat, meat, oils, and other temperate climate products. Total annual imports of agricultural products in 1964 and 1965 amounted to approximately US$150 million,[5] of which something more than half (about $82 million per year during the period 1961-63) are import substitutable.

[3] This weighted average was computed for the seven most important agricultural products, measured by money value, which altogether comprised 88 per cent of the total market value of output.

[4] Alvaro Marfan J., chief of the national planning office, ODEPLAN, pointed out (private communication) that by ignoring the policies of the present government designed to improve income distribution we have underestimated the growth in the demand for food. This is an appropriate correction, but one that cannot be incorporated into the model without additional information. The effect of this correction would be to increase further the needed efficiency of agricultural production or to increase the level of food imports, since, as shown later, the projected increase in agricultural output is constrained by land and water limitations.

[5] Statistics of the Departamento de Economía Agraria for August 1964, in the possession of Mr. Holsen, indicate that imports during 1961-63 averaged $137 million; the 1964-65 rate of importation is somewhat higher, according to preliminary estimates. Of total imports during 1961-63, about $82 million consisted of cereals, sugar, tobacco, meat, milk, wool, hides, and edible oils, all of which are produced in Chile.

If we accept Chilean plans as a basis of estimating output,[6] therefore, we should add to the growth of total demand another $85 million, or about 14 per cent of the 1960 level of production. Hence, even if per capita incomes should grow at the low rate of 1.29 per cent per year,[7] planned production would have to double in order to meet Chilean objectives.

Estimates made of the projected increase in demand—based upon the joint effects of income elasticity of demand, projected increase in family income, and change in size of population—translated, product by product and province by province, into required land under irrigation,[8] yielded a requirement of 2.6 million hectares of irrigated land under the assumption of the low rate of increase in GNP, and 3.0 million hectares at the high rate, without taking into account the reduction of imports or elimination of existing dietary deficiencies.[9]

[6] I make no attempt to evaluate the merits of Chile's objective of eliminating the importation of foods and fibers which they are "capable" of producing at home. "Capability" is, of course, a concept that is meaningful only within the context of comparative advantage and balance of payments restrictions. The feeling that Chile *should* produce its non-tropical agricultural "requirements" probably stems from the assumption that it could do so without strain (i.e., without unduly high marginal costs) if the agricultural sector were functioning at a reasonable level of efficiency. However, this assumption should itself be examined even though it may seem plausible. (See Chap. XVI, on implied increases in output per hectare.)

[7] On the assumption that growth in per capita income is the same as the growth in per capita GNP.

[8] On the assumption that irrigated land would increase in the same proportion as the projected increase in demand for products now produced on irrigated land. Estimates made by the Centro de Investigaciones Económicas, Universidad Católica, unpublished.

[9] An implied rise in per capita income would presumably afford a better diet. The dietary deficiency has not been translated into a fraction of total agricultural output, although this could be done with the data that are available. For specific food classes, average per capita dietary deficiencies were noted to be as follows as of 1961. (Because of the very unequal distribution of income in Chile, and the possibility that the well-off eat too much, the average deficiency may understate the degree of undernourishment that actually must be overcome.)

Food	Per Cent by which Available Per Capita Supply Falls Short (−) or Exceeds (+) Minimum Requirement
Milk, all forms except butter	−42%
Eggs	−13%
Legumes	−28%
Potatoes	−42%
Vegetables	−20%
Fruits	−28%
Sugar	+107%
Cereals	+17%
Meat	+8%
Fish	−75%
Butter, oil, and animal fat	+5%

(*For source, see next page.*)

It is assumed that at the low rate of income growth half of the dietary deficiency will be eliminated, and at the high rate of income growth, all. To the low rate of projected increase in demand one can add another 15 per cent[10] in needed additional output to account for dietary deficiency plus another 15 per cent to account for what is needed to eliminate the import deficit. Total demand would then be about 115 per cent above present levels at the low rate of income growth. Even if land requirements for elimination of dietary deficiencies and present imports are ignored, the requirements for irrigated land would be 2,644,000 in 1985 at the low rate of GNP growth (3.75 per cent) and 3,039,000 at the higher rate (5.5 per cent). The assumption that these requirements are distributed in proportion to present irrigated hectarage yields the distributions given in Table 20.

Land presently under irrigation, as noted previously, is not a precisely established figure. The photogrammetric survey classified 1,204,862 hectares as land "irrigated" and 708,332 hectares as land of mixed character, either because of low security of water supply or problems of micro-relief. CORFO estimated the amount of land under irrigation as being in the neighborhood of 1.4 million hectares. A figure somewhere between 1.2 and 1.9 million hectares is the measure of land under irrigation in a "normal" year. In a relatively wet year the amount would approach 1.9 million; in a relatively dry year, 1.2 million.

It is reasonable to assume a greater relative growth in cultivated irrigated land than cultivated dry land within the limits of land and water availability. If productivity per unit of land is to increase, more fertilizer, better seed, better weed control, and better methods of cultivation must be adopted. The increased investment per hectare that higher yields demand is likely to be placed on irrigated rather than dry land, because of the greater assurance of an adequate supply of water.[11] Unfortunately, Chile cannot expand output simply by putting dry land under irrigation. There is neither enough land nor enough water to allow irrigated areas to expand in proportion to the expected increase in required production. For

---

Source: CORFO (Programa Nacional de Desarrollo Económico, 1961-1970, p. 78) and Norman Hansen, H. Baeza, and J. Parker (Proyecciones de la Demanda de Agua y su Repartición Geográfica para los Próximos 20 Años. Ministerio de Obras Públicas, Dirección de Planeamiento, 1962, pp. 116-17) converted the dietary requirements into a weighted average of 0.55 hectares per inhabitant and concluded that instead of an expansion in irrigated area of about 809,000 hectares (by 1982), as revealed by governmental plans, the expansion should be greater by about 678,600 hectares. Since they assumed that 1.4 million hectares were already under irrigation, the additional required hectarage over the expansion already planned amounted to 678,600/2,209,000 or 33 per cent.

[10] In recognition of the $12\frac{1}{2}$ per cent increase in per capita demand that will remove roughly one-half of the dietary deficiency.

[11] This point is made by John Holsen.

Table 20
IRRIGABLE HECTARAGE REQUIRED ON BASIS OF
PROJECTED DEMAND, 1985

Province	Growth in GNP	
	3.75% Rate	5.5% Rate
Tarapacá	21,930	24,101
Antofagasta	8,478	9,542
Atacama	40,369	46,220
Coquimbo	198,580	235,014
Aconcagua	143,794	167,365
Valparaíso	91,284	106,960
Santiago	407,169	474,418
O'Higgins	316,636	368,762
Colchagua	151,517	173,453
Curicó	129,952	149,607
Talca	255,551	291,722
Maule	4,902	5,783
Linares	269,797	301,532
Ñuble	209,184	235,923
Concepción	137,142	159,373
Arauco	1,383	1,592
Bío-Bío	138,384	155,903
Malleco	84,139	91,133
Cautín	33,792	39,467
Total	2,643,983	3,037,870

this reason, a first approximation to the demand for water for agriculture can be made by assuming that all irrigable land will be irrigated in 1985.

This study takes as a measure of "all irrigable land" the total area of the following three groups of land capability classes in all provinces extending northward from Cautín.[12]

a) All land classified as Ir, IIr, IIIr, IVr—i.e., land already under irrigation with relatively secure water supply; about 1.2 million hectares.
b) All land in mixed irrigated-dry classes; about 700,000 hectares.
c) All land in Classes I, II, III (dry, arable); about 540,000 hectares.

The total of these groups is 2.5 million hectares, exclusive of land in the two northernmost provinces.[13] A figure of 2.5 million hectares is likely

[12] Based upon the air photogrammetric survey. Tables prepared by the Instituto de Investigaciones de Recursos Naturales. The survey excludes the two northernmost provinces. For these, estimates prepared by other agencies were adopted.
[13] Irrigable land in the provinces of Tarapacá and Antofagasta was estimated at 13,400 hectares by the Centro de Investigaciones Económicas of the Universidad Católica.

to be an overstatement, but the magnitude of overstatement cannot yet be ascertained.[14] At a guess, the overstatement is equal to 40 per cent of the land in Class III which would be about 200,000 hectares. Miguel Ruiz-Tagle P., Executive Director of the Instituto de Investigaciones de Recursos Naturales, has expressed an offhand opinion that total irrigable land is in the neighborhood of 2.0 million hectares. Plans of the Dirección de Riego for expansion of irrigation call for 546,000 hectares of "new" irrigated land and 855,000 hectares of "improved" irrigation,[15] which would imply 2.5 million hectares of irrigable land. In our model, the figure of 2.5 million hectares has been adopted,[16] as shown in Table 21.

An increase in irrigated area to 2.5 million hectares implies that irrigated hectarage will grow by approximately 66 per cent. This growth is at the expense of land now being put to other use—mostly natural pasture or dry land cultivation—except in the northernmost provinces, where production from dry land is zero. No data are available on the net change in total production that should be expected as land is transferred from dry to irrigated, nor are there enough data to estimate by how much per irrigated hectare and per dry hectare productivity must increase in order to meet projected goals. The estimates given below, therefore, have been constructed on the basis of indirect evidence.

Water requirements for irrigation were computed in the following manner. The so-called *tasa de riego* (rates of irrigation) supplied by the Centro de Investigaciones Económicas, Universidad Católica, measured the water requirements at the head of the "field" for six classes of crops and five zones. (See Table 22.) This figure gave neither the "diversion requirement" nor the "net consumption," since the *tasa de riego* was estimated to exceed the plant's evapotranspiration requirements by about 30 per cent but failed to include losses on the farm to the field and losses from the point of storage or diversion to the farm. In order to compute net and gross requirements, it was decided to follow the practice of the U.S. Department of Agriculture in their estimates of water requirements for irrigated farming in California; these were based on technology of water use expected in 1980.[17] Present water use in Chile is considered to be extravagant. The indicated *tasas* are designed to be conservative in the

---

[14] The Instituto de Investigaciones de Recursos Naturales is now attempting to measure the quantity of irrigable land without being distracted by the question of whether water is or is not available.

[15] Table prepared by Michael Nelson, Chile-California Program.

[16] This is a much smaller figure than has previously been used. For example, the CEPAL report estimated that "total irrigable land" that "required irrigation" amounted to 7.2 million hectares. CEPAL, pp.68-69.

[17] U.S. Senate Select Committee on National Water Resources, *Land and Future Requirements for Water*, Committee Print No. 12 (Washington: 1960), pp. 17-18, 67.

Table 21
IRRIGABLE LAND THAT REQUIRES IRRIGATION

Province	Hectares
Tarapacá	10,773
Antofagasta	2,626
Atacama	27,288
Coquimbo	113,023
Aconcagua	63,092
Valparaíso	65,549
Santiago	283,852
O'Higgins	170,280
Colchagua	152,114
Curicó	88,644
Talca	193,936
Maule	31,378
Linares	244,499
Ñuble	260,415
Concepción	65,956
Aruco	29,187
Bío-Bío	142,756
Malleco	259,140
Cautín	302,921
Total	2,507,429

Source: Prepared by Michael Nelson, Chile-California Program.

implied improvement in efficiency, but are clearly below estimates of current rates of water use. There are no estimates for Chile of diversion requirements or net losses.

Gross (or diversion) requirements were computed by applying the following adjustments:

tasa ÷ 1.3 = plant requirement;
plant requirement ÷ .55 = water required for delivery to the farm;
water required for delivery to the farm ÷ .55 = diversion requirement;
(diversion requirement − plant requirement) ÷ 2 = amount of water recovered for subsequent use;
diversion requirement − amount of water recovered for subsequent use = net loss.

By applying these computations to each crop class as weighted by the relative importance of estimated hectarage according to CORFO's

Table 22

TASA DE RIEGO

(*Thousand cubic meters per hectare per year*)

	Zone				
Crop	Tarapacá and Antofagasta	Atacama and Coquimbo	Aconcagua-Linares	Ñuble-Malleco	Cautín and South
Cereals	6.0	5.5	5.0	2.3	–
Vegetables	10.0	10.0	10.0	6.0	5.0
Fruits	12.0	10.0	9.0	8.9	5.0
Vineyards	–	12.0	9.0	–	–
Pasture	15.0	12.0	11.0	8.5	5.0
Rice	–	–	17.0	–	–

Source: Unofficial estimates supplied by the Centro de Investigaciones Económicas, Universidad Católica.

Table 23

PERCENTAGE DISTRIBUTION OF IRRIGATED LAND BY MAJOR CLASS OF CROP

Crop	Tarapacá and Antofagasta	Atacama-Linares	Maule-Bío-Bío	Arauco and Malleco [a]
	I. 1958-59 Crop Mix			
Cereals	–	36.5	34.7	22.4
Vegetables	17.1	4.4	2.0	16.0
Fruits	5.1	3.6	1.5	23.5
Vineyards	–	4.4	0.6	–
Artificial pasture	57.5	23.7	27.1	2.0
Natural pasture	20.3	27.4	34.1	36.1
	II. 1958-59 Crop Mix After Eliminating Natural Pasture			
Cereals	–	46.8	50.0	28.9
Vegetables	25.0	5.6	2.9	20.7
Fruits	7.4	4.6	2.2	30.4
Vineyards	–	5.6	0.8	–
Artificial pasture	67.6	37.4	44.1	20.0

[a] In Cautín Province the *tasa de riego* was 5,000 cubic meters per hectare per year for all crops. The regional division is slightly different from that used in Table 22, but this does not introduce a significant error.

Source: Table prepared by Maciej Zaleski from data in CORFO files.

Table 24
COMPUTATION OF DIVERSION AND NET LOSSES FROM
IRRIGATION BASED ON *TASA DE RIEGO*[a]
(*Thousand cubic meters per hectare per year*)

Zone	Weighted average Tasa de Riego	Plant use	Farm require- ment	Gross use	Net loss
	Rates I				
Tarapacá and					
Antofagasta	14.0	10.8	19.6	35.6	23.2
Atacama-Linares	9.1	7.0	12.7	23.1	15.1
Maule–Bío-Bío	6.3	4.8	8.7	15.8	10.3
Arauco and Malleco	6.8	5.2	9.5	17.3	11.3
Cautín	5.0	3.8	6.9	12.5	8.2
	Rates II				
Tarapacá and					
Antofagasta	13.5	10.4	18.9	34.4	22.4
Atacama-Linares	8.5	6.5	11.8	21.5	14.0
Maule–Bío-Bío	5.3	4.1	7.5	13.6	8.9
Arauco and Malleco	6.3	4.8	8.7	15.8	10.3
Cautín	5.0	3.8	6.9	12.5	8.2

[a] See text. These coefficients can be compared with those adopted in *Capacidad de Riego Actual de los Ríos de la Zone Central de Chile* (Santiago: Ministerio de Obras Públicas, Dirección de Riego, January 1967), in which it was assumed that "irrigation rates were taken that correspond to the strict necessities of the crops," that irrigation efficiency was 60% on the farm, delivery losses were 13%, and net recovery for further use was 12% of the amount diverted from the river. Beginning with a crop requirement of 6,000 m³/yr/ha, the gross amount diverted from the river was 11,500 m³/yr/ha, and net use was 10,125 m³/yr/ha. These coefficients were uniform for all provinces between Santiago and Ñuble. [A translation of the *Capacidad de Riego* report is included as Appendix C in the present volume.]

1958-59 estimated output,[18] it was possible to compute average gross and net water requirements per hectare by zone.[19] The figure for a zone was then assigned to all provinces in that zone, as shown in Table 25.

Since pasture requires more water than most other crops, a shortage of water might result in a greater reduction of pasture than other crops. Should Chilean farmers raise average output per hectare, the use of irrigated natural pasture would be reduced to a negligible quantity, since its productivity is much lower than that of artificial pasture. In order to

[18] Based on data prepared by Maciej Zaleski. (See Table 23.)
[19] Columns headed "Rates I" in Table 24.

Table 25
RATES OF WATER USE PER HECTARE PER YEAR
(*Thousand cubic meters*)

Province	Rates I		Rates II	
	Gross	Net	Gross	Net
Tarapacá	35.6	23.2	34.4	22.4
Antofagasta	35.6	23.2	34.4	22.4
Atacama	23.1	15.1	21.5	14.0
Coquimbo	23.1	15.1	21.5	14.0
Aconcagua	23.1	15.1	21.5	14.0
Valparaíso	23.1	15.1	21.5	14.0
Santiago	23.1	15.1	21.5	14.0
O'Higgins	23.1	15.1	21.5	14.0
Colchagua	23.1	15.1	21.5	14.0
Curicó	23.1	15.1	21.5	14.0
Talco	23.1	15.1	21.5	14.0
Maule	15.8	10.3	13.6	8.9
Linares	23.1	15.1	21.5	14.0
Ñuble	15.8	10.3	13.6	8.9
Concepción	15.8	10.3	13.6	8.9
Arauco	17.3	11.3	15.8	10.3
Bío-Bío	15.8	10.3	13.6	8.9
Malleco	17.3	11.3	15.8	10.3
Cautín	12.5	8.2	12.5	8.2

show what effects such changes might have on water requirements, revised gross and net rates per hectare[20] were estimated on the assumption that 1958-59 product mix was modified by eliminating natural pasture and dividing it equally between artificial pasture on the one hand and all other crops on the other. This change in product mix would reduce gross water requirements per hectare by amounts ranging between zero and 14 per cent; about 7 per cent in the central part of the Central Valley. Total water requirements for agriculture were computed by multiplying irrigable hectarage by the diversion and net requirements per hectare. The results are given in Table 26.

The resulting coefficients are roughly comparable to those computed by the U.S. Department of Agriculture for the State of California for 1954.[21] Gross use was estimated as 8.7 acre-feet per acre per year for Central

[20] See Rates II, Tables 24 and 25.
[21] Central Pacific and South Pacific water resource regions in U.S. Senate Committee Print No. 12.

Table 26
AGRICULTURE (IRRIGATION) DIVERSION REQUIREMENTS
AND NET LOSS FOR IRRIGABLE HECTARAGE
(*Thousand cubic meters per year*)

Province	Rates I 1958-59 mix		Rates II 1958-59 mix after eliminating natural pasture	
	Diversion	Net loss	Diversion	Net loss
Tarapacá	383,519	249,934	370,591	241,315
Antofagasta	93,486	60,923	90,334	58,822
Atacama	630,353	412,049	586,692	382,032
Coquimbo	2,610,831	1,706,647	2,429,995	1,582,322
Aconcagua	1,457,452	952,689	1,356,478	883,288
Valparaíso	1,514,182	989,790	1,409,304	917,686
Santiago	6,556,981	4,286,165	6,102,818	3,973,928
O'Higgins	3,933,468	2,571,228	3,661,020	2,383,920
Colchagua	3,513,833	2,296,921	3,270,451	2,129,596
Curicó	2,047,676	1,338,524	1,905,846	1,241,016
Talca	4,479,922	2,928,434	4,169,624	2,715,104
Maule	495,772	323,193	426,741	279,264
Linares	5,647,927	3,691,935	5,256,729	3,422,986
Ñuble	4,114,557	2,682,275	3,541,644	2,317,694
Concepción	1,042,105	679,347	897,002	587,008
Arauco	504,935	329,813	461,155	300,626
Bío-Bío	2,255,545	1,470,387	1,941,482	1,270,528
Malleco	4,483,122	2,928,282	4,094,412	2,669,142
Cautín	3,786,513	2,483,952	3,786,513	2,483,952
Total	49,552,179	32,382,488	45,758,831	29,840,229

Pacific and 9.3 acre-feet per acre per year for South Pacific. Net loss was
estimated at 5.1 acre-feet and 5.5 acre-feet, respectively. By comparison,
the figures in Table 24, Rates II, when converted to acre-feet per acre per
year, are as follows:

	Gross	Net
	(*acre-feet per acre*)	
Tarapacá and Antofagasta	11.3	7.3
Atacama-Linares	7.1	4.6
Maule-Bío-Bío	4.5	2.9
Arauco and Malleco	5.2	3.4
Cautín	4.1	2.7

In view of the extreme aridity and long growing season in Tarapacá and Antofagasta provinces, a figure above California's is not implausible. The coefficient for the very important Atacama-Linares zone—the heartland of Chilean agriculture—is, if anything, on the low side, and may have contributed to an overestimation of agricultural productivity.

By computing irrigation requirements on the basis of total irrigable land it is assumed that the area under irrigation in any province between Cautín and Tarapacá is a function of total national demand subject to land and water constraints, and not a function of local or provincial demand. This assumption conforms reasonably well to the present situation and is likely to be even more applicable in the future.

In addition to irrigation an estimate of water requirements for livestock has been included.[22] The requirements are very small in comparison with irrigation. (See Table 27.) It is assumed that water intake by livestock is

Table 27

REQUIREMENTS FOR THE WATERING OF LIVESTOCK, 1985

(*Thousand cubic meters per year*)

Tarapacá	781
Antofagasta	412
Atacama	946
Coquimbo	8,031
Aconcagua, Valparaíso	5,214
Santiago	9,345
O'Higgins, Colchagua	8,691
Curicó, Talco, Maule	13,312
Linares, Ñuble	4,065
Concepción, Arauco, Bío-Bío, Malleco, Cautín	33,150
Valdivia, Osorno, Llanquihue	28,739
Chiloé	4,652
Aysén	8,338
Magallanes	22,827
Total	148,503

Source: Centro de Investigaciones Económicas, Universidad Católica.

[22] Estimate prepared by the Centro de Investigaciones Económicas, Universidad Católica.

equal to water loss—i.e., no credit has been given for return flow. Also, it is assumed that livestock use was divided evenly over the year, and did not conform to the seasonal pattern set by irrigation.

Because of the wide swing in water use from season to season, and the fact that in some basins the natural variation in flow coincided with needs whereas in others it followed almost an inverse pattern, the quantity of required storage could not be computed directly as a function of required minimum flows. Total water requirements were computed separately for each month on the assumption that all uses except irrigation were evenly spread out over the year. The seasonal distribution used for irrigation is given in Table 28.

Table 28
MONTHLY DISTRIBUTION OF IRRIGATION REQUIREMENTS
(Percentage of annual total)

Province	Jan.	Feb.	March	April	May	June	July	Aug.	Sept.	Oct.	Nov.	Dec.
Tarapacá	15.8	10.2	8.2	2.7	2.3	1.1	–	5.8	9.1	10.4	15.0	19.4
Antofagasta	15.1	9.3	7.4	4.3	4.2	2.8	–	5.6	9.1	10.3	13.9	18.0
Atacama	13.8	8.8	6.7	3.3	5.4	2.1	–	7.0	10.5	12.2	12.8	17.4
Coquimbo	13.6	8.8	6.4	3.9	5.4	0.8	–	7.4	11.3	12.7	12.9	16.8
Aconcagua-Valparaíso	14.8	12.6	7.8	4.5	0.5	0.1	–	5.6	9.1	12.9	17.3	14.8
Santiago	15.6	14.3	10.6	7.4	1.5	0.7	0.6	2.7	7.3	10.4	13.9	15.0
O'Higgins-Colchagua	12.6	18.4	16.7	7.5	6.1	–	–	–	1.8	7.1	12.7	17.1
Curicó-Linares	16.5	15.1	8.0	5.4	–	–	–	1.7	8.4	11.9	16.3	16.7
Ñuble	13.6	12.3	10.5	7.1	–	–	–	2.4	9.3	13.3	18.2	13.3
Concepción-Cautín	16.7	14.5	9.0	5.9	–	–	–	2.1	9.5	13.9	15.8	12.6

Source: Basso, p. 52.

PRODUCTION FROM DRY AND IRRIGATED LAND

If we could estimate how Chile's agricultural output is at present divided between irrigated and dry land, and could estimate the possibilities of expanding land under cultivation—irrigated and dry—we could estimate the increase in output per hectare required to meet Chile's production goals.[23]

---

[23] We must also keep in mind the fact that Chile's internal price relationships have been subjected to controls, and that changes in such relationships will affect aggregate value of output either directly or by inducing a change in product mix, or both.

Rentabilidad[24] contains estimated weighted average productivities of irrigated and dry land converted into units of "wheat equivalent," which is the yield of each product in metric quintals[25] per hectare multiplied by the ratio of the price of the product over the price of wheat. Villarroel and Horn computed weighted average yields in this way for each irrigation project and adjacent dry land, based upon census data of hectares seeded and yields in each *comuna*. The objections raised above to the productivity measurements of Villarroel and Horn and the use of such measurements in determining the added productivity of land put under irrigation by the Dirección de Riego, do not apply to the use we are now making of their computations.[26]

Because Villarroel and Horn made no measurements for provinces south of Cautín, except for one small project in Aysén, it has been assumed that productivity on unirrigated land in the provinces of Valdivia, Osorno, and Llanquihue was the same as in the four provinces immediately to the north. The same productivity was assigned to Chilóe, Aysén, and Magallanes as Villarroel and Horn computed for the *comunas* adjacent to the canal Chile Chico in Aysén. The average for a zone was then assigned to each province in that zone. The resulting productivity measurements are shown in Table 29. They reflect not only the yield in physical terms but the prices that prevail for the crops that are grown. For this reason a change in crop mix or a change in price relationships among agricultural products can affect the productivity coefficient.

Productivity estimates reflect a difference of 100:1 between irrigated and dry land in the north (where the only dry land that can be used is the Andean slopes for seasonal grazing) and a difference of about 2.3:1 in the provinces at the southern limits of irrigated agriculture. In the six provinces centered around Santiago the ratio is approximately 5:1.

By applying the Villarroel and Horn productivity coefficients to land reported under cultivation in 1959, under the assumption that this figure is about the same today, we acquire some appreciation of the land constraint and the implied productivity changes that must be achieved in order to reach 1985 goals. Unfortunately, the accuracy of the basic measurements again comes into question, and our answer varies substantially depending upon which source is used.

According to CORFO's estimates of land under cultivation,[27] 1,389,084

[24] Villarroel and Horn, table on p. 39 and related discussion.

[25] One metric quintal (qqm) is equal to 100 kilograms in Chile. (Its size is not uniform in all countries.)

[26] The objection was that their measurements were *comuna* averages of all dry and irrigated land, respectively, and failed to give due regard to the differences in productivity of land specifically selected for the Dirección de Riego projects.

[27] Tables prepared by Maciej Zaleski from data in CORFO files.

Table 29
ESTIMATED PRODUCTIVITY OF IRRIGATED AND DRY LAND
(*Metric quintals of wheat equivalents per hectare*)

Province	Irrigated	Dry
Tarapacá	50.0	0.5
Antofagasta	50.0	0.5
Atacama	50.0	0.5
Coquimbo	30.0	2.0
Aconcagua	22.5	4.6
Valparaíso	22.5	4.6
Santiago	22.5	4.6
O'Higgins	22.5	4.6
Colchagua	22.5	4.6
Curicó	22.5	4.6
Talca	17.5	5.0
Maule	17.5	5.0
Linares	17.5	5.0
Ñuble	17.5	5.0
Concepción	17.5	5.0
Arauco	15.0	6.6
Bío-Bío	15.0	6.6
Malleco	15.0	6.6
Cautín	15.0	6.6
Valdivia	–	6.6
Osorno	–	6.6
Llanquihue	–	6.6
Chiloé	–	3.0
Aysén	–	3.0
Magallanes	–	3.0

Source: Adapted from Villarroel and Horn, pp. 39-40.

hectares were irrigated in 1959. This land produced 29,700,000 metric quintals of wheat equivalent, calculated with the use of the Villarroel and Horn coefficients. If all irrigable land is put under irrigation in 1985, the yield will be 49,000,000 metric quintals of wheat equivalent (see Table 30) at the productivity rates that now prevail. In other words, given no change in output per hectare, product mix, and price relationships, total production from irrigated land can increase by about 60 per cent.

Since, except in the North, the expansion of land under irrigation will take place at the expense of dry land now under cultivation, the net increase in agricultural output is less. Total potential output from dry land after expanding irrigable hectarage to its maximum depends, of course, on the quantity of arable land. If one assumes that CORFO's total of "dry land

Table 30
ESTIMATED PRODUCTION FROM IRRIGATED LAND

Province	Hectares irrigated 1959 [a]	Produc- tivity [b] (qqm WE/ha) [c]	Production 1959 (qqm WE) (1) × (2)	Hectares irrigable 1985 [d]	Production 1985 (qqm WE) (2) × (4)
	(1)	(2)	(3)	(4)	(5)
Tarapacá	7,000	50.0	350,000	10,773	538,650
Antofagasta	4,200	50.0	210,000	2,626 [e]	131,300
Atacama	26,081	50.0	1,304,050	27,288	1,364,400
Coquimbo	107,081	30.0	3,212,430	113,023	3,390,690
Aconcagua	38,181	22.5	814,073	63,092	1,419,570
Valparaíso	53,881	22.5	1,212,323	65,549	1,474,853
Santiago	228,412	22.5	5,139,270	283,852	6,386,670
O'Higgins	143,529	22.5	3,229,403	170,280	3,831,300
Colchagua	106,281	22.5	2,391,323	152,114	3,422,565
Curicó	79,885	22.5	1,797,413	88,644	1,994,490
Talca	125,881	17.5	2,202,918	193,936	3,393,880
Maule	41,181	17.5	720,668	31,378 [e]	549,115
Linares	148,831	17.5	2,604,543	244,499	4,278,733
Ñuble	100,000	17.5	1,750,000	260,415	4,557,263
Concepción	31,900	17.5	558,250	65,956	1,154,230
Arauco	5,000	15.0	75,000	29,187	437,805
Bío-Bío	82,650	15.0	1,239,750	142,756	2,141,340
Malleco	23,900	15.0	358,500	259,140	3,887,100
Cautín	35,210	15.0	528,150	302,921	4,543,815
Valdivia	–	–	–	–	–
Osorno	–	–	–	–	–
Llanquihue	–	–	–	–	–
Chiloé	–	–	–	–	–
Aysén	–	–	–	–	–
Magallanes	–	–	–	–	–
Total	1,389,084		29,698,064	2,507,429	48,897,769

[a] Tables prepared by Maciej Zaleski from CORFO files.
[b] From Villarroel and Horn.
[c] Metric quintals of wheat equivalent per hectare.
[d] Equal to all land now irrigated, plus mixed classes, plus Classes I, II, III of dry land, based on tables of Instituto de Investigaciones de Recursos Naturales.
[e] Apparent discrepancy in relationship to figure in first column not explained in source.

under cultivation" in 1958-59 is equal to the total amount of unirrigated land in Classes I-IV, the total amount of such land is about 4.1 million hectares, distributed among the provinces as shown in Table 31 (column headed "Dry land before reduction"). Multiplying dry land under culti-

vation by the Villarroel and Horn production coefficients gives an estimated 1958-59 output of 23.8 million metric quintals of wheat equivalent.
Total output in terms of the Villarroel and Horn unit, therefore, was about
53.5 million metric quintals of wheat equivalent. Projected agricultural
output without taking land or water constraints into account in 1985,
when expressed in wheat equivalent, would be somewhere between 97
million and 120 million metric quintals, depending upon the assumed
growth path and foreign trade policy within the range of behavior discussed
above. A doubling of output over the 1959-60 level of production is a
minimum estimate of projected requirements.

Projected output, based on CORFO's land figures would be equal to
48.9 million metric quintals of wheat equivalent from irrigated land and
17.3 million metric quintals of wheat equivalent from dry land, a drop
of 6.5 million quintals in dry land production in order to achieve an increase in irrigated production of 19.2 million metric quintals. It should be
noted that these estimates do not take into account the availability of
water.

If we use the figures on land capability released by the Instituto de
Investigaciones de Recursos Naturales, projected potential output is less.
The air photogrammetric survey shows only 2,951,266 hectares of dry land
in Classes I-IV, exclusive of land that is in the mixed, dry-irrigated classes,
compared with CORFO's figure of 4.1 million hectares of "dry land under
cultivation."[28] Since, when studying the photogrammetric survey's figures
on land capability, one cannot clearly distinguish between land that was
actually irrigated and land that was not, total arable dry land in 1985 was
estimated to be equal to the sum of land in Class IV in all provinces plus
land in Classes I-III in provinces south of Cautín. (All land in mixed
classes and all land in Classes I-III in provinces in and north of Cautín
were assumed to be land potentially irrigable by 1985.) The photogrammetric survey yields a total of 2,385,106 hectares of dry arable land after
expansion of irrigated area, in comparison with the figure of 3,008,039
based on CORFO's data. Applying the productivity coefficients to the
photogrammetric survey figure yields a potential output of 13.8 million
metric quintals of wheat equivalent, or a total, including production from
irrigated land, of 63.7 million metric quintals.[29]

[28] The two quantities need not coincide, but they presumably are designed to measure
the same thing. CORFO's figure includes arable land used for natural pasture.

[29] One cannot estimate the net change in output over current production on the basis
of photogrammetric survey figures because there is no way of knowing how much of
some 700,000 hectares of land in mixed classes was irrigated and how much was dry.
This information should be available some time in the future.

Table 31

ESTIMATED PRODUCTION FROM DRY LAND

Province	Reduction in dry land (hectares)	Productivity dry land[a] (qqm WE/ha)[b]	Dry land before reduction[c] (hectares)	Production before reduction (qqm WE)[b]	Dry land after reduction (hectares)	Production after reduction (qqm WE)[b]	Air photo non-irrigated land after expansion of irrigated area[d] (hectares)	Air photo production from dry land (qqm WE)[b]
Tarapacá	3,773	0.5	–	–	–	–	–	–
Antofagasta	–	0.5	–	–	–	–	–	–
Atacama	1,207	0.5	9,919	4,960	8,712	4,356	9	5
Coquimbo	5,942	2.0	32,919	65,838	26,977	53,954	6,533	13,066
Aconcagua	26,911	4.6	26,819	123,367	–	–	4,065	18,699
Valparaíso	11,668	4.6	34,119	156,947	22,451	103,275	17,933	82,492
Santiago	55,440	4.6	61,588	283,305	6,148	28,281	58,844	270,682
O'Higgins	26,751	4.6	18,471[e]	84,967	–	–	1,740	8,004
Colchagua	45,833	4.6	115,719	532,307	69,886	321,476	60,224	277,030

Curicó	8,759	4.6	28,115	129,329	19,356	89,038	9,251	42,555
Talca	68,055	5.0	91,119	455,595	23,064	115,320	18,342	91,710
Maule	—	5.0	110,819	554,095	110,819	554,095	51,615	258,075
Linares	95,668	5.0	128,169	640,845	32,501	162,505	16,347	81,735
Ñuble	160,415	5.0	421,000	2,105,000	260,585	1,302,925	195,784	978,920
Concepción	34,056	5.0	125,100	625,500	91,044	455,220	30,619	153,095
Arauco	24,187	6.6	196,000	1,293,600	171,813	1,133,966	46,623	307,712
Bío-Bío	60,106	6.6	195,350	1,289,310	135,244	892,610	170,345	1,124,277
Malleco	235,240	6.6	442,100	2,917,860	206,860	1,365,276	103,815	685,179
Cautín	267,711	6.6	692,790	4,572,414	425,079	2,805,521	329,964	2,177,762
Valdivia	—	6.6	502,000	3,313,200	502,000	3,313,200	367,273	2,424,002
Osorno	—	6.6	345,000	2,277,000	345,000	2,277,000	352,205	2,324,553
Llanquihue	—	6.6	195,000	1,287,000	195,000	1,287,000	231,953	1,530,890
Chiloé	—	3.0	97,000	291,000	97,000	291,000	53,122	159,366
Aysén	—	3.0	23,500	291,000	23,500	70,500	23,500	70,500
Magallanes	—	3.0	235,000	705,000	235,000	705,000	235,000	705,000
Total	1,131,722		4,127,616	23,778,939	3,008,039	17,331,518	2,385,106	13,785,309

a Villarroel and Horn.   b Metric quintals of wheat equivalent per hectare.
c Zaleski, CORFO.   d All of Class IV in Cautín and above, Classes I-IV, south of Cautín.
e Apparent discrepancy in relation to figure in first column not explained in source.

If water constraints are taken into account, estimated production would presumably be different. At the moment, however, it is assumed that all irrigable land is irrigated, all arable land is cultivated, and crop mix, prices, and productivity are as implied by the Villarroel and Horn coefficients. The estimates indicate that if the air photogrammetric survey is accurate, output can reach 63 million metric quintals by 1985. Since projected requirements are about 1.8 to 2.25 the current level of output, or from 97 to 120 million metric quintals of wheat equivalent, an average increase in output per hectare of from 50 per cent to 100 per cent is implied. When water constraints are taken into account, the implied required increase in productivity will be greater.

VII

MINING AND ELECTRIC POWER

Mining contributes to Chile on the order of 6 per cent of its national income, 4 per cent of "gross geographic product," and 85 per cent of its income from exports. A few large producers dominate the industry—copper and nitrates being the principal minerals. Some oil and gas in the far south, coal in the central zone, iron, and small amounts of gold, manganese, molybdenum, sulfur, and calcium complete the picture.

MINING

Production of coal, which is concentrated around Concepción, and of oil and gas, on the island of Tierra del Fuego, creates no foreseeable problems of water supply, conflicting demands, or serious threat of pollution. The story is different, however, for copper and nitrate, all of which come from regions of serious water shortage. One large copper mine, Braden's (Kennecott) El Teniente, is in the Central Zone on the headwaters of a tributary of the Rapel. There is a little production of copper in the North Central Zone and the southern part of the Norte Chico divided among a number of small mines. The bulk of production is in the Norte Grande. Chuquicamata, Chile's largest copper mine, is a huge open pit in the province of Antofagasta. Not far away are the major nitrate deposits.

In recent years Chile has produced in the neighborhood of 10-15 per cent of the world's copper. In 1963 production was 604,000 long tons of refined copper of which 84 per cent came from the *Gran Minería*—the mines of Anaconda in Antofagasta and Atacama and Kennecott in O'Higgins. Agreements have been negotiated between the executive branch of the government and the two major companies on a plan for expanding output, increasing total investment, and transferring to the Chilean government a share of financial and administrative responsibility. Since Chilean ores are both extensive and relatively rich,[1] a substantial expansion of the industry, with or without a corresponding expansion in the world market, appears to be reasonable.

Two projections of future output were made.[2] The lower assumed an industrial rate of growth equal to the historical average, but allowed small producers to grow more rapidly than large. Total output would rise from 604,000 tons to 1,222,000 tons in 1985. Output of the *Gran Minería* would fall from 84 per cent to 75 per cent. The higher projection assumed that the agreements now under discussion would be adopted, and that total production would be 2,000,000 tons by 1985 of which about 75 per cent would come from the *Gran Minería*. The growing relative share of small and medium producers means that mining demands for water will grow in Coquimbo, Aconcagua, Valparaíso, and Santiago as well as in the provinces dominated by Anaconda and Kennecott.

In recent years, output of nitrates has ranged between a million and a million and a half tons per year, with no clear trend. In 1963 production was 1,144,600 tons. The ten-year plan of CORFO assumed a moderate increase over the 1960 low to a level of production in 1970 that would still be less than output of the 1950's. If CORFO's assumed rate of growth is extended to 1985 output would be 1,600,000 tons. This level of production was used for both the low and high economic projections of the present study.

Estimates of water use were made by CEPAL and Hansen based on data supplied by the companies and coefficients taken from technical literature. The amount of water used per ton of refined ore depends on the method of beneficiation that is used, the type of ore, and the degree of recirculation. A flotation process is used for copper sulfide ores; a leaching process is used for copper oxide ores. Unit rates of gross use were estimated as follows:

Copper[3]

Chuquicamata: (Antofagasta)   Oxide ores—0.5 m³ per ton of ore. Sulfide ores—1.0 m³ per ton of ore or 91.5 m³ per ton of refined copper. Since the bulk of reserves are sulfide, this coefficient is used for projections.

El Teniente: (O'Higgins)   Same as Chuquicamata, sulfide ores, but with higher degree of recirculation: 83 m³ per ton of refined ore.

[1] According to Hansen *et al.*, Chuquicamata possesses the greatest single body of ore in the world. CEPAL says that Chilean costs of production are among the lowest in the world. An engineer for Kennecott said that their ores in Chile are about 1.8 per cent copper, compared with less than 1 per cent in the United States.

[2] By Centro de Investigaciones Económicas, Universidad Católica.

[3] CEPAL, Hansen *et al.*

Potrerillos and   No data. Estimated at 3.75 m³ per ton of ore treated
El Salvador: or 415 m³ per ton of refined copper.
(Atacama)

Medium Mines: No data. Estimated at 3 m³ per ton of ore treated.
              Leaching process estimated to require an intake of
              500 lts. per ton of ore treated.

Small Mines: No data.

Nitrates[4]

Brackish Water   Pedro de Valdivia and María Elena Mines: Current
of Loa and   use 180 lts/second or 15,500 m³/day. Expected total
Salvador   use after construction of 40 evaporation tanks—25,000
Rivers   m³/day.

Fresh Water   For domestic water supply and boiler feed. Current
                  use is 4,500 m³/day. No future increase is anticipated.

Tables 32 and 33 show projections of production and water use (intake)
as estimated by the Universidad Católica. Since no information was
supplied on quantities of water recoverable for further use, a loss rate of
15 per cent of intake was assumed.[5]

Table 32

COPPER PRODUCTION AND WATER REQUIREMENTS (INTAKE)

Province	Production (*1,000 tons*)			Water requirements (*1,000 m³/yr*)[a]		
		1985			1985	
	1963	Low	High	1963	Low	High
Tarapacá	[b]	[b]	4	[c]	[c]	160
Antofagasta	304.3	592	775	27,029	51,652	67,550
Atacama	107.7	220	437	38,391	72,035	166,326
Coquimbo	10.9	33	74	2,761	7,564	20,898
Aconcagua	17.6	54	188	807	2,477	14,168
Valparaíso	3.3	10	22	1,108	3,402	72,992
Santiago	15.5	48	76	3,925	12,050	19,294
O'Higgins	144.4	264	429	12,006	21,927	35,607
Total	603.7	1,221	2,005	86,027	171,107	396,995

[a] Assumed to be intake.
[b] Less than 500 tons.
[c] Less than 500 m³.
Source: Centro de Investigaciones Económicas, Universidad Católica.

[4] *Ibid.*
[5] See alternative computation of losses on the assumption that all intake is lost,
Chapter XI.

Table 33
NITRATE PRODUCTION AND INTAKE WATER REQUIREMENTS

	Production (*1,000 tons*)		Water use (*1,000 m³/year*)	
Province	1963	1985	1963	1985
Tarapacá	118.3	164	890	1,230
Antofagasta	1,026.3	1,436	7,290	10,765
Total	1,144.6	1,600	8,180	11,995

Source: Centro de Investigaciones Económicas, Universidad Católica.

ELECTRIC POWER

The use of water by steam-electric plants was estimated directly from data on current water use.[6] For the provinces below Atacama the rate of increase in production from thermal power projected by ENDESA was applied to current intake. In the three northern provinces, where most of the thermal power is produced by the mining companies, 1965 intake was divided between the power plants of the mining companies and all others on the basis of capacity. Water use by mining company plants was projected at the two alternative rates of growth used for the mining industry; other plants were projected at the rate of growth projected by ENDESA for power production in the country as a whole—thermal and hydro— on the assumption that hydro would supply a negligible share of increased power in the far north.

Losses were estimated at being equal to 0.42 per cent of intake, reflecting the experience of the Central Pacific and Southern Pacific regions of the United States (approximately equivalent to the state of California).

The loss rate for the United States is a measure of fresh water losses and, therefore, is affected by the use of ocean water as well as by the degree of recirculation that is practiced. However, a relatively large error in the coefficient is not likely to result in a significant difference in total of water requirements measured as losses, because under the most adverse conditions loss rates are a very small fraction of intake unless recirculation reaches a high level.

Table 34 shows that projected water use by thermal plants other than mining in Tarapacá, Antofagasta, and Atacama is 5.79 times current use. Power produced by the mines is estimated to increase by lesser amounts. South of Atacama, where the interconnected hydro and thermal grid

[6] Supplied by the Centro de Investigaciones Económicas, Universidad Católica.

Table 34
PROJECTED WATER USE IN THERMAL ELECTRIC POWER
(*Thousand cubic meters per year*)

		Intake 1985			
		Multiple of increase over 1965			
Province	1965	Medium A	Medium B	Medium A	Medium B
Tarapacá	*110*	*5.79*	*5.79*	*637*	*637*
Copper	–	–	–	–	–
Others	110	5.79	5.79	637	637
Antofagasta	*246,071*	3.08	4.02	*756,816*	*988,910*
Copper	177,171	2.02	3.33	357,885	589,979
Others	68,900	5.79	5.79	398,931	398,931
Atacama	*2,806*	3.53	4.31	*9,898*	*12,104*
Copper	1,684	2.02	3.33	3,402	5,608
Others	1,122	5.79	5.79	6,496	6,496
Coquimbo	8,885	1.39	1.39	12,350	12,350
Valparaíso	93,253	1.39	1.39	129,622	129,622
Santiago	56,293	1.39	1.39	78,247	78,247
Linares	1,421	1.39	1.39	1,975	1,975
Concepción	1,403	1.39	1.39	1,950	1,950
Bío-Bío	7,771	1.39	1.39	10,802	10,802
Llanquihue	553	1.39	1.39	769	769
Chiloé	1	1.39	1.39	1	1
Aysén	1	1.39	1.39	1	1
Magallanes	1,354	1.39	1.39	1,882	1,882

Source: Centro de Investigaciones Económicas, Universidad Católica.

exists, projected increase of thermal power water use is only 1.39 times present use. Within the area covered by the interconnected grid most of the new capacity is scheduled to come from hydroelectric plants.

ENDESA, which will be responsible for virtually all future public utility power additions within the country, plans to increase its hydroelectric capacity within the interconnected grid area (La Serena to Puerto Montt) from 537 megawatts to about 1,900 megawatts in 1978.[7] According to earlier plans reported by CEPAL,[8] ENDESA has expected to add

[7] From a table prepared by Michael Nelson, Chile-California Program.
[8] CEPAL, p. 77. CEPAL gives two figures for expected additional hydro capacity: 1,254,600 kw. (p. 77) and 1,124,600 kw. (p. 83).

about 1,255 megawatts by 1973 and another 2,744 megawatts by 1990, with the following regional distribution:

Region	1957	Installed Capacity (100 kw) Added by 1973	Added between 1973 and 1990
Norte Grande	1.4	9.0	–
Norte Chico	21.8	30.0	6.0
Chile Central	464.9	1,156.0	1,268.0
Sur Chico	25.2	59.6	1,470.0
Sur Grande	0.2	–	–
Total	513.5	1,254.6	2,744.0

Total hydroelectric capacity of 4,512 megawatts in 1990 represents 14 per cent of the country's gross potential of 31,880 megawatts, figured at average flow.

Eighty per cent of existing hydro capacity, and even more of produced energy, is run-of-the-river. Of 1.1 million kilowatts of new capacity under construction or under study, 50 to 60 per cent is to be regulated. (One project, Antuco on the Río Laja, is shown to be both run-of-the-river and regulated.)

An expansion in hydroelectric power installations in the Central Zone will compete with efforts to provide a higher degree of regularity in the supply of water for irrigation. In the Central Zone the rivers follow a mixed pluvio-glacial regimen, which means higher flows in the summer than in winter. If hydro installations are run-of-the-river, and if they are above the sites of irrigation, the two uses are neutral with respect to each other. If, however, the hydro installation is dependent upon a reservoir of such size that either season or annual flows are regularized, the uses will be competitive. For hydro, the main releases from a reservoir will be in the winter; summer flows will be stored. Irrigators, of course, need the water in spring and summer.

For the year 1990, installations utilizing 2,000 kilowatts of capacity out of a gross potential of 14,085,000 kilowatts are projected for the Sur Grande. The explanation for such vast underuse is the distance over which power would have to be transmitted. From the Río Baker, say, which has itself two-thirds of the gross potential of the sum of all rivers from the Aconcagua to and including the Toltén, to Puerto Montt, the southernmost city of the Central Valley, is roughly 450 miles. This does not exceed the distance over which power is being sent in other countries, but apparently topography and climate do not yet justify use of this source of energy in the near-term plans of Chile. ENDESA conceives of the hydroelectric resources of the South as a reserve for future exploitation.

The price of electric power per kilowatt-hour is about the same in Chile as in the United States, according to studies prepared for the Seminario Latinoamericano de Energía Eléctrica in 1962.[9] The average cost of Chilean hydroelectric plants built in the past was US$214 per kilowatt which compares with the less expensive of the hydro plants under construction or consideration in the 1950's in the United States;[10] the average cost of plants being planned or under construction is US$139 per kilowatt.[11] Fixed costs of ENDESA's plants are computed on the basis of 8 per cent interest and fifty-year depreciation.[12]

It is estimated that two new steam plants with a combined capacity of 200,000 kilowatts will cost $185 per kilowatt. The steam plants will require an outlay of foreign exchange to cover 66 per cent of the costs of construction, whereas only 30 per cent of the construction costs of hydro plants will be paid in foreign exchange. Operating costs of hydro plants are lower than operating costs of steam plants. Based on these figures, it is reasonable to anticipate a growth of hydroelectric power relative to steam even though the hydro power must be transmitted over greater distances. According to data prepared for the Seminario Latinoamericano de Energía Eléctrica,[13] for plants "under construction and projected," costs of transmission are included in the costs of generation but an additional cost of $32 per kilowatt on the average has to be added for interconnection. The cost advantage of hydro plants persists after taking interconnection costs into account. Except for one peaking plant with a construction cost of $162 per kilowatt and a plant factor of 26 per cent, the cost per kilowatt-hour of new hydropower should be no more than current costs, which range between 6.9 and 8.0 mills. In at least three plants the costs should be between 4 and 6 mills per kilowatt-hour.

One cannot infer that Chilean investment in hydroelectric power is economically justified merely because capital costs are as low or lower

[9] U.N., Comisión Económica para América Latina. Estudios Sobre la Electricidad en América Latina, Vol. 1 (Mexico City; 1962), p. 380.

[10] Bonneville ($211); added capacity TVA ($266). Computed from data on amounts allocated to electric power and installed capacity, Commission on Organization of the Executive Branch of the Government, Task Force Report on Water Resources and Power (Washington, June 1955), pp. 262, 423, 428, 453, 458, 555, 562.

[11] Estudios, Vol. I, p. 419. However, in this table escudos were converted into dollars at the parity rate of 1.314 escudos per dollar. Elsewhere in this same document the official conversion rate of E⁰ = $0.95 was used. The latter rate would raise the dollar equivalent by about 25 per cent.

[12] Ibid., p. 407.

[13] Ibid., pp. 388, 390.

than current capital costs in the United States.[14] The need for power is not a fact revealed solely by the cost of power. There is evidence, however,[15] that future capacity is planned to meet an anticipated growth in power use; rarely have facilities been constructed in the expectation that their availability would stimulate a demand. ENDESA's plans do, however, take into account any developmental programs of CORFO or other governmental or private activities.

Of the hydro installations in operation, under construction, or planned, only one, Rapel, is downstream, large, and dependent upon a relatively large reservoir. Fourteen installations are far enough downstream to offer some competition with other uses of water.[16] The installed capacity of twelve of these amounts to a total of 26,000 kilowatts. Rapel will have 350,000 kilowatts; no data are available for one. According to ENDESA engineers, Rapel should offer no competition with irrigation because of the limited amount of land capable of being irrigated. Water from the reservoir will be used to irrigate some new land to replace that which will be inundated by the lake behind the dam.

In a paper presented to the Seminario Latinoamericano de Energía Eléctrica, Raúl Saez, Manager of ENDESA, discussed various problems relating to the expansion of capacity, the choice of prime mover, and location of plants. Among the items with which he dealt were price policies applicable to fuels; import, export, and exchange rate policies as they related to fuels; the lack of stability in policies that has impeded adoption of a rational energy program; rates charged the user of electric energy; and the financing of new investment and criteria for justifying and selecting new projects, whether hydro or fuel.[17] He pointed out that Latin America faced three basic scarcities: trustworthy data, technically competent personnel, and financial resources. Consequently it was impossible to overcome simultaneously the absolute lack of electric service in some areas and the growing deficiency in other areas. The problem of priority in new investment was much more complex for public power enterprises than for private, since the latter needed only to consider profitability, whereas the former had to take into account a much wider range of factors

---

[14] Plant factors are relatively high in Chile. Of those in operation, the largest has a plant factor of 65.4 per cent. The lowest plant factor is 40 per cent. Of thirteen being constructed or still in the planning stage, three are expected to have a plant factor between 24 and 30 per cent; five will have plant factors of more than 60 per cent. *Ibid.*, p. 418.

[15] Conversations with ENDESA officials.

[16] Based on a map prepared by CEPAL from data supplied by ENDESA. See *Estudios*, Vol. I, pp. 164-67.

[17] Raúl Saez, "Criterios Económicos para la Selección y Desarrollo de Centrales y Sistemas Eléctricos," in *Estudios*, Vol. I, pp. 257-99.

relating to economic development within both regional and national perspectives. Saez emphasized the difficulties encountered in planning for the future that were created by lack of data—data needed to estimate future demand for power as well as data regarding the resources with which to meet the demand. "We know, moreover, of a case in which the decision to develop electric service for one zone rather than for another, was in part fundamentally based on the better state of basic information of consumption and resources."[18] The Central Sauzal was given priority because it had better hydrologic data than other projects of equal size built later.

In some cases priority was based upon the need to mesh an additional supply of power with other economic plans—such as development of a particular region or industry. In other cases priority rested upon an implicit or explicit scale of benefits, relative degrees of "urgency" such as the existence of power rationing, or distinctions between "productive" and "consumptive" uses.[19]

Another point touched upon by Saez was the choice between a few large plants coupled with an extensive distribution system and a large number of smaller plants serving smaller areas. A completely interconnected system has much merit in Chile because of the variety of river regimens. In the North high flows come in the summer from snow and ice melt, with clearly marked low flows in the winter. Farther south the regimen is mixed, since the winter trough is partly offset by rains. In the South, flows are relatively constant all year round, regulated by many natural lakes. However, because of the high cost of high-voltage lines, ENDESA, at least momentarily, is following a system of constructing separate plants for each region. Only two "modest" interconnections have been made, one of 110 kilovolts and 105 kilometers in length and another of 150 kilovolts and 242 kilometers. At present, and in the foreseeable future, interconnections are being made mainly within the Central Zone, between latitudes 27° and 42° among ENDESA's plants, other public utility plants, and industrial self-suppliers, and among hydro and thermal plants. This "preponderantly hydroelectric system" uses thermal power to supply the deficit of energy during the winter and in dry years.[20] The plans of

---

[18] *Ibid.*, p. 266. Saez noted that ENDESA's decision to give priority to the Pilmaiquén system over others of greater "economic urgency" was based in part on this consideration.

[19] *Ibid.*

[20] Renato E. Salazar and Carlos Croxatto, "Métodos Empleados por la Empresa Nacional de Electricidad S.A. para la Selección de Alternativas de Abastecimiento Eléctrico en el Sistema Interconectado de la Zona Central de Chile," in *Estudios*, Vol. II, p. 167.

ENDESA rest, not upon study of separate generating plants, but upon analysis of alternative systems of hydro run-of-the-river, hydro with regulating reservoirs, and thermal power plants. Hydro plants within a region are interconnected to make full use of complementary hydrologic regimens and to reduce to a minimum the deficit to be supplied by thermal power, taking into account transmission losses.

MULTIPLE-PURPOSE PROJECTS

There are very few multiple-purpose projects in use, under construction, or under consideration in Chile. The main reason given by ENDESA is the unfavorable topography whereby costs of reservoir construction in the Andean valleys is "extraordinarily expensive."[21] Of thirteen projects for which we have information, six have daily regulating ponds, five have larger reservoirs for seasonal regulation, and two have capacity for interannual regulation. In the lake country and beyond, to the south, natural regulation and the natural regimen of the rivers eliminate the need for artificial storage. For a number of hydro projects, e.g., Lago Laja, Canutillar, Pullinque, and Pilmaiquén, natural lakes are controlled at relatively low cost. There are a limited number of sites for production of power within the coastal cordillera close to the sea. Such are Rapel and Cabimbao. Here, again, because of terrain the possibilities of multiple-purpose reservoirs are limited.[22] No detailed studies were available that indicated the costs, benefits, and range of possibilities that had been considered and discarded in the process of making the final choice.[23]

A large multiple-purpose dam at Colbún in the Maule basin has recently come under scrutiny as a result of investigations carried on by the Chile-California Program. On the basis of very preliminary studies it has been ascertained that a dam could be erected with a capacity of 1,500 million cubic meters of water, which would support installed capacity of 208 megawatts, serve 70,000 hectares of new irrigated land, and supplement the water supply of an additional 30,000 hectares. In addition, return flows would support 20,000 hectares and other land would have the security of its water supplies raised from 85 per cent to 98 per cent. Since

[21] Alberto Bennet L. et al., "Influencia de la Magnitud y Características de una Central Hidroeléctrica en el Costa de las Obras." in Estudios, Vol. II, p. 327.

[22] The small irrigation project of Rapel was noted above.

[23] Chilean experience is not unique. Note the following comment in a slightly different context regarding Corps of Engineers projects in the United States: "Ordinarily it is impossible to tell whether the size of a project is correct, however, since data on the costs and benefits of marginal increments usually are not given in project reports." (Irving K. Fox and Orris C. Herfindahl, "Attainment of Efficiency in Satisfying Demands for Water Resources," Proceedings, American Economic Association, May 1964, p. 1201.)

Colbún could re-regulate water from Laguna del Maule now reserved for irrigation, an additional 192,000 kilowatts of capacity could be installed, bringing the total for this project to about 400,000 kilowatts. As has been said, if subsequent studies prove its merit, Colbún would be the largest project yet undertaken in Chile, the only major case in which a reservoir was used for re-regulation, and, since recreation would also be important, the only multipurpose project of any consequence.[24]

Except for reservoirs designed to supply daily regulation, ENDESA as yet produces no power from reservoirs that were artificially constructed,[25] but will do so at Rapel, the reservoir plant under construction. Seven other projects using artificial storage were reported as being under study: Cabimbao, Guaquirilo, Melado, Colbún, Porvenir, Ralco, and Collipulli. Total capacity is about 8,000 million cubic meters, of which Ralco Grande accounts for 4,100 million cubic meters. As we shall see later, estimates of storage capacity to meet offstream needs by 1985 in the same part of the country as these projects are located range between 8,500 and 22,000 million cubic meters. One might anticipate, therefore, a more intense effort than has been made up to now to plan dual- or multiple-purpose projects.

There is little further to say about hydroelectric power production. Without detailed systems studies one cannot anticipate how effectively storage for power will serve other uses. To the extent that regulatory storage can be used for power production, the costs of water allocated to non-power uses can be reduced. To that extent, therefore, a cost constraint on non-power users will be less binding than is assumed in a later chapter.

ENDESA has no plans at present for the production of hydroelectric power from regulated storage for any basins to the north of Santiago. Since projected requirements call for about 1,650 million cubic meters of storage capacity, the possibility of multiple-purpose uses should be fully explored. In this part of the country—i.e., Santiago northward—primary dedication of water to power production is probably unwise, but an allocation of costs and water on an incremental basis may justify hydroelectric installations.

EFFECT OF HYDROELECTRIC REQUIREMENTS ON ECONOMIC MODELS OF WATER USE

Although requirements for hydroelectric power are not part of the formal models developed later, the omission does not necessarily introduce a large error. Should the timing of flow requirements for hydroelectric power coincide with downstream irrigation and other uses, required flows

[24] Preliminary reports made available by Michael Nelson, Chile-California Program.
[25] Cipreses, Abanico, and Pilmaiquén use water of natural lakes.

are complementary, and the storage created for hydroelectric power can be counted as storage required to regularize flow in accordance with the model.

If hydroelectric uses are not complementary in time, and power installations are upstream from other uses, there would need to be re-regulation. In this case total storage will have been underestimated by the amount of hydroelectric storage or re-regulatory storage, whichever is greater.

If hydroelectric uses are downstream from other uses, and if because of upstream evapotranspiration there is inadequate water to meet hydroelectric requirements, and if it should turn out that hydroelectric power is given precedence over other uses, our model overstates the conceivable level of non-power uses but does not necessarily overstate total storage requirements. What was estimated as needed for non-power uses can be assigned to power production.

VIII

MANUFACTURING USES OF WATER

Chile's manufactures include "practically all the . . . non-durable consumer goods needed by the domestic market, . . . [and] substantial production of intermediate goods (pulp and paper, rubber, petroleum and coal products, non-metallic mineral products, and basic metal products). . . . The metal and metal-transorming industries are less developed. . . ."[1]

The present analysis of industrial uses of water has been directed mainly to the five major water-using and water-polluting industries: food, pulp and paper, chemicals, petroleum refining, and iron and steel production. All others have been aggregated into a single group.

The deficiency of data regarding the manufacturing uses of water is at least as acute as in other spheres. In four industries information was obtained directly from the companies themselves. In other instances it was necessary to estimate water requirements by a chain of inferences. There is practically no information on waste loads, level of waste treatment, and adverse effects of waste loads.

Published information regarding industrial water intake in Chile is found in the CEPAL study of 1960 and in Hansen's 1962 study brought out by the Dirección de Planeamiento del Ministerio de Obras Públicas.[2] The findings of both studies tend to be intertwined. Both studies estimated water requirements—current and future—by relying upon a relatively small amount of specific information supplied by Chilean manufacturers supplemented by coefficients taken from other countries, notably the United States.

As Hansen points out, ". . . there are no official statistics regarding the quantities of water used by industry in Chile," nor is there ". . . an official organization charged specifically with the problem of industrial water supply." While the Dirección de Riego ". . . indeed intervenes in the grant

[1] Unofficial statement, Instituto Latinoamericano de Planificación, March 1966.
[2] Hansen *et al.*

105

of water rights, this work, although necessary, is totally inadequate since it neither defines a clear policy to follow nor accomplishes any form of hydraulic planning."[3] Nor, Hansen might have added, does it gather information on industrial uses of water.

The distribution of manufacturing activity among industries and provinces can be ascertained for the year 1956 from *Industrias Año 1956*.[4] In 1956 the value of manufacturing output amounted to 407 billion pesos in 1956 prices. (This would be approximately 1.1 billion escudos at 1962 prices, and therefore, roughly equal to 1.1 billion U.S. dollars at the official 1962 exchange rate.) As Tables 35 and 36 show, most manufacturing output was concentrated in a few industries located in a few provinces. Of the twenty-five provinces, fourteen accounted for 5.6 per cent of total market value. At the other extreme, three provinces accounted for 83.8 per cent of which one, Santiago, accounted for 52.9 per cent. These three provinces, Valparaíso, Concepción, and Santiago, all border on the ocean, but whereas the cities of Valparaíso and Concepción are themselves located on the coast, the city of Santiago is in the interior, a circumstance that

Table 35

MANUFACTURING, PERCENTAGE DISTRIBUTION OF MARKET VALUE AMONG INDUSTRY CLASSES, CHILE, 1956

Industry	Per cent of total
Food	25.3
Beverages	3.0
Tobacco	2.8
Textiles	17.2
Shoes and clothing	5.8
Furniture and wood products	3.8
Paper and cellulose	2.9
Printing and publishing	2.2
Hides and leather	2.4
Rubber products	1.2
Chemical products	7.4
Petroleum refining and coal products	2.4
Cement, clay, glass, etc.	4.6
Basic metals	10.2
Metal manufactures, machinery, etc.	8.8
	100.0

Total market value, 1956 pesos, 407,093,267,000

Source: Dirección de Estadística y Censos, *Industrias, Año 1956* (Santiago, 1961).

[3] *Ibid.*, p. 17.
[4] Dirección de Estadística y Censos, Santiago.

Table 36
PERCENTAGE DISTRIBUTION OF MANUFACTURING OUTPUT
AMONG PROVINCES, BASED ON MARKET VALUE, 1956

Province	Per cent of national total
Tarapacá	0.6
Antofagasta	1.0
Atacama	a
Coquimbo	0.9
Aconcagua	0.8
Valparaíso	17.7
Santiago	53.0
O'Higgins	1.6
Colchagua	0.7
Curicó	0.4
Talca	1.6
Linares	0.3
Ñuble	0.6
Concepción	13.4
Arauco	0.1
Bío-Bío	0.7
Malleco	0.7
Cautín	0.9
Valdivia	2.4
Osorno	1.4
Llanquihue	0.6
Chiloé	a
Aysén	a
Magallanes	0.5

a Less than .05%.
Source: *Industrias, Año 1956.*

makes the problem of present and future pollution in the Maipo and Mapocho rivers especially acute. Food, textiles, and basic metals accounted for 53 per cent of total manufacturing value. Even though manufacturing is only in its infancy, there is no reason to expect a radical alteration in either geographic or industrial concentrations unless some unanticipated factor intervenes. (See table on next page.)[5]

[5] After the above was written the table below was unofficially prepared by the Instituto Latinoamericano de Planificación. According to the new table, between 1956 and 1964 the relative importance of consumer goods (mainly non-durable) fell from 62.5 per cent to 50.3 per cent of the total market value of manufacturing industries; intermediate goods (pulp and paper, rubber manufactures, chemicals, etc.) rose from 28.7 per cent to 35.2 per cent of total market value; and metal products and machinery industries rose from 8.8 per cent to 14.6 per cent of total market value. Since projections were based on industry plans as of 1965, the new figures do not affect the figures for estimated outputs in 1985, shown in Table 37.

Structure of Production of the Factory Sector of Manufacturing

(*Percentage Distribution of Market Value*)

Industrial branches according to the United Nations standard international trade classification	Existing situation (1964)[a]
Traditional Industries (principally producers of consumer goods, especially non-durable)	50.3
Food	18.1
Beverages	2.8
Tobacco	1.1
Textiles	14.4
Clothing and footwear	8.0
Furniture and fittings	1.4
Leather and leather manufactures	0.9
Printed matter	3.6
Intermediate Industries (principally producers of intermediate goods)	35.2
Pulp, paper, and manufactures thereof	3.4
Rubber manufactures	2.1
Chemicals	6.6
Petroleum and coal products	4.8
Non-metallic mineral manufactures	6.6
Basic metal manufactures	11.7
Metal and Metal Transforming Industries (principally producers of durable consumer goods and capital goods)	14.6
Metal manufactures	–
Machinery	–
Electrical machinery and equipment	13.3
Transport equipment	–
Miscellaneous	1.3
Total	100.0

[a] The factory (non-artisan) sector of industry is defined as including establishments that employ five workers or more. Based on the figures for value in the 1957 industrial census, adjusted to bring them up to date to 1964 according to the industrial production index of the Dirección de Estadística y Censos.

MANUFACTURING: PROJECTIONS OF OUTPUT

Manufacturing output was projected for the country as a whole and then allocated to provinces, and in some cases to cities. The methods that were used for making the projections and provincial distributions fell into two distinct categories:

1) Projections based upon plans of the enterprises themselves or of CORFO or of ODEPLAN for expansions of output in the future;
2) Estimates of future production based on the assumption that output would meet projected demand computed on the basis of estimated growth in population, income per capita, and income-elasticity of demand. Where appropriate, an estimated foreign trade balance was also taken into account.

Where income elasticities were used the following assumptions were adopted:

Annual rate of increase in:

Assumption	National Income	Population[6]
A	3.75%	2.43%
B	5.50%	2.43%

Per capita, the annual rates of growth in income were:

Assumption A: $3.75\% - 2.43\% = 1.32\%$
Assumption B: $5.50\% - 2.43\% = 3.07\%$.

Per capita demand was then projected as the product of the coefficient of income elasticity[7] multiplied by the rate of growth of per capita income. This product was augmented by the rate of population increase to yield the rate of growth of total demand for a given industry group, i.e., total demand was projected as growing at a rate equal to:

$.0132E + .0243$ for Assumption A
$.0307E + .0243$ for Assumption B

where E is the income elasticity of demand and .0243 is the medium rate of population growth. The way in which growth in production was related to growth in demand was established separately for each industry class. Projections were made for food and beverages, pulp and paper, chemicals,

---

[6] The "middle" rate of population growth was used for both assumptions; hence these projections are identified as "Medium A" and "Medium B." It is assumed that personal income grows at the same rate as GNP.

[7] Income elasticity coefficients were computed as linear in logarithms.

Table 37
PERCENTAGE DISTRIBUTION OF MANUFACTURING
OUTPUT AMONG PROVINCES, 1985

Province	Food[a]	Pulp[b]	Paper[c]	Chem.[d]	Petroleum chem.[e]	Petroleum Ref.[f]	Steel[g]	All others[h]
Tarapacá	1	–	–	2	–	–	–	–
Antofagasta	1	–	–	8	–	–	–	–
Atacama	–	–	–	–	–	–	–	–
Coquimbo	2	–	–	2	–	–	–	1
Aconcagua	2	–	–	–	–	–	–	1
Valparaíso	22	0.5	2	16	3	50	–	17
Santiago	36	2	22	63	–	30	5	64
O'Higgins	5	–	–	1	–	–	–	–
Colchagua	1	–	–	–	–	–	–	1
Curicó	1	–	–	–	–	–	–	–
Talca	4	0.5	2	2	–	–	–	1
Maule	–	15	–	–	–	–	–	–
Linares	1	–	–	–	–	–	–	–
Ñuble	1	–	–	–	–	–	–	–
Concepción	6	9	25	5	12	20	95	11
Arauco	–	15	–	–	–	–	–	–
Bío-Bío	2	57	45	–	–	–	–	–
Malleco	2	–	–	–	–	–	–	–
Cautín	2	–	–	–	–	–	–	1
Valdivia	4	1	4	–	–	–	–	2
Osorno	4	–	–	–	–	–	–	–
Llanquihue	2	–	–	–	–	–	–	–
Chiloé	–	–	–	–	–	–	–	–
Aysén	–	–	–	–	–	–	–	–
Magallanes	1	–	–	–	85	–	–	–
Total	100	100	100	100	100	100	100	100

[a] Based on the 1956 distribution of market value, as reported by *Industrias, Año 1956*.
[b] Based on the expected distribution of output in 1970, as reported by the FAO-CEPAL study "El Papel y la Celulosa en América Latina," E/CN, 12/570/Rev. 2, mimeo. (New York: United Nations, May 1965.)
[c] Same as [b].
[d] Same as [a]. Aconcagua, Ñuble, Bío-Bío, Cautín, Valdivia, Osorno, Llanquihue, and Magallanes together add up to 1%.
[e] This distribution is implied in company plans extended to 1985.
[f] Based on company plans for 1976.
[g] Based on 1961.
[h] Same as [a]. Tarapacá, Antofagasta, Atacama, O'Higgins, Curicó, Maule, Linares, Ñuble, Arauco, Bío-Bío, Malleco, Osorno, Llanquihue, Chiloé, Aysén, and Magallanes together add up to 1%.

petroleum refining, and steel. All other manufacturing activity was consolidated into a single category.

The method of determining regional distributions varied with the industry. In the case of food, it was assumed that the 1956 percentage distribution would be maintained. The same assumption was made for chemicals and "all others." For pulp and paper it was assumed that the planned relative distribution for 1970 -would be perpetuated to 1985. Petrochemicals and petroleum refining were based upon company plans as extended into the future. The distribution of steel production was based upon the 1961 percentage distribution. Table 37 shows the results.

FOOD AND BEVERAGES

The food industry is composed of a relatively large number of small enterprises, except in a few activities such as sugar refining, milk products, and beer. Output of the industry as a whole was projected by combining foods and beverages into a single group in order to make it comparable to the U.S. classification. This was done by weighting foods 85 per cent and beverages 15 per cent, reflecting the average respective market values of outputs during the period 1948-55. Separate income elasticities of demand were applied to each. The coefficient for food was taken as 0.5, based upon an estimate drawn from a study of the Centro de Investigaciones Económicas, Universidad Católica,[8] and an elasticity for beverages of 2.41 taken from an index of output of beverages prepared by Dirección de Estadística y Censos.[9] Weighting the two as indicated above yielded a combined income elasticity of demand of 0.8. In the absence of a clear policy regarding the imports and exports of foods, and in the presence of possible contradictory forces such as increased production of import-substitutables and increased consumption of imports such as tea, coffee, and tropical fruits as incomes rise, it was assumed that the absolute trade balance in food manufactures would remain unchanged and that production would follow the projection of demand.

Production was distributed by province in accordance with the 1956 distribution of market value.

PULP AND PAPER

A study of FAO-CEPAL[10] estimated pulp and paper production for 1970. From data in this study estimates of income elasticity of demand

[8] This elasticity was suggested by Mario Corbo of the Centro.
[9] That is, imports of beverages have been negligible and so it was assumed that output has met demand and that the effects of price elasticity could be ignored.
[10] FAO-CEPAL, "El Papel y la Celulosa en América Latina," E/CN, 12/570/Rev. 2, prepared for the Eleventh Session of CEPAL, Mexico. (Mimeo) (New York: United Nations, May 1965.)

were drawn and an export balance obtained for 1970. The absolute size of the 1970 export balance was assumed to persist through 1985 and production was assumed to grow in accordance with the rate of growth yielded by the growth of population, the change in per capita income, and the income elasticity of demand. Projections of paper and cardboard were separated from projections of pulp. The input of pulp per unit of paper was based upon the 1970 relationship given in the FAO-CEPAL study. Pulp exports were assumed to persist to 1985 at the level estimated for 1970. The relative distribution of output of pulp and paper among provinces was assumed to remain constant over the period 1970-85 in accordance with FAO-CEPAL estimates for 1970.

CHEMICALS

The chemicals category includes inorganic chemicals, miscellaneous organic chemicals, petrochemicals, and pharmaceuticals. At the time of writing this study there had been no production of petrochemicals in Chile. ENAP's[11] plans for production of petrochemicals through 1978 were adopted and extended to 1985 at an 8 per cent annual rate of growth, as estimated by ENAP. Their plans included data on aggregate output and location of plants.

Inorganic chemicals, miscellaneous organic chemicals, and pharmaceuticals have been produced in Chile. Output grew at 3.4 per cent per year during the period 1953-63. This was the low rate of growth projected to 1985. Because CORFO[12] expected a much higher rate of growth in the future, but without specific production plans, the industry's growth was also projected at 6 per cent per year, the rate used by CEPAL, as the high rate of growth.

Output was distributed among provinces on the basis of the 1956 distribution of market value produced.[13]

PETROLEUM REFINING

Demand for petroleum refining was projected on the basis of population and income growth, since ENAP's engineers indicated that refining operations would not exceed domestic consumption because of the shortage of domestic crude. Output was distributed among plants in accordance with ENAP plans for 1976.

[11] Empresa Nacional de Petróleo; interview with Estanislao Fabres, Ing.
[12] During an interview with Patricio Castro, he said that CORFO hoped to have the industry grow at 12 per cent per year to 1976.
[13] *Industrias, Año 1956.*

STEEL

Virtually the entire steel industry is within one establishment, Compañía de Acero del Pacífico (CAP). No change in the structure of the industry was envisioned. CAP has production plans to 1970. Domestic consumption was projected on the basis of population and income growth, except that income elasticity was computed by lagging consumption two years. The difference between projected demand for 1970 and CAP's planned production for 1970 was assumed to be exported. Exports were kept constant to 1985, and total production was assumed to grow in accordance with projected domestic demand.

ALL OTHER MANUFACTURING INDUSTRIES

The remaining industries are tobacco, textiles, apparel, lumber and wood products, printing, rubber products, leather and hides, stone, clay and glass, fabricated metal products, machinery, electrical machinery, transportation equipment, instruments, and miscellaneous. These were aggregated by value added and projected at two rates: (1) the historical rate of growth of the total manufacturing sector during the period 1953-63, namely, 6.1 per cent; (2) an expected rate of growth according to ODE-PLAN, of 8 per cent.[14]

The foregoing industrial projections (see Table 38) are not to be confused with serious industry location studies. Neither possible new marketing opportunities nor barriers created by unfavorable costs were investigated. Nor was it sought to establish the optimum location of an activity within the country. Instead, the projections are designed to approximate, roughly but rapidly, reasonable expectations on the basis of readily available evidence. There is the possibility also that some projections are inconsistent with others—such as implicit labor requirements of projected industrial outputs and the implicit labor supply of projected populations.

The implicit annual rate of growth projected to 1985 for manufacturing as a whole[15] is about 4.9 per cent for Assumption A and about 6.8 per cent for Assumption B, the latter being a rate slightly lower than the approximately 7 per cent growth rate in all manufacturing output between 1958 and 1963 reported by CEPAL.[16] Should the actual rate of growth follow the low path while planning follows the high path, by 1985 planned use of water will lead actual use by about five years. Most, but not all, major

---

[14] Interview with Eduardo García, Vice Director. ODEPLAN'S estimate for rate of growth during the period 1965-70 was extended to 1985.

[15] Exclusive of the petrochemical industry.

[16] *Boletín*, Vol. II, No. 1, p. 181.

Table 38
MANUFACTURING, OUTPUT PROJECTIONS, 1985

Industry	Growth rate (%) Medium A	Growth rate (%) Medium B	Output index (1964 = 100) Medium A	Output index (1964 = 100) Medium B	Output (1,000 metric tons) Medium A	Output (1,000 metric tons) Medium B
Paper	4.4	6.5	247	377	402.5	614.4
Pulp	6.0	7.3	343	439	610.4	781.7
Food and beverages	3.5	5.0	206	279	–	–
Chemicals	3.4	6.0	202	340	–	–
Petrochemicals [a]						
Ethylene	–	–	–	–	100.0	
Aromatics	–	–	–	–	25.0	
Ammonia	–	–	–	–	740.0	
Steel	4.5	6.2	252	355	1,513.6	2,131.2
Petroleum refining	4.7	7.7	262	475	7,619.9	14,176.3
All others	6.1	8.0	347	503	–	–

[a] There was no output of petrochemicals at the time of writing. Projection is based on data furnished by ENAP; interview with Estanislao Fabres, Ing.

water-using industries in Chile have been growing more rapidly than manufacturing as a whole, the main laggards being food, beverages, and chemicals. Current programs for food and chemicals envisage an acceleration in their growth, but by how much relative to manufacturing as a whole cannot be ascertained.

ESTIMATES OF WATER USE: REVISION OF 1957 WATER USE COEFFICIENTS IN MANUFACTURING

The Chilean census of manufactures (1957) collected information by industry and province covering employment, payrolls, installed horsepower, energy consumed, new investment, current expenses, total income, and value added. (See Table 39.) No data were tabulated or published on physical output. CEPAL based its projections of water use on its own survey of water use and physical output of major water-using industries. The procedure of the present study, benefitting somewhat by the passage of time, was the same as CEPAL's. Data on 1957 water use and production were obtained from pulp and paper, petroleum refining, steel, and sugar refining industries. The coefficients of water use so reported (see discussion of projections, above) fell within the range of coefficients given in studies

Table 39
MANUFACTURING, TOTAL INCOME AND VALUE ADDED,
CHILE, 1957
($E°\ 1,000$)

Industry	Income [a]	Value added [a]
Food	167,272	54,939
Beverages	22,682	13,709
Tobacco	18,591	16,327
Textiles	75,490	40,198
Shoes and clothing	50,010	23,642
Wood products and furniture	26,071	14,465
Paper and paper products	18,951	5,740
Printing and publishing	17,156	11,171
Hides and leather	9,973	3,814
Rubber products	8,333	3,765
Chemicals	48,436	23,763
Petroleum refining and coal products	23,343	9,643
Cement, clay, glass, etc.	28,316	15,858
Basic metals	58,025	33,016
Machinery and miscellaneous	55,217	33,348
Total	627,866	303,398

[a] Rounded.
Source: III Censo Nacional de Manufacturas.

prepared by the National Association of Manufacturers and the United Nations.[17]

Information given by the sugar refining industry[18] indicated that CEPAL's estimate for "food"—a two-digit class that included sugar refining—was probably too low by a substantial amount. There were differences between the figures reported to CEPAL and to us for steel, pulp and paper, and petroleum, as well, but these were differences of 10-15 per cent, small enough to be explained by the passage of time, inaccuracies of measurements, or source of information within the industry. In the case of food, however, the discrepancy was much greater. CEPAL estimated 1957 water intake as 2.5 million cubic meters, whereas the water use coefficient for the refining of sugar beets indicated that for sugar refining alone, after adding the refining of cane sugar, water use amounted to 8.4 million cubic meters.

[17] National Association of Manufacturers, Water in Industry (New York, December 1950). United Nations Department of Economic and Social Affairs, Water for Industrial Use (New York, 1958).
[18] Letter from Enzo Meschi, Chief, Departamento de Investigaciones, Industria Azucarera Nacional, S.A., April 21, 1965.

Since the coefficients of water use for the four industries about which direct information was available corresponded with experience in the United States, it seemed reasonable to use a U.S. coefficient when no other was available. This procedure was barred, however, by the absence of data on production measured in physical units. The possibility of using a U.S. water coefficient per unit of labor also was barred, because the ratio of productivity of Chilean workers to U.S. workers was probably different from the ratio of the respective water inputs per unit of product. Moreover, there was no reason to expect that physical product per unit of value added would be the same in both countries (after establishing a parity between US dollars 1954 value added and Chilean escudos 1957 value added).

The problem was especially important for foods and beverages, since these are highly water-polluting as well as water-using industries. The only component of the food and beverage industries in Chile for which we could get an estimate of water use was the refining of sugar beets. An official of Industria Azucarera Nacional, S.A. (IANSA)[19] estimated that the rate of water use was 1.5 liters per second per ton of sugar per day of operation. IANSA's refineries are in continuous operation for five months a year; water intake for the five-month year in 1957 was 3.2 million cubic meters. In that year sugar refined from cane amounted to 158,200 tons, and from beets to 24,200 tons. (Today the output of beet sugar is much higher, and has grown relative to cane.) No water use data were available for cane sugar. Using the 1954 U.S. coefficient for cane sugar yielded 34.4 cubic meters per ton or 5.4 million cubic meters per year. Thus, estimated partly from IANSA data and partly from the U.S. coefficient for cane sugar, the result was 8.6 million cubic meters per year. When Chilean water use was estimated by the value added method (see below) the answer was 7.5 million cubic meters. The figure for IANSA's water use, 3.2 million cubic meters, exceeded by 700,000 cubic meters the estimate made by CEPAL for the food category as a whole.

From the physical output and water input data provided by the four industries in Chile it was concluded that in the absence of direct information on water use a reasonably good estimate might be arrived at by using U.S. industry coefficients per unit of value added after establishing a monetary equivalence. A rate of parity, albeit subject to various infirmities, was suggested by the CEPAL study of Latin American price levels.[20]

[19] *Ibid.*
[20] U.N., Economic Commission for Latin America, "A Measurement of Price Levels and the Purchasing Power of Currencies in Latin America, 1960-1962," E/CN.12/653, mimeo. (New York: United Nations, 1963), p. 149.

Purchasing power parity of $1.05 for one escudo, as of June 1962, was established on the basis of a low-income consumer market basket priced in Santiago, representing Chile, and Los Angeles and Houston, representing the United States. At that date the official rate was $0.95 for one escudo. The U.S. 1954 values added were therefore adjusted to 1962 prices, Chilean 1957 values added to 1962 prices, converted from escudos to dollars at the rate of $1.05 per escudo; U.S. water intake coefficients per dollar of U.S. value added were applied to Chilean value added—all of which resulted in the following figures for the four industries supplying water intake data:

Water Intake, Selected Industries, Chile, 1957

(*millions of m³*)

Industry	Computed from value added	Computed from reported coefficients
Pulp and paper	13.8	13.3
Steel	114.6	75.1
Petroleum refining	41.3	30.9
Sugar (including cane)	7.5	8.6
Total	177.2	127.9

The agreement in pulp and paper as well as sugar was quite good. Since part of the reported sugar coefficient—that pertaining to cane sugar—was based on the U.S. coefficient, sugar could not be used to verify the value added method of computation. The results of steel and petroleum refining were quite poor. If one could explain this lack of correspondence, a further adjustment could be made that would permit the use of the U.S. coefficient of water use per unit of value added to estimate Chilean water use from Chilean value added.

Several reasons could explain the disparity between reported water intake and that estimated from value added. First, as noted above, physical output per unit of value added might be different in the two countries. Second, an inaccurate parity exchange rate might have been used. Third, there might be differences in rates of recirculation that would affect intake per unit of output. Fourth, there might be differences in production methods, apart from recirculation, that resulted in different amounts of water used per unit of product.

One could readily ascertain that physical output per unit of value added was, in fact, different in the two countries, assuming that the parity of $1.05 per escudo, after adjusting both prices to 1962 levels, was correct. (If it was not, no other source of information for a better parity was at hand.) Tons of product per dollar's worth of value added in the two countries compared as follows:

Tons of Product per $1.00 of Value Added[21]

Industry	U.S. (1954)	Chile (1957)	U.S./Chile
Pulp and paper	0.010	0.008	1.25
Steel	0.018	0.008	2.25
Petroleum refining	0.195	0.062	3.15
Sugar	0.024	0.031	0.77

If intake per physical unit of output was the same in both countries, the U.S. coefficient would overstate Chilean water use in three industries. The overstatement would be greatest for steel and petroleum refining. A possible offset of such overstatement would be the difference in recirculation rates, assuming that recirculation was greater in the United States than in Chile. The only information available on recirculation was an estimate by ENAP's petroleum refinery that water intake during the four months of low flow on the Aconcagua River was reduced to one-tenth normal intake, the balance being made up by recirculation. If intake in a "normal" month is 1 unit, total intake for the year would be 8.4 units to supply needs, without recirculation, of 12 units. The ratio of water intake in the absence of recirculation to water intake with recirculation, therefore, would be 1.4. For the United States the same ratio was 3.3. The "value added" estimate could be corrected by dividing by the ratio of U.S. to Chilean output per dollar of value added (or multiplying by the reciprocal) and multiplying by the ratio of U.S. to Chilean rates of recirculation, i.e.,

$$41.3 \times \frac{0.062}{0.195} \times \frac{3.3}{1.4} = 30.8 \text{ million m}^3$$

or a figure almost identical with what was reported directly. The result may indicate that all variables have been correctly accounted for or possibly only that several offsetting errors have been accumulated. The method has obvious limitations, because if we solve for the Chilean rate of recircu-

[21] Ignores quality and product mix within the specified industry class.

lation for steel, we get a value of 0.88, which is impossible.[22] However, it is only 12 per cent away from 1, which is correct. For pulp and paper, the Chilean inferred rate of recirculation rate is 2, and for sugar refining the rate is 1.1, computed by solving for the Chilean rate of recirculation in the above equation. (Direct information on recirculation rates was not available.)

If we accept the findings for petroleum refining, we can conclude that there is a relationship between the results obtained by multiplying the 1954 U.S. coefficient of water use per U.S. dollar of value added (adjusted to 1962 prices) by 1957 Chilean value added (adjusted to 1962 dollars) and that the estimate will deviate from reality by (a) the variation in output per $1 value added between U.S. and Chile, (b) the respective rates of recirculation, (c) unexplained factor or factors. If we assume that industry in general reflects the relationships revealed by averaging our findings for pulp and paper, steel, petroleum refining, and sugar (and there is no information that will support or contradict such hypothesis), we can estimate Chilean water intake by applying a U.S. water use coefficient to Chilean value added, reducing downward the results by 38 per cent to correspond to the average overstatement revealed by the four industries about which we have data. This, then, is what was done. The results are shown in Table 40. In the aggregate the difference between CEPAL's estimate and that of this study is on the order of 10 per cent, although in a number of particular industries the disparity is much greater. The effect of the differences in estimates is magnified several times if pollution is taken into account. Rates of water intake per unit of value added for 1957 were assumed to prevail in 1985.

Because recirculation can increase, intake is an unsatisfactory measure of water requirements. Furthermore, for a basin as a whole intake overstates total requirements. We therefore need to know how much water is lost. Since no Chilean data are available on the rate of loss per unit of output, it was necessary to adapt to Chilean conditions coefficients based on U.S. experience.

The relationship between intake and loss as given by U.S. Census data was adjusted to reflect the difference between the U.S. rate of recirculation and the estimated Chilean rate of recirculation. The loss rates per unit of intake that were used for Chile are shown along with the U.S. loss rates, both expressed as a per cent of intake in Table 41.

[22] The "rate of recirculation" is computed in this instance as equal to the total amount of water taken in in the absence of any recirculation divided by the amount of intake. In the absence of recirculation the "rate" is equal to 1.

THE WATER RESOURCES OF CHILE

Table 40

MANUFACTURING, WATER INTAKE, 1957

(*Million m³/yr.*)

Province	Food and beverages	Pulp[a]	Paper[a]	Chemicals[b]	Petroleum refining[c]	Steel	All others[d]	Total
Tarapacá	0.2	–	–	0.6	–	–	–	0.8
Antofagasta	0.2	–	–	2.6	–	–	–	2.8
Atacama	–	–	–	–	–	–	–	–
Coquimbo	0.3	–	–	0.6	–	–	0.2	1.1
Aconcagua	0.3	–	–	–	–	–	0.2	0.5
Valparaíso	3.7	0.1	–	5.2	15.4	–	4.1	28.5
Santiago	6.1	3.1	2.1	20.3	–	3.8	15.4	50.8
O'Higgins	0.9	–	–	0.3	–	–	–	1.2
Colchagua	0.2	–	–	–	–	–	0.2	0.4
Curicó	0.2	–	–	–	–	–	–	0.2
Talca	0.7	0.2	–	0.6	–	–	0.2	1.7
Maule	–	–	–	–	–	–	–	–
Linares	0.2	–	–	–	–	–	–	0.2
Ñuble	0.2	–	–	–	–	–	–	0.2
Concepción	1.0	2.8	3.9	1.6	–	71.3	2.6	83.2
Arauco	–	–	–	–	–	–	–	–
Bío-Bío	0.3	–	–	–	–	–	–	0.3
Malleco	0.3	–	–	–	–	–	–	0.3
Cautín	0.3	–	–	–	–	–	0.2	0.5
Valdivia	0.7	0.6	0.5	–	–	–	0.5	2.3
Osorno	0.7	–	–	–	–	–	–	0.7
Llanquihue	0.3	–	–	–	–	–	–	0.3
Chiloé	–	–	–	–	–	–	–	–
Aysén	–	–	–	–	–	–	–	–
Magallanes	0.2	–	–	–	–	–	–	0.2
Total	17.0	6.8	6.5	31.8	15.4	75.1	23.6	176.2

[a] For pulp and paper use was made of the 1958 provincial distribution of output, as reported by FAO-CEPAL's study, "El Papel y la Celulosa en América Latina," Rev. 1 (New York: United Nations, 1962).

[b] Intake in Aconcagua, Ñuble, Bío-Bío, Cautín, Valdivia, Osorno, Llanquihue, and Magallanes is estimated to add up to 0.5 million m³.

[c] Intake of ocean water at Concón was estimated at 15.5 million m³.

[d] Intake in all the other provinces adds up to 0.4 million m³.

Table 41
LOSS AS PER CENT OF INTAKE

Industry	United States	Correction factor [a]	Chile
Food and beverages	11	1.8	6
Pulp and paper	11	1.2	9
Chemicals	12	1.8	7
Petrochemicals	4	1.8	2
Petrol. refining	9	2.4	4
Steel	4	1.3	3
All others	13	1.8	7

[a] Correction factor: recirculation rate in U.S./recirculation rate in Chile. "Recirculation rate" is equal to estimated intake in absence of recirculation divided by actual intake. U.S. loss (as a per cent of intake) is multiplied by correction factor to yield Chilean loss as a per cent of Chilean intake.

Table 42
MANUFACTURING, RATES OF WATER USE PER UNIT
OF OUTPUT, CHILE

Industry	Unit	Water intake per unit (m³)	Losses per unit (m³)
Food	Value added [a]	0.13	0.01
Pulp	ton	272.6	24.5
Paper	ton	95.7	8.6
Chemicals	Value added [a]	0.69	0.05
Petrochemicals:			
Ethylene	ton	1,051.2	21.0
Aromatics	ton	1,576.8	31.5
Ammonia	ton	45.1	0.9
Petroleum refining	m³	26.6	1.1
Steel	ton	94.6	2.8
All others	Value added [a]	0.08	0.01

[a] Value added computed in escudos of 1962.

Although we probably overestimate intake in 1985 by using the same intake coefficient as prevails today,[23] we do not necessarily overestimate loss—at least relative to U.S. experience. Our ignorance of what will happen to loss rates (and dilution requirements) per unit of product as

[23] For steel the coefficient estimated for 1970 was used.

the rate of recirculation rises is no more profound for Chile than it is for the United States.

Table 42 shows both intake and loss rates per unit of output that were adopted for Chile. A change in the Chilean rate of recirculation that would lead to a change in intake per unit would not automatically imply a change in loss rate per unit of output.

We face a choice in the way in which losses are to be measured. If all plants recirculate water to the maximum degree practicable, total losses for a river basin (or province) are equal to the aggregate of losses sustained by all plants within the basin. If no plant adopts recirculation techniques, total losses for the basin are equal to losses sustained by upstream plants plus the fresh-water intake of plants whose wastes are discharged into estuarine or coastal waters. Since there is relatively little recirculation of water by Chilean manufacturers today, and since the acquisition of recirculation machinery adds to total capital and foreign exchange requirements, recirculation techniques may not be adopted unless compelled by absolute necessity. Because of this uncertainty losses have been computed in two ways: (1) as the sum of losses of upstream plants plus intake of coastal (downstream) plants; (2) as the sum of losses of all plants. Output was distributed between downstream and upstream locations for all manufacturing groups except foods and beverages by classifying each province on an all-or-none basis as "inland" or "coastal." This could be done because most manufacturing activity can be assigned to a single city or small region in each province, and an all-or-none classification introduces little additional error relative to the uncertainties that are already a part of the projections. In the case of food processing, however, the industry is diffuse and numerous and tends to be distributed in the same pattern as population. For this reason, food manufacturing was distributed in proportion to the estimated distribution of urban population between coastal and inland cities. Table 1 shows the all-or-none and percentage distributions that were used.

The results of these estimates are summarized in Table 43 for 1985. Loss I is computed on the assumption that seaside plants do not recirculate and that all intake is discharged into salt water. Loss II assumes that only evaporation, transpiration, and water incorporated into the product have to be taken into account in downstream plants as well as upstream. This assumes, in turn, that either there is complete plant recirculation or that all waste discharge is captured for other uses. Only one intake rate is given. One can, however, assume that the theoretical limit to which intake falls as recirculation rises is given by the column headed Loss II. The theoretical limit is not likely to be reached since process water is usually purged after it has reached a certain level of contamination.

Table 43
MANUFACTURING, INTAKE AND LOSSES I AND II, 1985,
MEDIUM A AND B

(Thousand m³/yr)

Province	Medium A			Medium B		
	Intake	Loss I [a]	Loss II [b]	Intake	Loss I [a]	Loss II [b]
Tarapacá	2,000	1,955	136	3,300	3,232	225
Antofagasta	7,000	6,842	486	11,400	11,163	792
Atacama	–	–	–	–	–	–
Coquimbo	3,700	3,277	250	5,700	5,136	387
Aconcagua	2,100	163	138	3,000	232	198
Valparaíso	141,800	139,036	6,203	211,500	210,534	9,610
Santiago	235,100	14,518	14,217	374,400	22,564	22,164
O'Higgins	3,000	188	188	4,400	278	278
Colchagua	1,800	140	121	2,400	185	162
Curicó	400	28	24	600	42	36
Talca	6,200	446	446	9,000	648	648
Maule	24,900	24,900	2,241	32,000	32,000	2,880
Linares	400	24	24	600	36	36
Ñuble	500	35	30	600	42	36
Concepción	331,500	331,348	11,625	444,200	444,003	16,312
Arauco	25,000	25,000	2,250	32,000	32,000	2,880
Bío-Bío	113,000	10,143	10,143	149,100	13,383	13,383
Malleco	900	54	54	1,100	66	66
Cautín	2,200	162	145	3,000	221	198
Valdivia	7,500	6,789	571	10,400	9,452	792
Osorno	1,800	108	108	2,400	144	144
Llanquihue	900	646	54	1,200	862	72
Chiloé	–	–	–	–	–	–
Aysén	–	–	–	–	–	–
Magallanes	33,800	33,800	692	34,000	34,000	704
Total provinces	945,500	599,602	50,146	1,336,300	820,223	72,003

[a] Loss I, manufacturing losses computed on the assumption that downstream plants do not recirculate and all downstream intake is lost.

[b] Loss II, manufacturing losses computed on the assumption that there is complete recirculation in downstream plants.

Table 43 shows the very large estimated effect on requirements that results from failure to adopt maximum recirculation efforts at coastal points of intake. The industrial region around the cities of Valparaíso and Concepción can reduce their intake of fresh water by a magnitude that approaches 95 per cent, if we can judge by the relationship between intake under present conditions of recirculation and estimated evaporation losses. Detailed tables for the Medium B projection are presented in Appendix A.

Substitution of saline water for fresh water for cooling, washing, and waste disposal would not materially reduce losses of fresh water computed as Loss II, but would, of course, have an absolute effect equal to the amount of fresh water displaced under Loss I. Loss II, therefore, is also indicative of minimum fresh-water requirements where there is maximum use of salt water.

IX

MUNICIPAL WATER USE

Municipal water requirements are treated as a homogeneous use although they are composed of several separate elements: household, commercial, light manufacturing, civic, and sanitary. The usual method of estimating municipal requirements is to start with a historical per capita figure for each class of use, project the trend, compute total requirements by multiplying by expected urban population, and sum up the results. There are a number of obstacles to the pursuit of such a method in Chile, yet no other is likely to yield better results.

Data on current use of water per capita from municipal systems are inexact because the number of people in each community served by the water system is not known. Projections for the future cannot be made on the basis of current quantities being used because of the restrictions imposed on users in "almost all of the large services." Also, "it has been statistically impossible to distinguish with precision the domestic use of water from other municipal uses."[1]

CEPAL estimated that muncipal water use was distributed as follows: domestic, 40 per cent; industrial, 10 per cent; and public services, 20 per cent. The destination of the remaining 30 per cent is not known, although it is suspected to be mostly leakage.[2]

ORGANIZATION OF MUNICIPAL SUPPLY

Domestic water supply in Chile is the responsibility of the Dirección de Obras Sanitarias of the Ministerio de Obras Públicas for all communities except Santiago, Antofagasta, and a few coastal and mining towns, which have their own systems. The rate schedule used by Obras Sanitarias is uniform for the entire country except for two groups of coastal communities, one of which pays a higher and the other a lower rate than the

[1] Hansen, p. 47.
[2] CEPAL, pp. 59-60.

125

country-wide schedule. Several of the coastal cities that pay lower than average rates are in the far North: Pisagua, Iquique, Tocopilla, and Taltal. Water is metered, and consumption beyond a stipulated quantity is subject to a progressive rate schedule that becomes constant after the second jump in unit price.

According to Chilean law, the rates charged water users are supposed to be fixed to cover all costs including an "adequate" return to capital. CEPAL concluded that in 1958 the "situation was very far from this objective," that rates did not cover a quarter of estimated costs, and that the deficiency in income was equivalent to the cost of supplying municipal water to 500,000 people annually.[3]

The deficiency in income today is apparently much greater. On the basis of an "average" Chilean household water bill,[4] the charge per cubic meter in 1965 was about three and a half times the charge computed by CEPAL for 1958 (about 53 pesos per cubic meter in 1965; about 15 pesos per cubic meter in 1958), an increase that falls short of the change in the consumer cost index (dominated by prices subject to control) by about 30 per cent.[5]

Varying estimates can be found of the present deficiency in domestic water supply. CEPAL[6] estimated that 3.2 million people, or 44.5 per cent of total population, had a public water supply in 1956. According to Hansen,[7] 3.5 million people in urban centers of 900 or more were served by public systems, but of this number 900,000, or about 25 per cent, were supplied by public spigots. Twenty-one per cent of urban residents lacked any type of service, and only 6 per cent of rural population (centers of less than 900 people) were served.

A background report of Dirección de Planeamiento of the Ministerio de Obras Públicas[8] showed that 56 per cent of dwellings in the country as a whole were supplied with plumbing in 1960. The highest percentage was in Santiago, with 81 per cent; the lowest was in Chiloé with 9.7 per cent. Current per capita water use supplied by municipal systems is relatively low. For the country as a whole Hansen quotes an estimate of 262 liters/per capita/per day. This can be compared with a per capita use of 480 liters per day in the United States in 1950.[9]

[3] *Ibid.*, p. 64.
[4] Based on the basic rate schedule of 30 m³ for 760 pesos, plus another 30 m³ at 40 pesos per cubic meter, plus 80 pesos per m³ for the remainder, computed bi-monthly, and assuming 35 m³ per person per day.
[5] One thousand pesos equals one escudo. The 1965 price is about US$0.05 per 1,000 gallons.
[6] *Ibid.*, p. 59.   [7] Hansen, p. 56.
[8] *Antecedentes para el Planeamiento Provincial de Obras Públicas*, Vol. I, *Generales e Inversiones* (Santiago, October 1963).
[9] Hansen, pp. 46, 47.

The rapid growth of urban population, the pressure of sanitary needs, and the programs of the Alliance for Progress, World Health Organization, and other international agencies will contribute to a rapid increase in domestic water use. Under legislation now in force in Chile, all urban centers of 1,000 and more are to have a public water system which "is equivalent to supplying practically the total urban population of the country."[10] The decennial plan of the Dirección de Obras Sanitarias calls for extending new facilities to 26,100 inhabitants located in centers of less than 1,000 inhabitants.

From the point of view of water adequacy, the extension of facilities to relatively small communities poses no significant problem. There still remain the questions of the minimum size that a community can be and still be given a public supply system, and what type of service should be rendered. These are important questions relative to the allocation of capital funds, even if unimportant relative to water as such. They are, however, outside the scope of this study.

PROJECTED MUNICIPAL INTAKE AND LOSS

Municipal water intake was estimated as a function of urban population and size of urban community (Table 44).[11] A distinction was also made among broad zones of the country. In common with estimates made by CEPAL and other authorities, per capita use in the four northern provinces was assumed to be less than in cities of the same size in the Central Zone—a reflection of the inadequate capacity of municipal systems to meet the demand for water. While this assumption mingles supply and demand forces, the Centro de Investigaciones concluded that any other assumption would be unrealistic for the period of the projection.

Estimated water use for domestic purposes by rural inhabitants is also given. This category covers communities below 1,000 inhabitants as well as isolated families.

The distinction between upstream (inland) and downstream (coastal) users, shown in Table 1, makes it possible to compute requirements for municipal purposes as equal to upstream losses plus downstream intake (Table 45). Evaporation-transpiration losses are assumed to be 20 per cent of intake in all cities. Wherever downstream waste discharge can be captured for industrial or agricultural use, the downstream flow requirement can be computed on the basis of downstream municipal losses rather than

[10] *Ibid.*, p. 57. See also memorandum of February 18, 1965, of the Director de Obras Sanitarias to the Director de Planeamiento of the Ministerio de Obras Públicas. This memorandum states, in addition, that sewage systems are being provided for all cities of 5,000 or more.

[11] Estimates made by Centro de Investigaciones Económicas, Universidad Católica.

intakes. All rural domestic intake was assumed to be lost, whether upstream or downstream.

Table 44
MUNICIPAL INTAKE PER CAPITA PER DAY[a]

(*Liters*)

Zone	Group				
	I	II	III	IV	V
I	150	200	250	–	–
II	200	250	290	370	400
III	160	230	260	350	–

Zone I	Tarapacá-Coquimbo
II	Aconcagua-Linares
III	Ñuble to the South

Group I	Cities up to 5,000 inhabitants
II	5,000- 10,000 inhabitants
III	10,000-100,000 inhabitants
IV	100,000-500,000 inhabitants
V	Over 500,000 inhabitants

[a] Rural domestic intake for all regions: 100 liters per capita per day.
Source: Centro de Investigaciones Económicas, Universidad Católica.

Table 45
MUNICIPAL REQUIREMENTS, 1985, MEDIUM

(Thousand m³/yr)

Province	Upstream				Downstream					Upstream losses plus down-stream intake	Total upstream and down-stream losses
	Total intake	Munic-ipal losses	Rural do-mestic intake	Total upstream losses	Intake	Munic-ipal losses	Rural do-mestic intake	Total intake	Total losses		
Tarapacá	17,091	393	341	734	14,440	2,888	342	14,782	3,230	15,516	3,964
Antofagasta	40,200	3,347	361	3,708	23,106	4,621	–	23,106	4,621	26,814	8,329
Atacama	23,440	3,671	1,844	5,515	2,988	598	251	3,239	849	8,754	6,364
Coquimbo	33,280	2,940	4,603	7,543	13,799	2,760	1,080	14,879	3,840	22,422	11,383
Aconcagua-Valparaíso	146,657	10,009	4,294	14,303	91,736	18,347	586	92,322	18,933	106,625	33,236
Santiago	885,954	170,840	14,037	184,877	17,433	3,487	286	17,719	3,773	202,596	188,650
O'Higgins-Colchagua	48,962	8,016	8,412	16,428	435	87	42	477	129	16,905	16,557
Curicó-Linares	70,367	11,078	12,310	23,388	1,890	378	786	2,676	1,164	26,064	24,552
Ñuble	24,730	3,421	7,453	10,874	173	35	–	173	35	11,047	10,909
Concepción-Cautín	203,343	13,508	22,485	35,993	111,374	22,275	937	112,311	23,212	148,304	59,205
Valdivia-Llanquihue	81,179	7,661	–	7,661	35,257	7,051	11,622	46,879	18,673	54,540	26,334
Chiloé	3,247	97	–	97	2,760	552	1,712	4,472	2,264	4,569	2,361
Aysén	5,545	–	–	–	5,545	1,109	1,241	6,786	2,350	6,786	2,350
Magallanes	19,163	–	–	–	19,163	3,833	748	19,911	4,581	19,911	4,581
Total	1,603,158	234,981	76,140	311,121	340,099	68,021	19,633	359,732	87,654	670,853	398,775

X

WASTE TREATMENT AND WASTE DILUTION

Data on pollution and water quality in Chile are particularly deficient. There is no information on volumes of waste produced, levels of treatment, effect of waste discharge on water quality, and effects, if any, of deterioration in water quality on subsequent uses.

The CEPAL report had this to say about pollution: "Currently the River Mapocho, because of large quantities of polluted water discharged from Santiago that go directly into the river, and the Rapel River, because of processing residues from the copper mine of El Teniente which are discharged into the Cachapoal, are contaminated or in danger of contamination, not withstanding the works designed to avoid this objectionable state of affairs. . . . The pulp mills under construction (San Rosendo) or that will be built on the Itata, Maule and Bío-Bío rivers will also be able to defile the waters."[1]

In addition to waste dilution, there is a requirement in many communities for a flow of water to flush the sewers. Some of the newer sewage systems have enough slope to eliminate the need for "washing" the sewers, but most, apparently, require either intermittent or continuous flushing. Most cities possess water rights for flushing. According to Hansen, the rights are usually for quantities in excess of needs: as sewage systems are improved or replaced the need for flushing will be reduced or eliminated. Flushing now represents a relatively small demand for water in each province, except for the city of Santiago, which in 1965 was still without a sewage treatment plant. According to CEPAL, only eleven cities, all relatively small, had treatment plants. At the time this study was prepared no information was available on the quality of coastal and estuarine waters and, except for the siltation of shell fishery beds in the South resulting from the 1960 earthquake, there was no information on the degree to which pollution might threaten the coastal fisheries.

[1] CEPAL, p. 100.

130

If the requirement for water is measured by loss to the atmosphere or incorporation in the product, it is implicitly assumed that recirculation can proceed indefinitely. The question still unsettled is the quality of intake water as each user discharges waste into the stream. In lieu of the exact knowledge acquired by routing water down the stream we shall assume that if the dissolved oxygen content of water in the river does not fall below a designated minimum after mixing with the decomposable organic matter discharged by cities and industrial users, the river will serve the usual range of purposes without exceptionally high costs of treatment or aesthetic offense. A commonly used standard is a dissolved oxygen content of four milligrams per liter of water.[2]

In computing waste dilution requirements it was assumed that if the outfall of waste was "downstream" no dilution was required. By failing to provide dilution water for waste discharged along the coast or in estuarine waters, it was implicitly assumed that coastal marine habitat would not suffer, nor would beaches used for recreation be adversely affected. It is impossible to say whether this assumption is valid.

In order to estimate what might happen in 1985 coefficients were used that were originally prepared for the Central Pacific region of the United States.[3] Dilution requirements were computed over a range of treatment levels extending from zero to 90 per cent removal of biochemical oxygen demanding (BOD) substances. According to Reid's formulas, dilution flows are linearly related to the quantity of waste discharged, given a desired level of dissolved oxygen in the stream after mixing with the waste. The dilution needed for waste that has had half its BOD removed (50 per cent treatment) is twice the dilution needed for 75 per cent treatment and half the quantity for no treatment.

Among the possible sources of error in translating Central Pacific conditions to Chile is the fact that dilution flows for the former are computed for summer low flows, when temperatures are high and velocities low—

---

[2] The choice of 4 mg/1 of dissolved oxygen as a standard of water quality does not rest upon knowledge that DO is a critical factor in the quality of Chilean waters or that DO is a satisfactory proxy in Chile for other qualitative characteristics. It has been adopted for this report because we shall make estimates of organic pollution—municipal and industrial—and required waste dilutions based upon U.S. coefficients. This discussion of water quality is limited to organic pollution in the absence of information regarding other pollutants. There is a salinity problem (but one does not know how much is natural and how much man-made, or how serious it is) as well as pollution by coliform bacteria, about which data also are incomplete.

[3] Estimates of waste produced and dilution requirements for various levels of treatment were taken from George Reid, "Water Requirements for Pollution Abatement," in *Water Resources Activities in the United States*, Committee Print No. 29 (Washington: U.S. Senate Select Committee on National Water Resources, 1960).

conditions under which the natural oxygenation capacity of the river is at its lowest point within the year. The degree to which the reoxygenation capacity, and therefore the waste assimilation capacity, of Chilean rivers behaves in corresponding fashion is not known. For example, if high temperatures are accompanied in Chile by peaks rather than troughs of flow and turbulence, as is the case in certain basins, dilution flows based upon U.S. experience will overstate Chilean requirements. Another possible source of overstatement is the fact that the gradient of most Chilean rivers is relatively steep, contributing to a relatively high average velocity. Furthermore, Reid's estimates are subject to an unknown range of error for rivers of the United States. His method of estimation is based upon the assumption that the discharge of waste along the river is proportional to the gradual increase in flow from headwaters to mouth, an assumption contrary to the point loading that is actually encountered. It cannot be emphasized too strongly that the estimates of dilution requirements made for the present study should be accepted only as a starting point for the necessary investigations that must be undertaken in Chile.

Reid concluded that treatment levels in excess of 90 per cent would contribute nitrogen and phosphorus to the rivers of the Central Pacific region in such quantity that algal blooms would create a secondary demand for oxygen and lead to an increase, rather than reduction, in dilution water requirements. Even at 90 per cent the effect of plant nutrients is visible in his estimates, since requirements at 90 per cent treatment are somewhat in excess of half the amount shown for 80 per cent. Whether Chilean rivers would respond in the same way to high levels of waste treatment is another question that must be settled specifically for Chile.[4] Another source of possible error is the fact that the present estimates make no distinction among rivers in various parts of Chile. In the North some of the rivers appear to behave as trickling filters, whereas in the South rivers carry large volumes of water, are much deeper, and seem to move more slowly.

In estimating Chilean waste dilution flows the same relationships were maintained between industrial intake water and pollution that were estimated for 1980 for the U.S. Central Pacific region, after adjusting for estimated differences in intake per unit of output. Thus, in the Central Pacific region 1980 water intake for food and beverages was estimated at 277 million gallons per day (MGD) and million population equivalents

---

[4] There is, also, the possibility of adopting treatment techniques, about which little is known at the level of practical operation, that would remove plant nutrients from waste liquor and eliminate the need for their dilution.

(P.E.) as 13.8 per day.[5] Converting 277 MGD to millions of cubic meters per year and multiplying by 1.8 to correct for less recirculation in Chile gave 2 P.E.'s per day per 100 million cubic meters of intake water per year. Applying this coefficient to Chile meant implicitly adopting the Central Pacific mix of the food processing industry—more accurately, the same waste-producing mix per unit of intake water. However, since there was no way of distinguishing among the various subgroups of the food industry according to their capacity to produce waste, no other course was possible.[6] The same procedure was followed when estimating the output of P.E.'s for pulp and paper and chemicals.

Petroleum refining wastes were handled differently because of the problem introduced by extensive use of salt water for cooling. Accordingly, Reid's implicit estimate for the United States was used: 4.4 P.E.'s per day for an annual output in 1954 of 403.1 million cubic meters of crude runs to stills, or 0.011 P.E.'s per day per million cubic meters of output. This figure was then applied to the estimated Chilean production.

To summarize: Pollution produced as a function of intake was estimated after adjusting U.S. intake to correspond with estimated Chilean recirculation rates. Then, after subtracting waste that was discharged directly into coastal waters, estimates of dilution flow were made as a function of P.E.'s discharged into rivers after treatment. All pollution was measured in "population equivalents."

By adopting a standard of instream water quality as 4 milligrams per liter of dissolved oxygen, it was implicitly assumed that other pollutants would also be adequately diluted to render unnecessary special cost of treating intake water. There may be, of course, special cases in which this assumption might not hold.

Table 46 shows the coefficients taken from the Central Pacific region of the United States, the special computation of waste load from petroleum refining, and the dilution requirements, expressed in millions of cubic meters per year per one million population equivalent discharged per day into the stream.

Using the coefficients of Table 46, estimates were made of P.E.'s produced in each province (Appendix Table A-11). P.E.'s discharged downstream (i.e., into brackish or salt water) were subtracted (Appendix Table

[5] "Population equivalents," a measure of industrial waste, in millions of units when in capital letters. One unit (p.e.) is the quantity of "oxygen required to completely reduce the organic oxygen demanding wastes of one population equivalent," Reid, p. 9.

[6] The same problem applies to the estimates of pollution in the various regions of the United States, since the "food industry" was conceived to be homogeneous throughout the country for the purpose of estimating gross pollution.

Table 46

ADAPTATION OF CENTRAL PACIFIC COEFFICIENTS TO CHILE

Industry	Central Pacific U.S.A., 1980		Adjusted to Chilean conditions		P.E. produced per day per 100 million m³/yr. of intake	Million m³ of petroleum refined	P.E. produced per day per million m³ of petroleum refined
	P.E. produced per day	Water intake (MGD)	Factor to correct for less recirc.	Million m³ after correction			
Food	13.8	277	1.8	689	2.00	–	–
Pulp and paper	0.8	73	1.2	121	0.66	–	–
Chemicals	4.4	442	1.8	1,098	0.40	–	–
Petroleum refined	0.4	394	2.4	1,305	0.03	–	–
Petroleum refined (U.S.)	4.4	–	–	–	–	403.1	0.011
Municipal[a]	–	–	–	–	–	–	–

Dilution requirements per P.E. produced per day Central Pacific, 4mg/l of D.O.

Level of treatment (per cent)	Dilution		
	MGD[b]	Million m³/yr	
0	2,300	3,179.2	
35	1,500	2,073.2	
70	690	952.7	
80	450	620.5	
90[c]	275	379.6	

[a] It was assumed that one urban resident produced one "population equivalent" of waste per day and therefore water intake was not used as the basis of estimating municipal P.E.'s.

[b] Rounded.

[c] Dilution requirements at 90 per cent treatment show effect of diluting for plant nutrients.

Source: Data for Central Pacific taken from George Reid, "Water Requirements for Pollution Abatement," in Comm. Print 29 (Washington: U.S. Senate Select Committee on National Water Resources, 1960).

Table 47

WASTE DILUTION REQUIREMENTS, 1985, MEDIUM B, 4 mg/l D.O.

(Million m³/yr)

Province	Zero			35 per cent			70 per cent			80 per cent			90 per cent		
	Municipal	Mfg.	Total	Municipal	Mfg.	Total	Municipal	Mgf.	Total	Municipal	Mfg.	Total	Municipal	Mfg.	Total
Tarapacá	86	3	89	56	2	58	26	1	27	17	1	18	10	a	11
Antofagasta	595	16	610	388	10	398	178	5	183	116	3	119	71	2	73
Atacama	505	–	505	330	–	330	151	–	151	99	–	99	60	–	60
Coquimbo	553	38	591	361	25	386	166	11	177	108	7	115	66	5	71
Aconcagua-Valparaíso	1,389	321	1,710	906	209	1,115	416	96	513	271	63	334	166	38	204
Santiago	15,305	2,938	18,242	9,980	1,916	11,896	4,586	880	5,467	2,987	573	3,560	1,827	351	2,178
O'Higgins-Colchagua	1,262	248	1,510	823	162	985	378	74	453	246	48	294	151	30	180
Curicó-Linares	1,488	308	1,796	970	201	1,171	446	92	538	290	60	350	178	37	214
Ñuble	750	38	788	489	25	514	225	11	236	146	7	153	90	5	94
Concepción-Cautín	2,124	3,338	5,462	1,385	2,177	3,562	636	1,000	1,637	414	652	1,066	254	399	652
Valdivia-Llanquihue	938	238	1,176	612	155	767	281	71	353	183	47	230	112	28	140
Chiloé	22	–	22	15	–	15	7	–	7	4	–	4	3	–	3
Aysén	–	–	–	–	–	–	–	–	–	–	–	–	–	–	–
Magallanes	–	–	–	–	–	–	–	–	–	–	–	–	–	–	–
Total	25,017	7,487	32,504	16,314	4,882	21,196	7,497	2,244	9,740	4,883	1,461	6,344	2,987	894	3,881

a Less than 500,000 m³ per year.

Note: Disparities in totals are due to rounding.

A-12), and dilution requirements as a function of the level of treatment were computed. Waste dilution flows are shown in Table 47 for the projection of manufacturing output based upon the higher, 5.5 per cent, rate of growth. Manufacturing waste dilution requirements for the lower rate of growth would be about 28 per cent lower. Since only manufacturing flows are affected by changing the assumed rate of growth in GNP,[7] the difference in total required flows, municipal as well as industrial, between the low and high rates of growth is only $6\frac{1}{2}$ per cent. (See Appendix Table A-13 for summary of Medium A waste dilution requirements.)

Table 47 reveals that estimated flows are divided roughly in the ratio of $3\frac{1}{2}$ for municipal to 1 for industrial requirements.[8] Dilution flows for the projected population and industrial output would be about 33 billion m³/year in the absence of treatment, about 21 billion m³/year if primary treatment is provided, about 10 billion m³/year if secondary treatment is provided, and about 4 billion m³/year if treatment is carried to 90 per cent removal of biochemical oxygen demanding substances. Should the stipulated oxygen level be higher or lower, required flows would be higher or lower, but not necessarily in direct proportion.

One province, Santiago, accounts for more than half of the total dilution flow, and most of the requirement is generated by municipal (rather than industrial) waste. Regions south of Santiago are also faced with the threat of quality deterioration, but compared with Santiago the threat is almost inconsequential.

[7] This assumption may very well be wrong, since the ratio of urban to rural population is likely to be related to the rate of economic growth.

[8] By contrast, projected requirements for the United States for 1980, medium growth rate, indicate a required flow of $1\frac{1}{2}$ for manufacturing to 1 for municipal waste dilution.

XI

TOTAL WATER REQUIREMENTS

We can now put together the projections of water requirements in industry, agriculture, mining, steam-electric power, and general municipal use, and compare the results of alternative assumptions regarding rate of income growth and the form in which "water requirement" is expressed. We can, after examining the water supply, compare projected requirements with available runoff and see what shortages, if any, should be anticipated, which activities contribute most to the shortage, and whether the need to meet downstream requirements will provide adequate dilution flows. We can also see how much regulation of surface flow is implied in the projections, and whether a regional redistribution of activity can significantly lower projected costs of water. We can compare projected agricultural output in the absence of water constraints with water resources available, and determine by how much productivity per hectare[1] will have to be increased in order to meet projected outputs. These matters will be discussed in this and succeeding chapters.

The reader must never lose sight of the fact that the empirical base on which all conclusions rest is a compound of meager bits of information, frequently contradictory, tentative measurements, and boldly adopted assumptions usually involving the transposition of a technical coefficient from one context to another. We have no way of knowing what range of error should be anticipated, not only because we deal with hypothetical conditions twenty years hence but because the error of measurement in the present cannot be established.

By water "requirements" we mean the amount of water of appropriate quality that must be available to a user whose output is included in the

---

[1] Because it has been assumed that a considerable improvement will take place over present practices in the use of water for agriculture, the main consumptive use, further economies in the use of water are unlikely to be achieved within the time horizon of this study.

projections for 1985 and whose product requires a water input plus the water required for municipal systems. The amount of water required for a particular bill of goods and services depends upon the technology of water use that prevails. (Possible variations in technology that one might theoretically consider are considerable, and include variation in the degree of recirculation, substitution of dry processes for wet processes and other changes in technique of production, and variation in the intensity of waste recovery. Except for what has already been stipulated we do not consider these possibilities.) To some degree changes in technology can take place without destroying the basis of our estimates. For example, an increase in the rate of recirculation practiced by upstream non-agricultural users should have little effect on our estimates of evapotranspiration loss, since the amount of water consumed during each cycle is presumably about the same as is consumed on a once-through basis. Intake would change considerably, but loss very little if at all.

When we talk of a region's "water requirements" we mean the amount of water that must be flowing in the stream in order to meet intake requirements of all users and at the same time satisfy instream uses. This is not an abstract idea if we know every point of use within a river basin and what relationships exist at any point among intake requirements, rate of flow, original quality, recoveries from previous users, quality changes, water treatment, and waste treatment.[2] In the absence of such detailed knowledge the convention of a two-point region has been adopted: an upstream point and a downstream point, between which all activity is divided. All water discharged from an upstream user is presumed to be recoverable for further use; water discharged from a downstream user is presumed to be irrecoverable unless it is intercepted before it mingles with waters of the estuary or sea.

In the formulation of alternative ways of measuring water requirements the term "intake" refers to a diversion of water from the stream channel to a separate hydraulic system such as a city water works, irrigation project, power plant, or foundry. The term "loss" refers to the disappearance of water to the atmosphere by evaporation, transpiration, incorporation in the product, or wetting of the soil or penetration of the subsoil in such fashion as to be irrecoverable. "Discharge" refers to waters turned back into a river or other receiving body of water after use; the drainage of irrigation water is a comparable phenomenon, but is usually described as "return flow" or "recovery of waters." The "loss" of water for all uses except irrigation is usually measured by the difference between intake and

[2] It is assumed that surface and ground water are interrelated and that one can speak of all water supply in terms of surface flow.

discharge. In the case of irrigation loss, it is equal to the difference between the amount of intake and the amount recovered by drainage to surface channels or recoverable from recharged aquifers. Fresh water that is discharged into brackish or salt water is "lost" from the fresh water supply of a region, but in our discussion we shall try to maintain the distinction between losses suffered within the process of use and losses suffered by virtue of the place in which used water was discharged. Both types of losses are subject to modification by variation in the technique of use or disposal.

INTAKE

Although the aggregation of intake requirements yields a figure that has little meaning, since it fails to account for the possibility that water can be used more than once, it is a common indicator of water use and will reveal, for a designated level of water supply, the implicit rate of basin-wide recirculation. Because of the relatively small differences revealed between projections A and B (see last two columns in Table 48) we shall limit ourselves for the most part to the results of the higher rate of income growth.

The figures on offstream use show the dominance of irrigation.[3] Of a projected total intake of 50.5 billion cubic meters per year, agriculture accounts for 45.9 billion cubic meters, or roughly 90 per cent. Mining, which is Chile's main export industry, accounts for less than 1 per cent. Manufacturing, municipal, and steam-electric power take roughly 3 per cent each.[4]

The geographic distribution of projected requirements, which, of course, is only distantly related to the geographic distribution of water resources, is determined by two major forces:

1) The availability of irrigable land;
2) The pattern of population and non-agricultural activity.

We cannot render any judgment regarding the likelihood that water shortages will make impossible the production of projected outputs so long as we look at gross requirements, but we can see what is implied in the way of average rates of basin-wide recirculation. If we assume "full"

[3] The total of 45,907 million cubic meters per year for agriculture and livestock is divided into 45,759 million cubic meters per year for irrigation and 149 (rounded) million for livestock watering.

[4] By contrast, projected water use in the United States for 1980 shows agricultural withdrawals accounting for about 30 per cent, steam-electric power accounting for almost 50 per cent, roughly 15 per cent for manufacturing, about 5 per cent for municipal use, and about 1 per cent for mining. Part of the difference between the two patterns of use is the result of the dominance of hydroelectric power in Chile.

Table 48

INTAKE (WITHDRAWALS), OFFSTREAM USES, 1985, MEDIUM B

(*Million m³/yr*)

Province	Agri-culture	Min-ing	Mfg.	Steam-Elec.	Munic-ipal	Total[a] Medium B	Total intake Medium A
Tarapacá	371	1	3	1	17	394	392
Antofagasta	91	78	11	989	40	1,210	957
Atacama	588	166	–	12	23	790	693
Coquimbo	2,438	21	6	12	33	2,510	2,495
Aconcagua-Valparaíso	2,771	87	215	130	147	3,349	3,197
Santiago	6,112	19	374	78	886	7,470	7,324
O'Higgins-Colchagua	6,940	36	7	–	49	7,032	7,016
Curicó-Linares	11,772	–	42	2	70	11,887	11,876
Ñuble	3,546	–	1	–	25	3,571	3,571
Concepción-Cautín	11,214	–	629	13	203	12,059	11,902
Valdivia-Llanquihue	29	–	14	1	81	125	121
Chiloé	5	–	–	–	3	8	8
Aysén	8	b	34	–	6	14	14
Magallanes	23	–	–	2	19	78	78
Total[a]	45,907	409	1,336	1,239	1,603	50,495	49,644

[a] Discrepancies due to rounding.
[b] Less than 500,000 m³/yr.

regulation—i.e., flows are regulated to yield a steady flow equal to esti-mated average flow[5]—and also assume that water is required in the same even manner, the implicit rate of basin-wide recirculation is as follows:

Tarapacá	4.6
Antofagasta	11.5
Atacama	3.4
Coquimbo	2.6
Aconcagua-Valparaíso	2.4
Santiago	2.2
O'Higgins-Colchagua	1.0

[5] Because of the likelihood that flow in a future period will not exactly repeat the experience of the period of record, "full" regulation is a hyperbolic phrase.

Elsewhere the rate is below one. Most of the implicit recirculation in these figures is attributable to agriculture. Only in Antofagasta does non-agricultural intake imply considerable reuse. In Atacama non-agricultural intake is approximately equal to average flow.

The significance of implicit basin-wide recirculation is in the relationship that might exist between repeated intake and discharge and change in water quality. If the cycle is attributable to agriculture, water is likely to become mineralized; if the cycle is attributable to domestic use, water will accumulate organic material and some salts as well; if the cycle is attributable to mining or manufacturing, water may accumulate a wide variety of organic and inorganic substances, depending on specific activities; if the cycle is attributable to steam-electric power, water can accumulate heat. Manufacturing uses can also add heat. Except for the estimates made regarding biochemical oxygen demand of industrial and municipal pollution, the obviously important question of whether projected uses will have serious qualitative effects has been ignored.

LOSSES

If we assume that all water can be used until it is lost to the atmosphere or incorporated in the product (which implies that all discharged water can be recaptured for further use), the measure of loss is as given in Table 49. If we assume that certain downstream users or class of users discharge used water into estuaries or coastal waters, so that such water is no longer recoverable as "fresh" water, "losses" must be raised to account for such discharge. Under these latter circumstances, the fresh-water supply that is lost is equal to evaporation and transpiration losses, water incorporated into the product, and, for designated users or classes of users, gross intake or withdrawal of fresh water. Table 50 shows alternative estimates of losses when:

1) all downstream municipal and agricultural intake is considered to be lost,
2) all downstream intakes are considered to be lost.

Also, because of uncertainty regarding the estimates of mining water use, we have made an alternative computation on the assumption that all mining intake is lost.

The projected "requirement" for water can be framed either in terms of all losses, certain losses plus certain intakes, or certain losses and intakes plus waste dilution flows, depending upon options that a country may have regarding instream uses of water, recirculation, treatment at point of intake vs. treatment at point of discharge, and substitution of

Table 49

LOSSES, OFFSTREAM USES, 1985, MEDIUM B

(*Million m³/yr*)

Province	Agri-culture	Min-ing	Mfg.	Steam-elec.	Munic-ipal	Total[a]	Average supply
Tarapacá	242	b	b	b	3	245	86
Antofagasta	59	12	1	4	8	84	105
Atacama	383	25	–	b	5	413	229
Coquimbo	1,590	3	b	b	7	1,600	953
Aconcagua-Valparaíso	1,806	13	10	1	29	1,859	1,423
Santiago	3,983	3	22	b	177	4,185	3,371
O'Higgins-Colchagua	4,522	5	b	–	10	4,537	6,973
Curicó-Linares	7,672	–	4	b	14	7,690	23,302
Ñuble	2,322	–	b	–	5	2,327	6,749
Concepción-Cautín	7,344	–	33	b	41	7,417	61,487
Valdivia-Llanquihue	29	–	1	b	16	46	71,164
Subtotal average supply							176,203
Chiloé	5	–	–	–	1	6 ⎫	
Aysén	8	b	–	–	1	9 ⎬	269,317 c
Magallanes	23	–	1	b	4	28 ⎭	
Total	29,989	61	72	5	320	30,446	

a Disparities due to rounding.

b Less than 500,000 m³/year.

c Sum of flows in seven major rivers of three southern provinces (CEPAL, p. 31).

Note: In this table losses are limited to evaporation-transpiration, disappearance into the product and into irrecoverable ground water.

dilution flow by treatment or vice versa. In particular instances some options may not be available because of limited supplies of water and constraints upon the expenditure of funds on water resources.

Table 49 shows what losses would be sustained on the assumption that no discharges took place into salt water. That is, losses of downstream users, including agriculture, are computed as though they were upstream users (or as though all users recirculated their water until it disappeared.) Such an estimate of losses is, of course, an underestimation in comparison with practices that are now current, but does reveal what might be considered a minimum water requirement for projected activity

Table 50
SUMMARY: ALTERNATIVE WAYS FOR COMPUTING
FLOW REQUIREMENTS, 1985, MEDIUM B
(*Million m³/yr*)

Province	Case I[a] Municipal and agriculture downstream intake plus all other losses	Case II[a] (Case I with mining intake instead of loss)	Case III Upstream losses, all intakes downstream	Case IV Waste dilution at 90% treatment + losses
Tarapacá	311	312	328	256
Antofagasta	103	169	344	157
Atacama	439	580	493	473
Coquimbo	1,766	1,784	1,794	1,671
Aconcagua-Valparaíso	1,979	2,053	2,456	2,063
Santiago	4,240	4,287	4,254	6,363
O'Higgins-Colchagua	4,557	4,587	4,557	4,717
Curicó-Linares	7,946	7,946	7,977	7,904
Ñuble	2,333	2,333	2,333	2,421
Concepción-Cautín	7,591	7,591	8,150	8,069
Valdivia-Llanquihue	56	56	95	186
Chiloé	7	7	9	9
Aysén	11	11	15	9
Magallanes	28	28	79	28
Total	31,366	31,714	32,883	34,327

[a] Agricultural intake is the excess over municipal discharge.

on the basis of production technology in use or readily available. These losses are estimated in all cases from coefficients derived from U.S. experience and therefore may be in error because of errors of translation. It is likely that the errors are on the side of underestimation.[6]

The figures reveal that about 98½ per cent of losses so computed are from irrigation; mining, manufacturing and steam-electric power together account for about ½ per cent and municipal losses for about 1 per cent. In comparison, projected losses for 1980 in the United States indicate that agriculture will account for 55 per cent of the total, municipal losses for 1½ per cent and manufacturing for about 2 per cent.[7]

[6] Mainly because of the relatively inefficient canal system in Chile that would contribute to higher delivery losses of irrigation water.
[7] Total losses in the United States are affected by inclusion of items for which no provision has been made in Chile, but which accounted for 37 per cent of U.S. losses: soil and moisture conservation programs and expansion of fish and wildlife habitat. Further study might reveal comparable requirements in Chile.

These figures indicate that in the process of economic development very small changes in the extent of irrigated agriculture can have very large effects on the relative quantities of water available for non-agricultural use, whether such use is measured by intake or by loss. Since our estimates of agricultural use in 1985 are based upon a combination of Chilean coefficients and coefficients expected to prevail in California in 1980, rather than upon rates of use that now prevail in Chile—which are much higher according to various authorities—the probability of being able to transfer water from 1985 agricultural uses to 1985 non-agricultural uses, without a reduction in irrigated area, is relatively low. At least, it is lower than it would have been if the coefficients of water use had been based on current Chilean experience.[8] We can at this time introduce the question of supply in its simplest dimension, namely average annual flow, and relate it to projected losses. These relationships, elementary as they are, indicate the basic incompatibilities between the distribution of water resources in Chile and projected demands upon them. (See last column in Table 49.)

The deficit of water cumulates progressively as we go from Tarapacá to the province of Santiago. Because of their large irrigation requirements, Coquimbo and Santiago reveal the largest deficit. Among all seven northern provinces Antofagasta alone shows a slight surplus. This surplus disappears, and the deficit of the other six regions increases, if losses are computed according to one of the other options that are considered. Regardless of the alternative ways that are considered in the computation of water requirements the basic pattern as revealed by Table 49 persists.

WATER REQUIREMENT AS A COMBINATION OF INTAKE AND LOSS

A water requirement specified by the sum of intakes within a basin overstates what is needed if uses are arranged in tandem and water is not contaminated too severely for reuse. A water requirement specified by the sum of losses within a basin is the theoretical minimum amount of water that will suffice. However, such a measure is likely to be an understatement of what is practically attainable. For example, cities resist reusing their own sewage water. If, therefore, a city is located at the discharge point of a basin and draws its water supply from the river, directly or through the ground, the minimum flow requirement is equal to upstream losses plus municipal intake. If an irrigation project is located

---

[8] However, even on the assumption that the likelihood of achieving economies greater than already assumed is nil, some saving in water without corresponding reduction in irrigated area would be possible by concentrating production in water-short regions on crops with the lowest water requirements.

adjacent to the city and shares the river with the city at its downstream point, the minimum flow requirement is equal to upstream losses plus municipal and agricultural intake. If the irrigation project can intercept the discharged waters of the municipality before they reach the sea, the minimum requirement is equal to upstream losses plus municipal intake, plus the excess of downstream agricultural intake over municipal discharge (assuming that downstream agricultural intake exceeds downstream municipal discharge), which is equal to downstream agricultural intake plus all other losses. If downstream industries, mines, and power plants do not recirculate their water and there is no interception of municipal discharge, total flow requirements within a basin are equal to upstream losses plus the sum of downstream intakes. (It is implicit in the definition of "downstream" that the discharge [i.e., return flow] of a downstream irrigation project cannot be recovered for further use.) If water is in shorter supply than irrigable land, we shall assume that irrigation will be limited to upstream land unless the agricultural productivity per unit of gross input of water downstream is greater than the agricultural productivity per unit of net input of water upstream, other inputs being equal.

In general, the minimum flow requirement (without considering dilution flows) is equal to all losses plus the intake of the last user regardless of whether the last user is in an upstream or downstream position. The maximum flow requirement, without considering quality maintenance flows, is equal to upstream losses plus all downstream intake.

In order to simplify further exposition we shall compare three alternatives, all in the absence of a water constraint. We shall compare these cases with an alternative that takes waste dilution into account. We shall then examine the question of water supply and the regulation of flow by means of storage (see Chapter XII), after which we can study the effects of costs of water on projected outputs (see Chapter XIII).

The three cases that are examined in detail are the following:

Case I. Downstream municipal discharge is assumed to be captured for use for downstream irrigation. All other downstream users recirculate completely. In effect, requirements are equal to the sum of all losses plus downstream agricultural intake.

Case II. Case I is modified by assuming that mining requirements are measured by intake instead of loss. There are no data for Chile on the amount of water that is reusable when discharged from a mining, beneficiation, and refining complex. We know that about 94 per cent of intake at El Teniente is discharged, but we do not know how much is to lagoons where the liquid is evaporated, and how much is to treatment facilities for ultimate return to the river. Case II is clearly incompatible with plans for an increase in copper production unless relatively large quantities of water are imported into Antofagasta and Atacama. We shall not have more to say about Case II.

Case III. In this case water requirements are measured as the sum of upstream losses and downstream intakes. If Case I is at one extreme of the water-economizing spectrum, Case III is at the other (without consideration of dilution flows).

Detailed computations of Cases I, II, and III are shown in Appendix Tables A-14, A-15, A-16, and A-17. Summary results are shown in Table 50.

The difference between adopting reasonably complete water-economizing techniques (Case I) and no economizing techniques (Case III)[9] is of no significance for the country as a whole (31.4 billion cubic meters per year vs. 32.9 billion cubic meters per year), but is of importance in Antofagasta, Atacama, and Aconcagua-Valparaíso.

Presumably, the main effect of assuming that downstream municipal discharge is recovered for use is in the additional area capable of being irrigated. Whether additional land would in fact be irrigated would depend upon the availability of irrigable land at suitable elevation and distance from the point of municipal discharge. If we assume that all downstream municipal discharge is recaptured, the areas capable of being irrigated by the discharge are as follows:

Tarapacá	340 hectares
Antofagasta	540 hectares
Atacama	110 hectares
Coquimbo	510 hectares
Aconcagua-Valparaíso	3,410 hectares
Santiago	650 hectares
Total	5,560 hectares

These figures do not indicate how much water is available from a single municipal system, nor whether the benefits would justify the costs. Such determinations would have to be made separately for each locality. Another possibility is the use of treated municipal discharge for industrial

---

[9] Presumably treatment levels are high enough to allow reuse of water for offstream purposes even if no dilution is provided.

purposes. Except in the Aconcagua-Valparaíso region, estimated municipal discharge exceeds estimated manufacturing intake in all of the regions from O'Higgins-Colchagua to the north. This option would be attractive if there were no downstream lands for irrigation or if upstream lands of better quality than those available downstream had been withdrawn from use in order to meet downstream manufacturing intake. In any case, by computing municipal losses on the assumption that all municipal discharge were recoverable, as is done in Table 49, we automatically increase the total use that can be made of the water supply within each region.

At present not only is there no recapture of downstream municipal discharge, except experimentally in the Antofagasta area, but also very little recirculation of manufacturing water. As a consequence, virtually all downstream manufacturing intake is lost.

One should note that since the most likely effects of water shortage will be a reduction of land under irrigation, the failure of downstream manufacturing users to recirculate will compel further contraction of irrigated agriculture. In Antofagasta this means another 300 hectares. In the Aconcagua-Valparaíso region it means 9,350 hectares. In the case of Aconcagua-Valparaíso, if 50 per cent of manufacturing intake is saved by recirculation and 50 per cent of municipal discharge can be reused for irrigation, 6,600 hectares could be irrigated.

Taking a more realistic account of downstream municipal and agricultural requirements than is given by considering only evapotranspiration losses has this effect: It pushes southward into the Curicó-Linares region the line at which average annual supply, accumulated in going southward from Tarapacá, balances annual losses, as one adds requirements and flows. If we cumulate losses shown in Table 49, without accounting for irrecoverable downstream use, the surplus of the O'Higgins-Colchagua region offsets, with a little to spare, the deficit accumulated to the north. If the deficit is computed on the basis of Case I, the surplus of O'Higgins-Colchagua falls short of meeting the deficit in the provinces to the north. Chile from its northern boundary to the southern boundary of Colchagua Province would be a net deficit region on the basis of projections for 1985. The deficit computed on the basis of Case III is approximately 1,000 million cubic meters per year greater.

Case IV: Losses Plus Waste Dilution. An alternative measure of water requirements is the sum of losses and waste dilution. By fixing the water requirement as waste dilution plus total losses rather than upstream losses, we are assured of an outflow to the sea equal to the quantity of waste dilution.

Losses plus waste dilution serve as a satisfactory measure of required flows if waste dilutions are always large relative to intake at any single point. Although this condition most likely holds for the United States, it may not for a country such as Chile, where upstream reaches are relatively short and, except for Santiago and several minor inland points, most polluting activities take place on the coast.

Required flows depend upon the level to which treatment is carried. If a quality standard were imposed in water-short regions, it is most likely that treatment would be raised to the point that minimized the requirement for dilution water: in the present instance, to 90 per cent. The use of total loss plus waste dilution flow introduces a slight overstatement of water requirements, since downstream loss could be met out of waste dilution flow. However, the overstatement is negligible. (See Table 51.)

If treatment were 90 per cent in all regions, losses plus waste dilution flows for all provinces from Santiago to the north would be 10,983 million cubic meters per year compared with an average annual flow of 6,170

Table 51
LOSSES PLUS WASTE DILUTION, 1985, MEDIUM B, 4 mg/l
(*Million m³/yr*)

Province	Losses only	0%	35%	70%	90%	Average supply
Tarapacá	245	334	303	272	256	86
Antofagasta	84	694	482	267	157	105
Atacama	413	918	743	564	473	229
Coquimbo	1,600	2,191	1,986	1,777	1,671	953
Aconcagua-Valparaíso	1,859	3,569	2,974	2,372	2,063	1,423
Santiago	4,185	22,427	16,081	9,652	6,363	3,371
O'Higgins-Colchagua	4,537	6,047	5,522	4,990	4,717	6,973
Curicó-Linares	7,690	9,486	8,861	8,228	7,904	23,302
Ñuble	2,327	3,115	2,841	2,563	2,421	6,749
Concepción-Cautín	7,417	12,879	10,979	9,054	8,069	61,487
Valdivia-Llanquihue	46	1,222	813	399	186	71,164
Chiloé	6	28	21	13	9	269,317
Aysén	9	9	9	9	9	
Magallanes	28	28	28	28	28	
Total	30,446	62,950	51,642	40,186	34,327	

Level of treatment spans 0%, 35%, 70%, 90%.

million cubic meters. Every province down to and including Santiago contributes to the total deficit, but more than half comes from Santiago. At zero treatment no additional regions are in short supply, but the net deficit is, of course, much greater. Without treatment the balance between cumulated demand and cumulated supply, moving southward from Tarapacá, is not achieved until virtually the entire average flow of the Curicó-Linares region is used.

So long as the use of water downstream from major points of pollution is mainly for irrigation, there is little reason to believe that dilution of wastes will become important unless the waters become heavily mineralized or polluted with persistent chemicals. Without additional information there is no way of assessing the impact of this form of pollution. If it is established that waste dilution flows are unnecessary, the required flow is equal to one of the alternative measurements of upstream losses plus downstream intake.

XII

▰▰▰▰▰▰▰▰▰▰▰▰▰▰▰▰▰▰▰▰▰▰▰▰▰▰▰▰▰▰▰▰▰▰▰▰

THE COST OF WATER [1]

▰▰▰▰▰▰▰▰▰▰▰▰▰▰▰▰▰▰▰▰▰▰▰▰▰▰▰▰▰▰▰▰▰▰▰▰

The "cost of water" is the cost of assuring a designated degree of control over stream flow by construction of surface storage. Many of the inefficiencies of Chilean agriculture, e.g., cropping patterns and water use, reflect the existing low state of security of water supplies. This chapter is concerned with the costs of raising existing minimum flows to successively higher levels up to average flow or "required" flow, whichever is lower.[2]

As a first step in calculating the cost of water in Chile, river basins and provinces were grouped into regions for which coterminous boundaries could be drawn. (See Table 52.) A few small rivers included in the table made such small contributions to total regional runoff and suffered from such deficiencies in data, that they were ignored, as were several small coastal streams. In all, the exclusions account for a few per cent of total surface runoff.

No account was taken of ground water except that which is discharged into streams and is measured by stream gauges. The quantity of water that escapes measurement may be significant, but data on the volume of underground reservoirs, the rate of recharge, and the linkage with measured

---

[1] Data on flows of Chilean rivers and storage requirements required to achieve varying levels of regulation were prepared by the Centro de Planeamiento of the Facultad de Ciencias Físicas y Matemáticas, Universidad de Chile (Professor Fernán Ibáñez, chief of the project, Ricardo Harboe and Juan Antonio Poblete, research associates), supported by a grant from Resources for the Future, Inc. See Ibáñez, Harboe, and Poblete, *Estudio de la Disponibilidad de Recursos Hidráulicos en Chile* (Publication No. 65-5/B, [Santiago: Universidad de Chile, July 1965]) for details of estimates and limitations in quality of data.

[2] The reader should not confuse the method followed in this report with such studies as *Capacidad de Riego Actual de los Ríos de la Zona Central de Chile* (Santiago: Dirección de Riego, Ministerio de Obras Públicas, January 1967) in which irrigation capacity in the various basins of the Central Zone (Santiago-Ñuble) was fixed by the low flows experienced under the *existing pattern* of storage and regulation. [See Appendix C for a translation of the *Capacidad de Riego* study.]

surface flow are not available. A few sample studies portend a greater relative importance of ground water in the northern desert provinces.

Basic data are incomplete in several ways. (1) Virgin flows cannot be accurately ascertained because diversions are not measured. (2) It is difficult to separate the effect of irrigation return flows from independent contributions of underground aquifers. (3) The period of record is too short to provide a reasonably accurate flow duration curve for most rivers.[3] (4) Gauging stations are far too few in number and are rarely placed at those points that allow reconstruction of virgin discharge into the sea. Because of these limitations many flows were estimated indirectly, based on correlations with meteorological data and the behavior of rivers for which more complete information was available. The authors of the cited hydrologic study caution the reader to accept the flow data and flow storage relationships as approximations, and not as suitable for detailed planning.

Ibáñez, Harboe, and Poblete concluded that on the basis of the hydrologic balance of the main longitudinal Central Valley between the provinces of Aconcagua and Llanquihue, underground supplies where rivers come from the cordillera into the Central Valley are not important. Underground supplies increase further downstream through infiltration from the river bed, return flow from irrigation, and rainfall in the Central Valley. For this reason, measurements of flow in the foothills of the Andes would account for most (98–99 per cent) of the supply, including ground-water recharge, in the summer months. Then, the contribution from rain over the lowlands is negligible, as is the case in the glacial and pluvio-glacial basins more to the north. In winter the station near the mouth of the river measures supply since it records all contributions and is not appreciably altered by consumptive uses, which at this time of the year are at a minimum. Farther to the south the measure of supply, or of virgin flow, is given by gauging stations near the mouth of the river, after correcting the data for the "use" season by correlation with data of the "no-use" season.[4]

Flows in cubic meters per second were averaged for each month of record and the flows equalling or exceeding 95, 90, 70, and 50 per cent of the time *for each separate month* were identified, as well as the long-run average flow for the entire period of record.

Storage requirements needed to raise the present low flow (the flow equalled or exceeded 95 per cent of the time for the month that had the lowest flow) to successively higher minimum flows up to the average flow

---

[3] As noted elsewhere, the period of record for computed virgin flows ranges between three and thirty-four years, and averages twelve years.

[4] Ibáñez, Harboe, and Poblete, pp. 19-27.

Table 52
WATER RESOURCE REGIONS

Province	River Basins
1. Tarapacá	Lluta, Lauca, Azapa
2. Antofagasta	Loa
3. Atacama	Copiapó, Huasco
4. Coquimbo	Elqui, Limarí, Choapa
5. Aconcagua Valparaíso	Petorca, Ligua, Aconcagua
6. Santiago	Maipo
7. O'Higgins Colchagua	Rapel
8. Curicó Talca Maule Linares	Mataquito, Maule
9. Ñuble	Itata
10. Concepción Arauco Bío-Bío Malleco Cautín	Bío-Bío, Paicaví, Imperial, Toltén
11. Valdivia Osorno Llanquihue	Valdivia, Bueno, Maullín, Chamiza, Petrohue, Puelo
12. Chiloé	Yelcho
13. Aysén	Palena, Cisnes, Aysén, Baker, Bravo, Pascua
14. Magallanes	Serrano

were computed for three levels of certainty: 100, 95, and 85 per cent.[5] Table 53 shows storage requirements to assure designated flows with a security of 85 per cent. We concentrate on storage requirements needed to yield 85 per cent security—i.e., the flow will equal or exceed the specified flow in seventeen years out of twenty—because this is the level of security

[5] Regulation to achieve average flow at 100 per cent certainty is theoretically impossible unless future flows duplicate the historical record.

Table 53

FLOW-STORAGE RELATIONSHIP: 85 PER CENT SECURITY

(Flow equalled or exceeded indicated per cent of time in million m³/yr; storage in million m³)

Province	Flow now equalled or exceeded 95 per cent of time	70 per cent[a]		50 per cent[b]		Long-run average	
		Flow	Storage	Flow	Storage	Flow	Storage
Tarapacá	41	45.7	0.37	47.2	0.37	85.5	44.7
Antofagasta	81	92.1	1.8	94.6	1.8	104.7	8.8
Atacama	81	120.1	12.8	154.2	86.5	229.2	374.3
Coquimbo	199	335.8	42.9	434.6	118.2	952.6	2,526.0
Aconcagua-Valparaíso	373	492.2	18.5	537.3	33.5	1,423.2	2,552.0
Santiago	1,220	1,567.3	67.5	1,781.8	196.0	3,371.2	3,385.0
O'Higgins-Colchagua	1,602	2,106.6	41.0	2,601.7	96.0	6,972.6	6,175.0
Curicó-Linares	3,264	4,837.6	167.6	5,714.4	314.0	23,301.9	32,801.0
Ñuble	1,009	1,482.2	35.0	1,545.3	48.0	6,748.7	11,250.0
Concepción-Cautín	10,925	16,096.9	799.4	18,040.3	1,177.3	61,487.0	45,361.0
Valdivia-Llanquihue[c]	22,088	30,722.7	2,069.0	37,225.2	4,021.0	71,164.2	41,228.0
Chiloé-Magallanes	83,488[d]	—	—	—	—	269,317.0[e]	—

[a] Lowest of monthly flows now equalled or exceeded 70% of the time (see Appendix Tables A18-A28).
[b] Lowest of monthly flows now equalled or exceeded 50% of the time (see Appendix Tables A18-A28).
[c] 95% security from indicated storage.
[d] Estimated at same ratio of flow equalled or exceeded 95% of the time to average flow found in Valdivia-Llanquihue. Average flow taken from CEPAL, p. 31.
[e] Estimated.

which has been used by Dirección de Riego in planning its projects.[6] Later we shall discuss the implications of a higher degree of security.

STORAGE REQUIREMENTS TO MEET SEASONAL VARIATION IN DEMAND

Seasonal requirements for irrigation reach a peak in the summer and drop to as little as zero during the winter months. After projected requirements for all uses had been ascertained, Ricardo Harboe compared the amount of storage needed to meet the seasonal pattern of use with the amount of storage needed to provide a constant flow, on the assumption that regulation was extended to the theoretical limits of average annual flow in the seven northern provinces and to projected requirements in the rest. Storage requirements for seasonal needs were greater than storage requirements for a constant flow in all regions except Aconcagua-Valparaíso and Santiago. In some regions storage volume to meet seasonal irrigation needs was more than twice the volume needed to assure a specified minimum flow. The ratio of storage required for seasonal needs to storage required for a constant flow is referred to as the "storage coefficient."

In computing the costs of storage it was first assumed that irrigation requirements could be expressed as an annual amount (i.e., ignoring seasonal variation). After storage was computed on this basis, volume and costs were adjusted by using the storage coefficient for each region. In this way one could use a cost-of-flow schedule designed to show the costs of increments of minimum flow and adjust the results to conform to the seasonal requirements of each region.

In several of the preliminary models, no distinction was made between storage for constant flows (non-agricultural uses) and storage for seasonally variable flows, since the former usually constituted a relatively small fraction of the total. Storage requirements were therefore computed on the assumption that all followed the same seasonal pattern. In the more detailed cases, where variation in marginal costs was the concern, a separation was made between the two. A detail omitted from all models was the determination of additional evaporation losses from additional seasonal storage requirement. Research is needed on the question of reservoir evaporation generally, but beyond this one also needs to know how evaporation losses would be affected by the seasonal patterns of storage and release.

We shall use the multiplier derived from a comparison between constant *average* flow and seasonally regulated flows even when we deal with

---

[6] More exactly, in three years out of twenty the flow in one or more months can be less than the amount indicated.

lower flows. This procedure may understate required storage at less-than-average flow. Computations for the Río Elqui show that the multiplier to meet seasonal variation tends to be higher for less-than-average flows than it is for the average flow (see Table 54). This may partly explain the relatively high coefficients for the four regions south of Santiago. If, in northern regions, regulation were introduced for a lower level of water use than represented by average annual flow, presumably based upon results derived from the Río Elqui, the multiplier coefficient would rise. However, a reduction in water use would probably be accompanied by a reduction in the relative importance of agriculture, and therefore a reduction in seasonal variability of requirement, which would tend to reduce the multiplier in all regions except Aconcagua-Valparaíso and Santiago, where

Table 54

COEFFICIENT TO ADJUST STORAGE FROM
CONSTANT MINIMUM FLOW TO SEASONALLY
VARIABLE REQUIRED FLOW[a]

Tarapacá	1.24
Antofagasta	2.28
Atacama	1.13
Coquimbo	1.13
Aconcagua-Valparaíso	0.95
Santiago	0.92
O'Higgins-Colchagua	1.85
Curicó-Linares	2.82
Ñuble	2.88
Concepción-Cautín	b
Valdivia-Osorno	no irrigation

Río Elqui: Multipliers for Flows Less Than Average
Storage (*mil. m³*)

Flow (mil. m³/yr)	Constant	Seasonal	Multiplier for seasonal
262	403	408	1.01
205	76	142	1.87
165	30	48	1.6
350 (average)	1,285	1,420	1.1

[a] Based upon storage requirements to meet seasonal pattern of flow at "full regulation" for first six regions, and for projected water requirements for remaining four regions.

[b] For projected requirements at 85 % security no storage would be needed if flow were constant. Storage to meet seasonal variability or required flow was computed as 473 million m³.

the multiplier would rise. We shall not, however, take these refinements systematically into account for any of the hypothetical variations in regional production with which we shall be concerned.

We shall assume that the effect of the coefficient is to change total costs by the same factor as the indicated change in the storage coefficient. This assumes that the size-distribution of storage sites to meet requirements for seasonal flows is the same as the distribution to meet requirements for a given minimum flow. In regions in which less-than-average flow is required—i.e., O'Higgins-Colchagua and south—we shall follow the same procedure, rather than "move up" the schedule.[7]

RESERVOIR EVAPORATION LOSSES

The Centro de Planeamiento study did not include in its flow-storage relationships an adjustment to account for the net increase in evaporation from the basin resulting from added water surface exposed to the atmosphere as the volume of surface storage would be increased. Relatively little is known about the relationships that would be found between operation of the reservoirs and exposed area. Estimated annual net rates of evaporation from water surfaces in the areas where reservoirs are likely to be range from 400 millimeters in the vicinity of Valdivia to 1,400 millimeters and higher in the Norte Grande.[8] In order to give some expression to the potential loss by evaporation and the effect on marginal costs of flow, it was assumed that average reservoir heights were directly related to volumes up to a point (see Table 55) and that rates of evaporation were as given in Table 56. With these assumed values, the procedure was to reduce each increment in minimum flow by the amount of estimated added evaporation from storage.

Table 55
ASSUMED RELATIONSHIPS BETWEEN HEIGHTS AND
VOLUMES OF RESERVOIRS

Volume (*million m³*)	Height (*meters*)
0-100	15
100-200	20
200-400	25
400 and over	35

[7] In making detailed plans one further adjustment would have to be taken into account which is ignored here, namely, the additional evaporation.

[8] Unofficial estimates supplied by Centro de Planeamiento.

Table 56
ESTIMATED AVERAGE RATE OF EVAPORATION
(*Meters per square meter of reservoir surface*)

Tarapacá	1.4
Antofagasta	2.5
Atacama	1.2
Coquimbo	1.5
Aconcagua-Valparaíso	1.0
Santiago	1.0
O'Higgins-Colchagua	0.9
Curicó-Linares	0.7
Ñuble	0.6
Concepción-Cautín	0.5
Valdivia-Llanquihue	0.4

THE COSTS OF REGULATING SURFACE FLOW

On the basis of data on reservoirs already built, under construction, and under study, Ibáñez, Harboe, and Poblete constructed cost curves for rock-fill and earth dams, showing costs of water impounded as a function of the size of the reservoir.[9] It was on the basis of these curves that the cost schedule shown in Table 57 was adopted. The values selected for the smaller size-classes tend to be closer to the curve for earth-fill, which is the lower of the two, than for rock-fill; and coincide exactly with the earth-fill curve for the largest size-class. Based on current experience, the selected values understate by 50 per cent the costs of large rock-fill dams. It is difficult to predict which form of dam will dominate future construction. One point in favor of an earth dam is the fact that a clay core tends to resist tremor damage a little better than a more rigid structure. Most dams already built or in one stage or another of being under way are earth-fill. A single size-class unit-cost curve is used for the entire country.

There still remains the question of how one should distribute future reservoir capacity among the various size-classes. Presumably all reservoirs cannot be of the largest size-class, since the availability of sites, the places where water will be used, the flow of the river, the degree of regulation already attained, and the additional degree of regulation desired will vary from basin to basin and, in fact, tributary to tributary. It is reasonable, therefore, to assume that reservoirs of all size-classes will be built as total storage capacity is increased.

One can, of course, assume several ways in which total storage in a basin grows: (1) by first using the largest reservoir sites; (2) by first using the

[9] Ibáñez, Harboe, and Poblete, Graph 2, p. 39.

Table 57
UNIT COST SCHEDULE ACCORDING TO SIZE-CLASS

Size-class of reservoir (million m³)	Cost per 1,000 m³ (E⁰ 1964)
A 0- 49	200
B 50- 99	150
C 100-199	100
D 200-399	80
E 400 and over	50

smallest sites; (3) by random or studied additions that do not follow an order by size-class. The history of Dirección de Riego indicates that it is following the third course, but with an ascertainable trend such that, on the average, future reservoirs will be larger than past reservoirs.

Of forty-five reservoirs built, under construction, and under study, as of 1958, the mean sizes varied as follows:[10]

reservoirs already built	31 million m³
reservoirs under construction	450 million m³
reservoirs under study	310 million m³

Of the twenty-one reservoirs under study in 1958, five had a capacity of less than 49 million m³, and twelve a capacity of less than 200 million m³. The capacity of the largest under study was 2,750 million m³, that of the largest already built was 150 million m³, and that of the largest under construction was 1,570 million m³.

Synthetic cost curves were constructed wholly on an intuitive basis, on the assumptions that, wherever appropriate, large rather than small reservoirs would be used; that to reach the capacity needed for complete regulation some reservoirs of all size-classes would be used; and that storage capacity would be increased by first building large reservoirs followed by smaller ones.[11] The order in which reservoirs of different size-classes are assumed to be constructed has a significant effect on the steepness of a curve that describes the marginal cost of minimum flow. This curve will rise on the basis of "diminishing marginal physical productivity of storage"—a reflection of the fact that it takes more and more storage capacity to raise minimum flow by equal successive increments. If,

[10] CEPAL, pp. 65, 72.
[11] A number of large reservoirs in Chile consist of natural lakes with regulated outlets. These were excluded, insofar as they could be identified, from the mean figures given above.

in addition, we assume that "later" (i.e., smaller) reservoirs cost more per cubic meter of capacity than "earlier" (i.e., larger), the marginal cost of flow is subject to a double upward thrust. Our cost curves are constructed on the assumption that this double thrust will prevail and that every basin will use at least a few small reservoirs if it regulates at full capacity. In order to make these assumptions specific, total reservoir capacity at assumed full regulation in each basin was divided among reservoir classes of different sizes in accordance with the values specified in Table 58.[12]

Table 58
ASSUMED DISTRIBUTION OF RESERVOIR CAPACITY
BY SIZE-CLASS

Where full regulation requires: (*million m³*)	Distribution
0-49	All of size-class A [a]
50-399	First 50% of capacity, C Next 25%, B Last 25%, A
400-2,999	50%—E 20%—D 10%—C 10%—B 10%—A
3,000–up	75%—E 15%—D 5%—C 3%—B 2%—A

[a] See Table 57 for size-classes and costs per unit of capacity.

By applying this distribution to the unit costs indicated by Table 57 it was possible to construct for each basin a set of schedules showing increments of storage, successively higher levels of minimum flow, costs of increments of storage, costs of increments of flow, and cumulative costs.

Capital costs were converted to annual costs on the assumption that the rate of interest applicable to a loan of fixed real value (or one for which the capital sum was subject to revaluation with changes in the price level)

[12] The distribution roughly reflects what is happening in the country as a whole after taking into account reservoirs built, under construction, and under study.

was 8 per cent and that the life of a reservoir was fifty years. The results for each water resource region are shown in the Appendix Tables A18–A28. The effect of the storage coefficient for seasonal requirements on the costs of storage for the six northern regions in the aggregate is negligible. Increases in the first four regions are slightly overbalanced by decreases in Aconcagua-Valparaíso and Santiago.

XIII

~~~~~~

THE EFFECTS OF WATER SHORTAGE

~~~~~~

Three conclusions emerge when we compare projected water requirements with the natural availability of flows:

1) If nothing is done to modify the natural seasonal and annual variability of flows, there will be periods of shortage in all regions from the province of Cautín to the northern boundary of the country.

2) There is no way the distribution of activity can be modified in order to overcome the scarcity of water in the North and the scarcity of arable (irrigable and non-irrigable) land in the South except by diversions of water from surplus to deficit areas. Each region, from Tarapacá to and including the province of Santiago (the Maipo-Mapocho basin) has an average flow that is less than projected requirements. The first region with a projected surplus is O'Higgins-Colchagua (the Rapel and several minor streams), but the surplus is less than the deficit cumulated to that point, even if requirements are measured conservatively (i.e., as being equal to downstream municipal intake and agricultural intake in excess of municipal discharge plus all other losses [Case I]), or as the sum of losses plus waste dilution flows at 90 per cent treatment (Case IV). In order to bring the available supply into balance with projected requirements, streams would not only have to be regulated to the maximum degree possible[1] but a series of northward transbasin movements would also have to be undertaken. This movement would be comparable to diverting half the average annual flow of the Rapel northward plus replacing the deficit that would then appear in O'Higgins-Colchagua. The cumulated deficit including that of the O'Higgins-Colchagua region is 252 million cubic meters per year for Case I, 1,083 million

---

[1] See below for description of regulation needed. Flows would have to be controlled to meet the seasonal variability of requirements, which means, for most streams, a larger volume of storage capacity than would be needed to yield constant flows at the historical average.

162

cubic meters per year for Case III, and 2,557 million cubic meters per year for losses plus waste dilution after 90 per cent treatment. If requirements are measured only as losses, and there is no provision for waste dilution, the projected surplus of O'Higgins-Colchagua almost matches the deficit accumulated to the north.

3) *In the absence of transbasin movements, there is no way of meeting projected outputs except by increasing the agricultural productivity of land beyond the increase implicitly assumed up to this point in the analysis.*

FIRST ESTIMATE OF THE COSTS OF STORAGE

The closest we can come to meeting Case I[2] without disturbing the pattern of non-agricultural activity projected for 1985 is by providing maximum regulation in all regions from Santiago to the northern border.[3] In the remaining regions regulation is assumed to proceed up to projected requirements. The deficiency of water will mean that some irrigable land in the north will not be irrigated.

Table 59 is basic, since in the discussion that follows we shall be concerned with possible changes in the regional distribution of activity that will induce changes in this table. It shows the costs of maximum regulation of all streams in the northern part of Chile (Maipo and northward) and the costs of meeting projected requirements in the remainder. Additional storage needed to meet seasonal requirements is also given.

Under these conditions total additional investment cumulated for the next twenty years is about E°1 billion (about US$250 million at the October 1965 official rate) or about E°50 million per year.[4] Equivalent annual cost of the cumulated capital investment (including interest and amortization) at full development would be about E°84 million.

---

[2] The reader will recall that Cases I, II, III, and IV are alternative ways of stipulating the water requirements of a single economic projection—the medium rate of population growth and the high rate of growth of GNP (Medium B). Water requirements of the four cases are specified as follows (see Chap. XI, Table 50):

Case I   – Municipal and agricultural downstream intake plus all other losses;
Case II   – Case I with mining intake instead of mining loss;
Case III – Upstream losses; all intake downstream;
Case IV – Evaporation-transpiration losses from all uses plus waste dilution to yield 4 mg/l of dissolved oxygen after 90 per cent removal of BOD by waste treatment.

[3] By "maximum regulation" is meant the amount of storage that would raise minimum flow to average flow on the assumption that future runoff would duplicate the experience of the period of record. This is also what is meant when "100 per cent" or "complete" regulation is specified.

[4] This compares with E°24 million budgeted in 1964 by Dirección de Riego for reservoir construction.

Table 59

CASE I: COSTS OF FLOW REGULATION (85 PER CENT SECURITY)

Province	Required flow (million m³/yr)	Storage (million m³)	Coefficient for seasonal requirements	Storage for seasonal requirements (mil. m³)	Cost before applying storage coefficient (E°1,000-1964)			Cost after applying storage coefficient (E°1,000-1964)		
					Annual equivalent	Cumulative capital	Marginal[c]	Annual equivalent	Cumulative capital	Marginal[c]
Tarapacá	311[a]	45	1.24	55	730	8,940	96	905	11,086	119
Antofagasta	103[a]	9	2.28	20	144	1,760	22	328	4,013	50
Atacama	439[a]	374	1.13	422	4,126	50,500	817	4,662	57,065	923
Coquimbo	1,766[a]	2,526	1.13	2,858	17,647	216,000	551	19,941	244,080	623
Aconcagua-Valparaíso	1,979[a]	2,552	0.95	2,413	17,892	219,000	481	16,997	208,050	457
Santiago	4,240[a]	3,385	0.92	3,114	19,461	238,200	117	17,904	219,144	108
Subtotal		8,891		8,882	60,000	734,400		60,737	743,438	
O'Higgins-Colchagua	4,557	1,075	1.85	1,990	4,391	53,750	1	8,123	99,438	2
Curicó-Linares	7,946	934	2.82	2,634	3,815	46,700	d	10,758	131,694	1
Ñuble	2,333	210	2.88	605	858	10,500	d	2,471	30,240	1
Concepción-Cautín	7,591	—	—	473[b]	—	—	—	1,932	23,650	d
Valdivia-Llanquihue	56	—	—	—	—	—	—	—	—	—
Subtotal		2,219		5,702	9,064	110,950		23,284	285,022	
Chiloé	7	—	—	—	—	—	—	—	—	—
Aysén	11	—	—	—	—	—	—	—	—	—
Magallanes	28	—	—	—	—	—	—	—	—	—
Total	31,367	11,110		14,584	69,064	845,350		84,021	1,028,460	

[a] Required flow exceeds average flow. Storage is for average flow.
[b] Centro de Planeamiento, separate estimate.
[c] Per million cubic meters per year of flow.
[d] Interpolated cost is less than E°1,000.

The distribution of total costs among the various regions depends upon the use or non-use of the seasonal variation coefficient. Without the coefficient, northern regions account for 87 per cent of total costs; with the coefficient, the North accounts for 72 per cent. Marginal costs of water, important for regional planning purposes, are very much higher in the North than in the South.

Since there is a projected shortage of land nationwide (relative to expansion of cultivated area needed to meet projected outputs at current rates of production per hectare) and a projected shortage of water in the seven northern provinces, the question remains of how land and water resources should be used. One possibility is to retain as much agriculture as possible in the North, moving all other mobile activity to regions of water surplus. If all water in northern provinces were used for agriculture, the following amounts of irrigated area, roughly speaking, could be supplied with water:

Province	Hectares
Tarapacá	3,620
Antofagasta	2,626[5]
Atacama	14,350
Coquimbo	57,000
Aconcagua-Valparaíso	93,300
Santiago	232,000
Total (rounded)	403,000

In general we know that output per unit of water (loss or intake), measured by value added, is greater for non-agricultural than for agricultural products, especially if no allowance is made for dilution of discharge. Therefore, if water is allocated among competing uses in such a way as to maximize the region's gross product, non-agricultural uses will force out agricultural uses. The same result usually occurs if the objective is to maximize a region's employment. Under these circumstances, if we assume that all non-agricultural requirements of Case I are met in water-short regions, and streams are fully regulated, the water supply that remains for agriculture will allow irrigation of about 372,500 hectares. (In other words, using Case I as the basis for computing requirements, to meet all non-agricultural requirements means taking about 30,500 hectares out of cultivation. Cases II or III would require larger reductions in irrigated area.)

[5] All irrigable land. Some water would remain for other uses.

MARGINAL COST OF WATER CONSTRAINTS

If water in the seven northern regions is fully developed, marginal costs of regulated flow reach very high levels. It is doubtful whether agriculture or manufacturing could afford to pay more than a fraction of such costs. What, then, would be the effect on the distribution of economic activity of charging a price for water equal to its marginal product? Although the data necessary for the answer to this question do not exist, we can speculate about the results by using proxy information.

Since there is no reason to expect productivity per unit of water to differ materially among regions for non-agricultural uses, we shall examine only the available evidence for agriculture. There are no data available on marginal productivity. Relative prices of agricultural land would be a useful index of net value productivity (adjusting for transportation costs) but these are not available. We can, however, make use of a scale of values of Class IIIr land issued for tax assessment purposes, on the assumption that it reflects relative productivities among communities. (Assessed values are given by *comuna*.)

The unweighted average of assessed valuation for each *comuna* was converted to a scale of values for provinces and water resource regions. The scale was based upon Class IIIr land because this class is the largest of the irrigated classes and because it maintained a constant relationship with other classes of irrigated land in each *comuna*. The highest values are for Aconcagua and Santiago provinces. Since an additional assessment factor was to be applied to these valuations to account for the quality of transportation facilities, only part of locational, as distinct from physical productivity characteristics, are included in the indexes. How much the assessments reflect speculative changes in value induced by prospective transfer from agricultural to urban use cannot be ascertained.

The assessed valuation indexes do not correspond very closely to marginal costs of water that are implied when regulation is extended to the limits indicated in Table 59. Presumably, the valuation indexes reveal the relative prices for water that owners of the land could pay. If, for example, development could proceed economically up to a marginal outlay of E°20,000 per million cubic meters per year in the province of Santiago, we might say that investment could proceed to a marginal outlay of E°15,000 per million cubic meters per year in Tarapacá and Antofagasta, and to E°7,600 in Concepción-Cautín. The amount of water required per hectare would affect this relationship, moderating it if inputs of water were directly correlated with land values and reinforcing it if inversely correlated. The results of these adjustments are shown in Table 60. The indexes must be considered as illustrative only. We have no information regarding the factors that went into the original assessments, nor do we know what distortion was introduced by averaging values by *comuna* without weighting by the amount of land per *comuna*. The final column displays an interesting symmetry of values north and south of Santiago. The low value for the Curicó-Linares region, which is a deviation from this symmetry, reflects the depressed quality of the region's economy.

Table 60

AVERAGE VALUES FOR CLASS IIIr LAND FOR TAX ASSESSMENT AND ADJUSTMENT FOR WATER USE

| Province | Unweighted average of comunas (E^o/ha)ᵃ | Index of land values | | Index of water use (*Santiago* = 100) | Index o land value adjusted for index of water use |
		Index (*Santiago* = 100)	Weighted by irrigated area		
Tarapacá	1,055	75	75	160	47
Antofagasta	1,065	75	75	160	47
Atacama	960	68	68	100	68
Coquimbo	1,065	75	75	100	75
Aconcagua	1,285	91	–	–	–
Valparaíso	1,090	77	–	–	–
Aconcagua-Valparaíso	–	–	84	100	84
Santiago	1,415	100	100	100	100
O'Higgins	1,120	79	–	–	–
Colchagua	977	69	–	–	–
O'Higgins-Colchagua	–	–	74	100	74
Curicó	839	59	–	–	–
Talca	701	50	–	–	–
Maule	384	27	–	–	–
Linares	587	41	–	–	–
Curicó-Linares	–	–	46	98	47
Ñuble	631	45	45	64	70
Concepción	615	43	–	–	–
Arauco	227	16	–	–	–
Bío-Bío	524	37	–	–	–
Malleco	475	34	–	–	–
Cautín	418	30	–	–	–
Concepción-Cautín	–	–	33	65	51

ᵃ *El Mercurio*, Supplement, August 15, 1965, Graph 3 (New values for property), Servicio de Impuestos Internos.

Table 61

EFFECT OF CONSTRAINT ON MARGINAL COST OF WATER

(Flows in million cubic meters per year)

Province	Present minimum flow	Index of land value adjusted for water use	Marginal cost of water ($E°/mil. m³/yr$)	Storage coefficient	Minimum flow marginal cost ($E°/mil. m³/yr$)	Effect of marginal cost limit: agriculture in residuary position						Flow for agriculture after meeting non-agricultural requirements, Case I
						Storage ($mil. m³$)	Minimum flow	Capital costs ($1964 E°1,000$) Minimum flow	× coefficient	Annual costs ($1964 E°1,000$) Minimum flow	× coefficient	
Tarapacá	41	47	4,180	1.24	3,370	2	56	400	496	33	41	40
Antofagasta	81	47	4,180 [a]	2.28	2,684 [a]	1	88	236	538	19	43	44
Atacama	81	68	6,050	1.13	5,350 [a]	63	113	6,310	7,130	516	583	79
Coquimbo	199	75	6,680	1.13	5,910 [a]	665	601	33,250	37,573	2,717	3,070	575
Aconcagua-Valparaíso	373	84	7,480	0.95	7,870	919	1,093	45,950	43,653	3,754	3,566	963
Santiago	1,222	100	8,900	0.92	9,670	1,848	2,920	92,400	85,008	7,549	6,945	2,692
Subtotal	–	–	–	–	–	3,498	4,871	178,546	174,398	14,588	14,248	4,393
O'Higgins-Colchagua		74	6,590									
Curicó-Linares		47	4,180	No reduction in use				All flow adjusted for seasonal variation.				
Ñuble		70	6,230									
Concepción-Cautín		51	4,540									

Table 61—Continued

Using all flow up to marginal constraint for agriculture plus Case I non-agriculture

Province	Hectares served	Hectares served	Case I non-agricultural flow required	Required minimum flow	Storage and costs based on constant minimum flow				Hectarage adjusted for Antofagasta	Costs adjusted for storage coefficient (E°1,000)	
					Storage (mil. m³)	Capital cost (E°1,000)	Annual cost (E°1,000)	Marginal annual cost per mil. m³/yr (E°1964)		Capital	Annual
Tarapacá	1,786	2,500	16	72	14	2,833	232	25,059	2,500	3,513	288
Antofagasta	1,965	3,929	44	132[b]	9	1,760	144	21,787	2,626	4,013	328
Atacama	5,643	8,071	34	147	130	13,000	1,062	11,000	8,071	14,690	1,200
Coquimbo	41,071	42,929	26	627	706	35,300	2,884	6,270	42,929	39,889	3,259
Aconcagua-Valparaíso	68,786	78,071	130	1,223	1,560	86,400	7,059	43,549	78,071	82,080	6,706
Santiago	192,286	208,571	228	3,148	2,868	161,500	13,195	42,900	208,571	148,580	12,139
Subtotal	311,537	344,071	478	5,349	5,287	300,793	24,576	–	342,768	292,765	23,920
O'Higgins-Colchagua											
Curicó-Linares											
Ñuble											
Concepción-Cautín											

Note that this flow is assumed to be available as an even flow—not adjusted for seasonal variations.

See page 170 for footnotes.

What value can we assign to the marginal cost of water in Santiago, on the basis of which "reasonable" marginal outlays elsewhere can be determined? In the absence of benefit-cost studies for specific projects, one can only hazard a guess. Let us assume that a marginal annual outlay of $E^{o}8,900$ per million cubic meters per year is economically feasible.[6] The marginal value in each region, based upon the indexes of Table 60, are shown in Table 61. Also shown is the level of development as measured by minimum flow which such marginal cost would support. These flows have been translated into the hectarage that would be supplied with irrigation water with 85 per cent security, on the assumption that non-agricultural needs as measured by Case I would first be met. Costs of storage have been multiplied by the coefficient that represents additional storage to meet seasonal variations in requirements.[7]

Footnotes for Table 61

[a] See *note.*

[b] Exceeds maximum; storage and costs are for maximum. Available water supply meets one-third of non-agricultural needs; remaining two-thirds (equal to 29 million m^3/yr) must be transferred to another province or hectarage must be reduced to 2,630 as shown in last column. Storage is for constant minimum flow.

Note: The relation between constrained marginal cost and available flow was estimated on the assumption that the marginal cost curve was equal to zero at the existing minimum flow and rose linearly to the first point in the schedule. This is a simple and possibly incorrect assumption and was not used for Antofagasta, as will be explained in a moment. It seemed perfectly reasonable for Coquimbo because the constrained marginal cost was almost equal to the computed marginal cost for the first interval of storage. For Atacama, the first interval gives a marginal cost of $E^{o}16,119$ per million m^3 of minimum flow, yet if we build the 6.4 million m^3 of storage estimated to raise minimum flow by 32 million m^3/yr, average annual cost per million cubic meters of added flow would be $E^{o}3,270$. If anything, for Atacama, the assumption that one can interpolate linearly is conservative—i.e., flow is biased downward for a given marginal expenditure.

For Antofagasta, if we estimate additional storage to raise flow from 81 to 88 million m^3/yr as requiring 1.15 million m^3 of storage, and build this at the highest unit cost used, namely $E^{o}200$ per 1,000 m^3 of capacity (since the largest reservoir to handle this required storage falls into the smallest size-class), average annual cost per million cubic meters of added annual flow would be $E^{o}2,684$. This figure was adopted as the marginal cost of flow. (At the computed constraint of $E^{o}1,840$, only the minimum flow would be supplied.) It was assumed that flow would be raised to the amount indicated by a marginal cost of $E^{o}2,684$ by interpolating on a marginal cost curve that is assumed to rise linearly from zero at present minimum flow to the point given by the first interval in the table of costs.

The behavior of marginal cost when the size-order of reservoirs is reversed is discussed later in the text.

[6] This would be about $3.42 per acre-foot, converted at the rate of $E^{o}3.2$ per dollar, which was the official average rate for 1964. Farmers would also have to pay for delivery (canals, siphons, etc.) and on-the-farm costs.

[7] The marginal productivity of water, where water clearly meets a supplemental rather than full-time need, can be much higher than is revealed by comparative land values. This consideration is especially relevant for the southern provinces.

By introducing a marginal cost limitation the following changes are introduced relative to "complete" regulation:

1) Flows would be regulated to levels ranging, roughly, between 60 per cent and 90 per cent of "complete" regulation in water-short regions.

2) Reduction in irrigated hectarage is 60,000 (relative to Case I), or approximately two and one half per cent of irrigated area in the country as a whole. The loss in irrigated area would be, of course, relatively more critical with respect to the local economy. Also, the reduction in output would be relatively greater than the reduction in irrigated area.

3) The savings in capital costs, after adjusting by the seasonal storage coefficient, is E°443 million, or 24 per cent of "full development" costs. For the six regions of the North considered by themselves the saving is about 60 per cent. Savings in annual costs would be about E°37 million.

4) The costs of going *from* the level of development represented by accepting the marginal cost limitations of Table 61 *to* full development under Case I, would represent a capital cost per hectare of new irrigated area amounting to about E°23,000, and an annual cost of about E°1,875. These are only the costs of regulation and do not include annual on-the-farm costs (about E°500 per hectare)[8] or costs of major canals (about E°40–50 per hectare[9] after adjusting 1962 escudos to 1964 values).

5) The chosen marginal cost limit for flow regulation, which ranges between E°8,900 (1964 escudos) for Santiago and E°4,200 for Tarapacá and Antofagasta compares quite favorably with average costs incurred by the Dirección de Riego for past reservoirs. On the basis of data in the Villarroel and Horn study, annual capital cost computed at 8 per cent interest and fifty-year amortization, ranged between E°67 (1962) and E°158 per hectare for past reservoir projects constructed by Dirección de Riego. These values should be doubled to convert to 1964 escudos, the price level on which our costs are based. For Atacama, for which a marginal cost of E°6,050 per million cubic meters of flow was fixed, this means (at net loss rates, since return flow is usable) an annual capital cost of about E°84 per hectare, a figure that is low when compared with past investments converted to 1964 prices. The marginal cost limits of Table 61 appear to be within the limits of credibility, on the assumption that historical average costs do not materially differ from historical marginal costs.

8 According to Villarroel and Horn, p. 52.   9 *Ibid.*

It is possible to construct models of water use based on other assumptions. What, for example, are the implications of regulating water resources in each region only up to the level at which regulated flow never falls below the flow available 50 per cent of the time, or, alternatively, never falls below one-half the average annual flow? In either case the total amount of regulation would be lower than is given by the marginal cost limit used in Table 61.

An interesting speculation is the effect on total costs of water if projected growth of municipal and manufacturing activity in water-short regions were transferred to water-surplus regions. The level of water resource development by agriculture would also have to be settled in order to ascertain the savings in the costs of water used by the displaced non-agricultural activity in the water-short regions. In fact, encouragement of activity in a water-short region, given national production goals, can be facilitated by "assigning" as much as possible of the high-cost water to non-agricultural users for whom water costs are a relatively small part of total costs and who could adopt water-economizing techniques at costs that are not prohibitively high. We can, therefore, assume that if the level of agricultural development is given by the marginal costs of water in Table 61, non-agricultural water use is met by the more expensive increments of supply beyond the indicated marginal cost. Costs of non-agricultural users, as well as savings in expenditures on water if non-agricultural activity is moved to regions of lower water costs, can be determined on this basis.

According to Case I, which implies maximum recirculation in use of non-agricultural water, non-agricultural flow requirements in the six northern regions amount to 478 million cubic meters per year. To supply this flow in the regions in which the uses are projected (except that in Antofagasta maximum regulation falls short of meeting projected requirements) would require an additional E°122 million in original capital outlay and about E°10 million in equivalent annual cost over the costs required to meet flows subjected to a marginal cost constraint out of which non-agricultural needs had to be supplied. The computations are given in Table 61.[10]

[10] In examining Table 61, the reader must bear in mind the fact that neither the flow-storage curve nor the shape of the marginal cost of flow curve is well established at the lower end of the scale, especially for flows with a security of 85 per cent, since for these flows the Centro de Planeamiento supplied fewer points from which to construct a flow-storage curve. In applying the idea of a marginal cost constraint, it was assumed that the marginal cost curve was zero at zero increments to existing minimum flow, and that the curve rose linearly from this point to the first interval computed in Appendix Tables A-18 to A-28. If, in fact, the movement of the marginal cost curve is discrete, and the first increment in regulation (which is not necessarily the first step in Tables A-18 to A-28) indicates that marginal costs have a minimum value that exceeds

Table 61 also reveals that for the northern regions taken as a whole, the effect of adjusting required storage to meet seasonal requirements is negligible. Requirements are increased in Tarapacá, Antofagasta, Atacama and Coquimbo, but are reduced in Aconcagua-Valparaíso and Santiago. The net effect is an aggregate reduction, relative to storage designed to yield a constant flow, of about 2 $\frac{1}{2}$ per cent. An effect of greater consequence that should be incorporated in more detailed studies is the increased evaporation that must be taken into account—especially in Antofagasta, where the evaporation rates are high and the seasonal coefficient large—and the added regulation needed to meet seasonal requirements.

The effect of yielding to agriculture all flow that is provided by storage after introducing the marginal cost limits of Table 61 implies that marginal costs of water for non-agricultural purposes would range between E°6,000 and E°44,000[11] per million cubic meters per year, depending upon the water resource region. Antofagasta is the only province that would exhaust its water supply before supplying all projected requirements, implying, therefore, a reduction in irrigated hectarage below the projected amount. It is this reduced level of irrigation that is implied in Table 59, Case I (no marginal cost constraint), a level that falls between the two alternative situations described in Table 61 (marginal cost constraint). Total hectarage in Antofagasta would fall to 2,626, thereby reducing the northern regional total by 1,300. A rounded figure of 343,000 hectares being supplied with water for irrigation in the northern provinces appears reasonable in terms of a land constraint and estimates (very crude) of marginal costs of water.

The significance of this reduction in irrigated area is quite a bit greater when converted into agricultural output. (See Table 63.) If all land that was irrigable were supplied with water, estimated production (at current rates of output per hectare) would be about 48.9 million metric quintals of wheat equivalent, and production from arable dry land would be 13.8 million metric quintals: a total of 62.7 million metric quintals of wheat

---

the constrained values of Table 61, then the flows shown in Table 61 are overstated. For each basin in which the constrained marginal cost is less than the minimum marginal cost that would be experienced by the first unit of storage, the existing minimum flow would have to be substituted for the indicated flow.

[11] These are prices equivalent to a range of US$2.31 to $17.50 per acre-foot at 1964 official rates of exchange, or between seven-tenths of a cent per 1,000 gallons and 5.5 cents per 1,000 gallons, prices that would be within the economic range of municipal users in general, even with additional costs of purification and delivery that would have to be incurred. Furthermore, the high marginal costs are in the Aconcagua-Valparaíso and Santiago regions, the two regions that are most urbanized and most able, by virtue of the concentration of urban activity, to bear relatively high costs of water.

Table 62
HECTARAGE, IRRIGATED AND PROJECTED

Province	Irrigated 1959 [a]	Irrigable area (basic projection)	Case I Full regulation (agriculture residuary)	Case III Full regulation (agriculture residuary)	Marginal cost constraint		If all water went to irrigation [b]
					Agriculture residuary	Non-agricultural beyond marginal constraint	
Tarapacá	7,000	10,773	2,900	2,680	1,786	2,500	3,620
Antofagasta	4,200	2,626	2,626	0	1,965	2,626	2,626
Atacama	26,081	27,288	11,930	8,390	5,643	8,071	14,360
Coquimbo	107,081	113,023	55,140	53,930	41,071	42,929	57,000
Aconcagua-Valparaíso	92,062	128,641	84,000	55,140	68,786	78,071	93,290
Santiago	228,412	283,852	215,860	215,860	192,286	208,571	232,140
Subtotal	464,836	566,203	372,456	336,000	311,537	342,768	403,036
O'Higgins-Colchagua	249,810	322,394	322,394	322,394	322,394	322,394	322,394
Curicó-Linares	395,778	558,457	558,457	558,457	558,457	558,457	558,457
Ñuble	100,000	260,415	260,415	260,415	260,415	260,415	260,415
Concepción-Cautín Valdivia-Llanquihue	178,660	799,960	799,960	799,960	799,960	799,960	799,960
Total	1,389,084	2,507,429	2,313,682	2,278,226	2,252,763	2,283,994	2,344,262

[a] CORFO, unpublished data.
[b] See p. 165. Water restriction applies only to seven northern provinces,

equivalent. If agriculture is extended in all water-short regions to the full extent of the available water supply, after meeting non-agricultural projected requirements according to the conditions of Case I, output would be reduced by 4.8 million metric quintals of wheat equivalent, or a reduction of 8.3 per cent. If irrigated hectarage were further limited by a marginal cost constraint, giving agriculture all water up to the amounts supplied within the constraint, total output would drop another 800,000 metric quintals to an output of 57.1 million metric quintals of wheat equivalent.[12] If we supposed that the marginal cost constraint applied to all water and that agriculture received what was left after meeting Case I non-agricultural requirements, total production in the northern regions would be 700,000 metric quintals less. In both cases, if we were to assign all costs of regulation to agriculture, an extreme step, the average cost of storage would be E⁰12.5 per metric quintal of wheat equivalent. At full regulation under the same assumed allocation of cost, average cost would be E⁰15.3 per metric quintal. The marginal cost of water, expressed in relation to agricultural output, mounts rapidly if we go from a cost constrained supply to full regulation. In going from the condition in which agriculture is a residual claimant to being a full claimant of the cost constrained supply, the water cost per marginal metric quintal of wheat equivalent is E⁰13.8; in going to full regulation, water cost per metric quintal of wheat equivalent rises to E⁰46.6.[13]

With the data we have, it is very difficult to know how much production originates on irrigated land of the northern part of the country (Santiago northward), since an area that is shown as "irrigated" is not necessarily producing as effectively as an area that enjoys the 85 per cent security implied in the projected storage figures. Thus, the presumed levels of present output in metric quintals of wheat equivalent constitute a measurement that ought to be abandoned in favor of something better at the earliest opportunity. The use of such arbitrary values for determining present (1959) output is likely to be more misleading than when used to compare one hypothetical model with another, in which the *relative changes* are significant enough to sustain interest in the model even if the absolute values are incorrect. According to all Case I models, whether full regulation or cost constrained, total irrigated hectarage in the six northern regions would fall below 1959 levels. Production would probably rise merely as a

[12] See Appendix Table A-29 for further example of adjustments. Outputs from non-irrigated land is increased as irrigable hectarage is converted to dry land.

[13] In 1964 the average wholesale price of wheat was about E⁰21 per metric quintal. The fraction represented by costs of water is unknown but must have been quite small. A comparable outlay for water presumably would hold, with minor variation, for other products when expressed as "wheat equivalent."

Table 63

COMPARISON OF OUTPUTS AND COSTS OF WATER,
ALTERNATIVE PROJECTIONS FOR AGRICULTURE, 1985

Projection	Output (qqm/wheat equivalent)[a]	Annual costs of stream regulations (1964 E°1,000)
Basic, all irrigable land	62,683,078	Beyond limits of water supply without trans-basin movements
Case I, full regulation	57,892,352	84,021
Case I, water supplied to agriculture up to specified marginal cost	57,102,823	47,204
Case I, water supplied to all users up to specified marginal cost, agriculture's needs met after all non-agricultural requirements	56,404,210	37,532

[a] Metric quintals of wheat equivalent.

matter of higher security of water, but without more information we cannot say by how much. For this reason we cannot indicate what would be
the marginal changes in production (relative to present levels of production) as a result of specified levels of expenditure on stream regulation.
The need for such information is paramount. At the moment we shall
assume that one or another of our cost-constrained models will meet the
test of economic feasibility.

In spite of the qualifications with which we must hedge any measure of
current output from dry and irrigated land, we shall proceed with its use.
The reader will recall that projected increased demand over the present
for agricultural products, on the basis of Medium B rates of growth, were
as follows:

Increase in demand with no change in import balance	118%
Increase in production to eliminate substitutable imports	14%
Total projected increase over present	132%

Present output was estimated as being equal to 53.5 million metric
quintals wheat equivalent. In order to meet projected requirements, output in 1985 must be equal to 124.12 million metric quintals. If Chile
develops all flows to their theoretical limit, output would be 57.9 million
metric quintals at current rates of productivity per hectare. Output per
hectare would have to be 2.14 times recent levels for projected require-

ments to be met. If Chile applies the marginal cost constraint used in our illustration, and agriculture is put into a residual position (i.e., non-agricultural water requirements are fully met first), total output would be 56.4 million metric quintals. Productivity per hectare would then have to be 2.2 times greater. The difference between these alternative water resource policies would have a negligible effect on the required increase in productivity. Other water resource policies might be stipulated, but implied effects on the required increase in productivity would not yield results that materially differ from those already indicated. In short, without more than a doubling of output per hectare, Chile cannot meet its production goals even after all steps have been taken to expand the area of irrigated land.

Another inference to be drawn from the estimates is also significant. The difference in annual costs of water between full utilization and a marginal cost constraint is about E°46 million. This amount, supplemented by the additional delivery and on-the-farm costs of bringing the larger amount of land under irrigation, is an alternative to the cost of raising output per hectare from 2.14 times its present level to 2.2 times its present level—i.e., an alternative to the marginal cost of raising output per hectare by another 4 per cent after it had already been doubled.

One final note: The water supply available for agriculture, on the assumption of full regulation and after meeting non-agricultural requirements of Case III (all downstream intake lost), is about the same as is available to agriculture if it receives all water after applying the marginal cost constraint. Output and implied increases in productivity fall between the cases we have just discussed.

The economic consequences of these adjustments can be stated in simple terms:

1) It is impossible to irrigate all irrigable land without transbasin movement of water (given the coefficients that we have used).

2) Full regulation under conditions of Case I, allocating to agriculture the water that is available after meeting non-agricultural requirements, would allow production of 57.9 million metric quintals of wheat equivalent, at a total annual cost of stream regulation of E°84 million (1964 prices) and a cumulated capital investment of E°1.0 billion.

3) Imposing a marginal cost limit to the conditions of Case I, allocating to agriculture all water available within the specified limit (except in Antofagasta, where non-agricultural needs exceed the balance and agriculture's use is reduced), implies a total output of 57.1 million metric quintals of wheat equivalent, at a total annual cost of stream regulation of E°47 million, and a cumulated investment of E°578 million. (See Table 64.)

Table 64
COSTS OF STORAGE FOR ALTERNATIVE MODELS,
WITH STORAGE COEFFICIENT
(*1964 E°1,000*)

	Annual			Capital		
	Case I	Marginal cost constraint		Case I	Marginal cost constraint	
Provinces	Full regul.	Agric. all	Agric. resid.	Full regul.	Agric. all	Agric. resid.
Subtotal of 7 northern provinces	60,737	23,920	14,248	743,438	292,765	174,398
Subtotal of O'Higgins-Llanquihue	23,284	23,284	23,284	285,022	285,022	285,022
Total	84,021	47,204	37,532	1,028,460	577,787	459,420

The saving of E°36.8 million (1964) per year is accompanied by a re-duction in agricultural output of 789,529 metric quintals of wheat equivalent. This is tantamount to saying that the extension of irrigable hectarage to the full limit of runoff (with 85 per cent security) involves a marginal water cost of E°46.6 per metric quintal of wheat equivalent. Given the structure of agricultural and non-agricultural prices, in the world as well as in Chile, the extension of irrigable area to the limit of full regulation is not warranted.

By adopting the marginal costs of water that are implied when non-agricultural requirements are met after agriculture receives all water up to the marginal cost constraint, we can ascertain the savings that would result from moving non-agricultural activity from water-short to water-surplus regions. Since we do not know exactly what is or is not footloose, we shall assume that one-half of the non-agricultural requirements in the four northern provinces and three-quarters of the requirements in Aconcagua-Valparaíso and Santiago could be transferred to another region.[14] Total movable water requirements computed in this way would be 329 million cubic meters per year. This quantity could be supplied at zero cost of

[14] Given the existing Chilean preference for domicile in the Santiago area this is probably an extreme assumption. We ignore the problem of generating excess capacity of overhead services in the losing region and shortage of overhead services in the gaining region.

regulation at 85 per cent security (or more) in the Valdivia-Llanquihue region, and at relatively low marginal costs (roughly, between E°1,000 and E°4,000 per million cubic meters per year) in the other regions. Marginal costs of storage of the displaced water in the northern regions ranges, for this model, between E°6,270 and E°43,549 per million cubic meters per year. For the six regions in the aggregate the savings would be an estimated E°12.5 million (1964) annually,[15] of which E°11.5 million originated in the Aconcagua-Valparaíso and Santiago regions. At the 1964 official rate of exchange, this amounts to about US$3 million per year, an amount that seems relatively small in comparison with the violent shifts in population and activity implied. If, however, to the costs of regulation are added costs of high-level treatment, the savings in costs of water by transferring urban activity to water-surplus regions grow considerably.

The assumption that three-fourths of non-agricultural activity in the Valparaíso-Santiago area can be moved implies a decline in population over present levels. Let us, then, reduce this percentage to 50 per cent, implying thereby the maintenance of existing population and urban activity (since projected urban population for Santiago in 1985 is approximately double the present population). The most extreme measure of potential saving is provided by moving all footloose activity into the Valdivia-Llanquihue region. Here agricultural demands are negligible,[16] if not zero, and projected non-agricultural requirements range between 56 and 186 milllion cubic meters per year, depending upon the model. The flow equalled or exceeded 95 per cent of the time is 22,088 million cubic meters per year. The amount of storage necessary to raise the level of security for that flow to 100 per cent would be 475 million cubic meters.[17]

If waste dilution requirements are proportional to non-agricultural water uses transferred, we can conclude that at zero treatment flow requirements for waste dilution of the six northern regions would be about 11,000 million cubic meters per year. This quantity, plus the intake requirements of 239 million cubic meters per year (one-half the projected Case I non-agricultural requirements), is well within the capability of the

---

[15] Apart from local distribution and treatment costs. If long-line transmission costs are required in the North, as in some cases they are, this should be added, because such requirement would not be necessary in the South.

[16] The photogrammetric survey shows 16.4 hectares irrigated in Osorno, 0.7 hectares in Llanquihue, and 541.4 hectares of mixed classification in Osorno. It was assumed that no demand for irrigation existed in the three provinces—Valdivia, Osorno, and Llanquihue.

[17] Ibáñez, Harboe, and Poblete. This can be compared with the 3.5 billion cubic meters needed to raise the minimum flow in the six northern regions to 4,871 million cubic meters per year with 85 per cent security.

Valdivia-Llanquihue region at zero costs of regulation for 95 per cent security. Consequently, in addition to saving $E^o8.7$ million (less than the E^o13 million discussed above because only one-half of non-agricultural water use in the Aconcagua-Valparaíso and Santiago regions is transferred), $E^o22.7$ million (including collection costs) in treatment costs at 90 per cent treatment would be saved.[18] Total savings would be about $E^o31.4$ million, or approximately US$8 million, annually. Cumulated capital savings would be on the order of US$100 million, since we have assumed annual costs to be 8.17 per cent of capital costs.

Net capital (and annual) savings would be somewhat less, because of the additional housing costs that would be incurred against a slightly lower average winter temperature and considerably greater rainfall. There might be a net change in transportation costs, but whether positive or negative cannot be ascertained without further investigation. There might also be a net change in per capita costs of other urban services; but again the direction and magnitude of difference cannot be determined without additional study. The possibility of saving a capital sum of about E^o377 million in costs of water (regulation of supply plus treatment) over the next twenty years is, however, attractive enough to warrant further detailed study. Chile might decide that the benefits of living in the Valparaíso-Santiago area are worth the costs (either in the form of capital costs to provide an adequate quantity of water of suitable quality or in the form of deterioration in the quality of water and regularity of supply), but the benefits of investing this large sum in alternative activities has an attraction of its own.

[18] Savings at 35 per cent treatment would be $E^o12.8$ million, but since Santiago accounts for 84 per cent of the treatment costs, and because its inland position will probably compel high-level treatment, it is more reasonable to assume 90 per cent.

XIV

THE QUESTION OF WATER QUALITY

In the previous chapter it was noted that if water quality became a matter of such concern that a standard were adopted, whether formally or informally, and whether by zoning or other type of regulation, substantial savings would be made by inducing the migration of non-agricultural activity from the water-short to the water-surplus regions, especially to such cities as Valdivia and Puerto Montt, located on tidal waters. However, it is in this southern region, plus Cautín Province immediately to the north of Valdivia, that instream quality maintenance is likely to be of greatest consequence. Here is the famed lake region of Chile, one of the outstanding fresh-water sport fisheries of the world. While the rivers of the region can assimilate a certain amount of waste, their natural beauty would undoubtedly be defiled by a substantial increase of waste-producing activity along their banks, even on the assumption that treatment would reach a high level. For this reason, and because the reversal of the "natural" extrapolation of events from the past to the future that is implied in such population redistribution raises forbidding obstacles, we shall return to our basic projections as modified by Case I in order to examine the conditions under which water quality can be maintained. Our analysis will be limited to the maintenance of quality at a level of 4 milligrams per liter of dissolved oxygen.[1] The output of pollution and dilution requirements after treatment were inferred from coefficients based upon studies prepared for the United States.

Costs of treatment were inferred from data taken from the United States, but reduced by 50 per cent in agreement with some slight evidence

---

[1] The choice of 4 mg/1 of dissolved oxygen is arbitrary. Should further investigation reveal that a lower (or higher) oxygen content is appropriate for planning purposes, it would not be difficult to change all relevant flow and cost figures.

181

regarding construction costs in Chile vis-à-vis those in the United States.[2] Treatment costs were estimated for 35 per cent, 70 per cent, and 90 per cent levels of BOD removal. Collection costs were assigned only to municipal treatment and were assumed to be one-half the U.S. per capita figure. Annual costs were assumed to be based on an 8 per cent interest rate rather than the 2½ per cent used for the United States.

The costs of maintaining water quality are the sum of treatment costs and costs of waste dilution flows—i.e., the costs of maintaining a flow greater than is necessary to meet offstream intake or losses. In order to estimate these costs as conservatively as possible (i.e., by adopting a model for which the marginal costs of flow would be as low as possible), all cost estimates have been based on the marginal cost constraining variant of Case I for which agriculture was a residual claimant after non-agricultural water needs were met.

In order to make the most of a given flow we shall assume that all water not consumed upstream is available for both waste dilution and downstream intake. Therefore, only the excess of waste dilution over downstream intake is charged against quality maintenance. (In computing upstream losses and irrigated hectarage, all agriculture was assumed to be upstream, since a limited amount of water will go farthest if irrigated areas are far enough upstream to allow recovery of return flow.)[3]

Tables 65 through 67 and Appendix Tables A-30, A-31, and A-32, show estimated costs of collection, treatment, and flow augmentation for various treatment levels. (Industrial waste treatment costs are based upon the number of population equivalents produced for Medium B projections.)

What should one do in Antofagasta and Santiago, where the supply of water is too low to maintain a dissolved oxygen content of 4 milligrams per liter even if subjected to complete regulation, and treatment is extended to 90 per cent BOD removed? Should regulation be carried to the limit anyway? Should treatment be carried to 90 per cent? At full regulation and 90 per cent treatment, about 60 per cent of Antofagasta's flow dilution requirement can be met, but only about 16 per cent of Santiago's. For the purpose of Table 66 it has been assumed that a maximum effort is

[2] According to Walter A. Castagnino, Engineering Adviser, Programa de Recursos Naturales y Electricidad, CEPAL, capital costs of plants providing primary and secondary treatment are about $37.50 per capita in the United States and about $20.00 per capita in Chile.

[3] In the northern regions irrigation return flow will probably contain dissolved minerals. We may, therefore, be overstating the possible usability of water downstream, both for agricultural and non-agricultural purposes. Subsequent investigation may reveal that a more accurate picture is yielded by assuming that all irrigation is downstream—i.e., all intake is lost.

Table 65

TREATMENT COSTS PER MUNICIPAL AND INDUSTRIAL POPULATION EQUIVALENT

	U.S. South Pacific					Chile				
Treatment level (per cent)	Annual costs without collection (1960 $)	Capital costs without collection (1) × 22.22 (1960 $)	Municipal annual costs without collection (2) × .0817 (1960 $)	Collection costs (1960 $)	Total municipal annual costs (1960 $)	Total municipal annual costs (5) × 1.6 (1964 E°)	Industrial annual costs (2) × .0937 (1960 $)	Industrial annual costs (7) × 1.6 (1964 E°)	Collection costs (4) × 1.6 (1964 E°)	Municipal annual costs without collection (6) − (9) (1964 E°)
	(1)	(2)	(3)[a]	(4)	(5)	(6)[b]	(7)[c]	(8)	(9)	(10)
35	.67	14.89	1.22	1.30	2.52	4.03	1.40	2.24	2.08	1.95
70	1.22	27.11	2.21	1.30	3.51	5.62	2.54	4.06	2.08	3.54
90	1.64	36.44	2.98	1.30	4.28	6.85	3.41	5.46	2.08	4.77

[a] 8% interest and 50 years' amortization.
[b] US$1 = E°3.2 = official 1964 average rate. Chilean costs were taken to be half of U.S. costs.
[c] 8% interest and 25 years' amortization.

Table 66

ESTIMATED COSTS OF QUALITY MAINTENANCE (4 mg/l of D.O.):
CASE I—AGRICULTURE RESIDUAL, MARGINAL COST CONSTRAINT 1985, MEDIUM B

(1964 E°1,000)

Province	Annual treatment cost (excluding collection costs)			Additional annual cost of flow			Annual cost of quality maintenance treatment plus flow		
	35%	70%	90%	35%	70%	90%	35%	70%	90%
Tarapacá	55	100	134	a	109	–	a	209	134
Antofagasta	376	682	919	a	a	(138)a	a	a	1,057
Atacama	310	563	758	a	a	774	a	a	1,532
Coquimbo	366	665	896	a	3,909	376	a	4,574	1,272
Aconcagua-Valparaíso	1,078	1,957	2,636	a	a	1,446	a	a	4,082
Santiago	11,457	20,793	28,008	a	a	(11,900)a	a	a	39,908
O'Higgins-Colchagua	949	1,722	2,320	2,987	1,314	456	3,936	3,036	2,776
Curicó-Linares	1,130	2,051	2,762	1,875	–	–	3,005	2,051	2,762
Ñuble	487	884	1,191	2,405	1,104	440	2,892	1,988	1,631
Concepción-Cautín	3,655	6,628	8,919	–	–	–	3,655b	6,628	8,919
Valdivia-Llanquihue	Minimum flow dilutes at zero treatment			–	–	–	–	–	–
Total of above provinces	19,863	36,045	48,543	7,267	6,436	3,330 (15,230)c	13,488	18,486	64,073

a Flows are beyond average annual flow. Figures in parentheses are additional cost to achieve full regulation.
b At zero treatment, the added cost of waste dilution flow would be E°3,330,000—roughly the cost of 35% treatment.
c Includes added costs of full regulation in two regions, although water quality would fall short of 4 mg/l of dissolved oxygen.
Note: See Appendix Table A-32 for detail.

Table 67

LEAST COST COMBINATION OF QUALITY MAINTENANCE

(Annual costs in 1964 E°1,000)

Province	Level of treatment (per cent)	Total annual cost excluding collection	Annual treatment cost excluding collection	Annual storage cost	Extra flows required (million m³/yr)	Agricultural gross use (m³/yr/ha)	Added area irrigable (hectares)	Total annual cost including collection
Tarapacá	90	134	134	–	–	34,000	–	190
Antofagasta	90 [a]	1,057	919	138	15 [a]	34,400	436 [b]	1,446
Atacama	90	1,532	758	774	48	21,500	2,233	1,863
Coquimbo	90	1,272	896	376	55	21,500	2,558	1,634
Aconcagua-Valparaíso	90	4,082	2,636	1,446	89	21,500	4,140	4,991
Santiago	90 [a]	39,908	28,008	11,900	330 [a]	21,500	15,349	49,921
O'Higgins-Colchagua	90	2,776	2,320	456	145	–	–	3,602
Curicó-Linares	70	2,051	2,051	–	–	–	–	3,024
Ñuble	90	1,631	1,191	440	94	–	–	2,122
Concepción-Cautín	35	3,655	3,655	–	–	–	–	5,044
Valdivia-Llanquihue	–	–	–	–	–	–	–	614
Chiloé	–	–	–	–	–	–	–	15
Aysén	–	–	–	–	–	–	–	–
Magallanes	–	–	–	–	–	–	–	–
Total	–	58,098	42,568	15,530	776	–	24,716	74,466

[a] Assumes that flows are raised to full regulation and treatment carried to 90%; flows so marked are quantities available, not quantities required.

[b] The figure appears to be questionable.

made; thus, the possibility of 35 per cent and 70 per cent levels of treatment have been ignored, since at these lower levels of treatment flows would be hopelessly inadequate. In regions of limited supply, only the costs of 90 per cent treatment and full regulation were estimated. *A reasonable alternative for the seven northern provinces would be 90 per cent treatment without flow regulation, because the cost of augmenting flow is very high relative to the probable additional benefit of maintaining instream water quality.*

Costs of treatment were assumed to be incurred only for wastes discharged at inland points. Wastes produced along the coast, domestic and industrial, were assumed to be discharged into the sea without treatment. It was not possible to establish what effect this would have on the usability of beaches for recreation and the productivity of coastal fisheries. The assumption coincides with present practice. In coastal areas that are summer resorts it is likely that at least primary treatment will become necessary. Hence, treatment costs for the Aconcagua-Valparaíso provinces are probably underestimated.

Annual treatment and collection costs for the country as a whole were estimated to be E°37 million for 35 per cent treatment, E°54 million for 70 per cent treatment, and E°67 million for 90 per cent treatment. Of these totals, about 60 per cent were attributed to the Aconcagua-Valparaíso and Santiago regions. Santiago itself accounted for more than half the national total.

The growth of collection costs is inevitable even with little or no treatment or dilution. Water-borne diseases in Chile are more likely to be caused by pollution of ground waters (that then infiltrate into water pipelines) and by inadequate sewage systems than by inadequate treatment of municipal water. Many sewage systems are relatively primitive—e.g., in Santiago they must be flushed—and are likely to be replaced as soon as possible. Hence, it has been assumed that collection costs are a direct function of total urban population rather than of the increase between now and 1985 in urban population.[4]

No additional factor was introduced for the costs of collecting industrial wastes. Altogether, collection costs were estimated at about E°16 million annually (1964 prices). They do not vary with the level of treatment.

In Table 66 the costs of treatment (without collection) and costs of additional flow are added together to measure the costs of quality maintenance.

_____
[4] Most likely this assumption results in some overstatement of required sewage outlays.

Each region has its own response to the maintenance of a quality standard. Tarapacá, for example, in spite of being a water-short region, needs no additional dilution if treatment of upstream wastes is carried to 90 per cent BOD removal. Neither Antofagasta nor Santiago can meet a standard of 4 milligrams per liter of dissolved oxygen, even with full regulation. This suggests that not only will treatment have to be carried to high levels but that other techniques, such as artificial aeration, might be necessary. Atacama and Aconcagua-Valparaíso can maintain water quality only if treatment is carried to 90 per cent; Coquimbo and Tarapacá can maintain water quality with treatment as low as 70 per cent.

All regions from O'Higgins-Colchagua southward can meet the dissolved oxygen standard by various combinations of treatment and flow. Where there is such a choice, presumably the selection will depend upon the combination that costs the least unless the possibility of earning income warrants a more expensive alternative (e.g., hydroelectric power revenues). In Curicó-Linares the least cost combination is at 70 per cent treatment, and in Concepción-Cautín, at 35 per cent. (Zero treatment with augmented flow would cost about the same.) In the Valdivia-Llanquihue region the projected discharge of untreated wastes would not reduce instream content of dissolved oxygen below 4 milligrams per liter even at zero treatment and present minimum flows.

If we assume that whenever full regulation falls far short of meeting required flows no expenditure is incurred for waste dilution but that otherwise such expenditure is made, annual costs of dilution range between E°1.3 million for 35 per cent treatment (but all northern regions fail to meet the quality standard) to E°3.5 million at 90 per cent treatment, at which all regions except two meet the standard.

The least cost combination of flow and treatment is shown in Table 67. Altogether, quality maintenance would cost E°58.1 million per year (exclusive of collection costs), of which E°42.6 million are treatment costs and E°15.5 million are storage costs. The "minimum cost" quality maintenance program[5] is estimated to cost about one-half of the amount that would be required to regulate flows for all other purposes. If only treatment were provided, the total costs of quality maintenance would fall by 27 per cent. Including collection and dilution, total costs of quality maintenance are estimated at about E°75 million (1964) annually.

Except for Ñuble and O'Higgins-Colchagua, which together account for only 6 per cent of total waste dilution costs, all required waste dilution

[5] This is "minimum" only within the limits of the underlying assumptions of waste produced and the technology of waste treatment. If these assumed conditions are changed another combination might be "minimum."

flows of the minimum cost model are to be found in the northern part of the country where they could serve agriculture if recaptured before discharge to the sea. Land area so served would be determined by gross rather than net water requirement per hectare, since the land would be downstream rather than upstream. Dilution flows required in O'Higgins-Colchagua and Ñuble would have no additional use, unless such flows were part of a regulated release for hydroelectric power, since there is no irrigable land that would not already be irrigated. (All Ñuble requirements are computed at loss rates since Ñuble is upstream. O'Higgins-Colchagua downstream intake requirements have already been taken into account in fixing the "extra" waste dilution flows at 144 million cubic meters per year. Of course, new developments not anticipated in the model might make use of the water.)

Total irrigable area that could be served by waste dilution flows amounts to 24,700 hectares, *provided* additional downstream regulatory storage were available. Conceivably such reregulation might be met by small on-the-farm ponds, since the amounts of water and irrigable area are not large. The additional area supported by dilution flows would not offset the relatively high cost of dilution water. (The cost of waste, excluding O'Higgins-Colchagua and Ñuble, is about E°27,300 per million cubic meters per year, or, if assigned wholly to agriculture, E°590 per hectare per year.)

The question of water quality involves the two kinds of action that have been discussed: treatment of wastes before discharge and dilution of the discharged, treated effluent. Because of Chile's limited experience with matters pertaining to water quality, there are few supports for any extrapolation of policy into the future, and because of past unconcern there is little information. The figures used and the conclusions reached here are wholly inferential and based upon translations of foreign experience and data to Chilean waters.

Nothing has been said about the cumulated capital investment that maintaining high-quality water would require. Capital costs are assumed to be approximately twelve times annual costs, based upon 8 per cent interest and fifty-year amortization. A collection system alone (whose costs have not been included in several of the previous tables), would require a total investment by 1985 of approximately E°200 million (1964). Treatment plants, for the least cost combination of treatment and flow, would require another E°500 million. The added cost of flow would require another E°186 million. Altogether, the cumulated capital cost by 1985 amounts to about E°900 million (1964)—about US$300 million at 1964 official exchange rates.

A minimum program (as distinct from the minimum cost program discussed above) that would provide primary treatment to all domestic and industrial wastes discharged upstream, except where present minimum flows would adequately dilute untreated wastes, would cost E°16 million annually for collection and about E°20 million annually for treatment—or about one-half the cost of a program designed to meet a dissolved oxygen standard of 4 milligrams per liter. Its capital costs would be about E°432 million.

XV

VARIATIONS ON THE MAJOR THEME

All estimates of storage costs are based on the assumption that a certainty of 85 per cent was assured for the indicated flows. This means that three years out of twenty, on the average, flows will fall below the specified quantity.

Our data enable us to give approximate answers to two additional questions: (1) What would be required to raise the level of security to 100 per cent? (2) What flows have a certainty of 100 per cent when the indicated flows have a security of 85 per cent?[1]

HIGHER DEGREES OF SECURITY

If existing flows equalled or exceeded 95 per cent of the time are raised to 100 per cent certainty, non-agricultural requirements, assuming high levels of recirculation for industrial uses, can be met with no difficulty (at the expense, of course, of agriculture). This can be accomplished with less storage than is specified for Case I (marginal cost constraint, agriculture as residuary).

If, on the other hand, there is a desire to raise the level of security of all users from 85 per cent to 95 per cent or 100 per cent, the amount of storage is significantly increased. Table 68 shows the percentage changes in storage that would be needed beyond that required for 85 per cent security. Storage volumes would have to be raised by amounts ranging between 2 per cent and 55 per cent in order to reach 95 per cent certainty; and by amounts ranging between 3 per cent and 68 per cent to reach 100 per cent certainty. In several regions the additional storage requirement appears to be insignificant, relative to all other uncertainties with which our estimates deal. These regions are Tarapacá, Antofagasta, Aconcagua-Valparaíso (for 95 per cent certainty), Santiago, and Ñuble. Elsewhere, where storage

[1] See earlier comments, pp. 163, on "100 per cent certainty."

Table 68
STORAGE REQUIREMENTS FOR HIGHER LEVELS OF SECURITY

Province	Storage to raise 95% flow to 100% security[a] (mil. m³)	Percentage increase over storage for 85% security to assure security of:[b]		Minimum flow at marginal cost constraint, agriculture residual	
		95%	100%	85% security (mil. m³/yr)	100% security (mil. m³/yr)
Tarapacá	0.3	2	3	56	53
Antofagasta	0.52	3	18	88	83 [c]
Atacama	2.34	29	52	113	100
Coquimbo	9.1	33	53	601	480
Aconcagua-Valparaíso	13.0	16	28	1,093	980
Santiago	65.0	5	8	2,920	2,830
O'Higgins-Colchagua	26.0	55	68	4,557	4,040
Curicó-Linares	130.0	32	51	7,946	6,300
Ñuble	39.0	11	15	2,333	1,830
Concepción-Cautín	118.0	42	61	10,940	10,000 [c]
Valdivia-Llanquihue	476.0	–	–	22,088	22,000 [c]

[a] Centro de Planeamiento, Universidad de Chile—i.e., storage to assure at 100% certainty flow now equalled or exceeded 95% of the time.
[b] Centro de Planeamiento, based on storage for average flow.
[c] Rough estimate; curves converging.

volumes would have to be increased by amounts ranging between 30 per cent and 60 per cent, the economic effect, when translated to marginal cost, would be quite constricting.

The amount of storage required for Case I (marginal cost constraint, agriculture residual) will provide flows with 100 per cent security that are roughly 90 per cent of the amount provided with 85 per cent security.[2]

Non-agricultural requirements fall well within these quantities unless all downstream industries, foundries and power plants, as well as municipal systems, use water on a once-through basis. If, however, steam power plants and mining activities recirculate, so that their intake is equal to their losses, downstream flow, when highly regulated, is ample enough to allow

[2] Estimated from curves derived from flow-storage relationships supplied by Ricardo Harboe.

manufacturing plants and municipalities to use water without recirculation. A further safety margin for non-agricultural uses is provided by the
additional storage to meet seasonal irrigation requirements.[3] Whether the
storage does in fact provide a safety margin for non-agricultural uses will
depend, of course, on the amount of advance notice that is in possession
of those responsible for controlling releases from storage and on their
authority to withhold the water for agriculture.[4]

SEQUENCE AND TIMING OF ADDITIONS TO STORAGE[5]

Nothing has been said about problems of selecting the time when
particular increments to storage capacity will be supplied, except the
obvious fact that we have been discussing assumed conditions in 1985;
nor, except by passing reference, have we discussed the possibility of
alternative sequences by which reservoirs of different capacity could be
added. Costs of storage were based upon *ex ante* schedules constructed by
following the rule that large reservoirs would be built first and reservoirs
of successively smaller size later. It was assumed that reservoirs would
vary in size as the total volume of storage would grow toward full regulation, but this assumption is itself subject to correction by better information.

Since the storage and treatment capacity with which our models deal
are capacities in addition to what now exist, and since certain deficiencies
—such as in food production and the water quality of certain regions—
already exist, our models include requirements for water to meet a backlog
of need beyond the amounts that are dependent only upon future growth
of population and demand. In order to overcome backlog "need," therefore, a relatively high rate of investment in the near future would have to
be undertaken, after which the growth of investment in water resources
facilities could be based upon projected growth rates of water use. Because
the planning, design, and construction of river basin projects usually
require a lead time expressed in years rather than months, and because the
deficiencies in data needed for rational planning require, in many instances,
decades before they are remedied, the planning and data collection proc-

---

[3] Except in Aconcagua-Valparaíso and Santiago.
[4] The fact that the runoff record is relatively short in many regions means that our
estimates of flow-storage relationships may be in error. Furthermore, a given volume of
storage will provide 100 per cent security of a given flow only if the administration of
releases follows a rule consistent with such objective over many years, and not only
during a period of water shortage.
[5] I am grateful for the opportunities I have had to discuss with Orris C. Herfindahl
many of the theoretical problems treated in this and other sections of the study. Mr.
Herfindahl not only helped to clarify a number of relationships but suggested others as
well.

esses must reach a peak as soon as possible. Where adequate hydrologic records require more time than is available between now and the date that designs will be fixed and construction begun, substitute forms of information must be sought that will bridge the gap without incurring large risk of error. Not only are river basin projects expensive and long in gestation; they usually result in irreversible changes of a river's regimen and should not be undertaken until the risk of error is reduced to tolerable size.

Problems of timing are related to the general problem of capital shortage and the possibility of using alternative techniques, at least in the short run, to meet a given objective. For example, increases in agricultural productivity can be quickly achieved by adopting appropriate on-the-farm practices within the limits of available water supplies. Changes such as increased use of fertilizer, which are complementary with investment in water resources, can be undertaken immediately without danger that later findings will prove them wasteful.

Beyond these obvious observations, which are made only to avert the accusation that they have been ignored, I shall not go. Further studies in greater detail are needed in order to yield more specific conclusions. However, a little can be added to what has already been presented regarding the sequence in which reservoirs of different size are added.

Suppose the order in which reservoirs are added is reversed, beginning with the smallest instead of the largest. Presumably there is no effect on total costs if regulation is extended to the theoretical limit. But if regulation falls short of the hydrologic limit because an economic limit is encountered, and if the economic limit is determined by the marginal costs of storage, there can be a significant difference in costs between the two sequences. By beginning with large reservoirs[6] and proceeding to the

---

[6] The term "large reservoirs" is a proxy for low-cost reservoirs; by "low cost" is meant reservoirs whose cost per unit of impounded water is low. These circumlocutions reflect the fact that we do not have for each water resource region a schedule of reservoir sites whose costs of storage can be related to the total amount of regulation achieved at any given time. In the absence of such schedule it has been arbitrarily assumed that there is an inverse relation between capacity of a reservoir and cost per unit of capacity. Furthermore, the analysis has rested upon the aggregation of flows of all rivers in a water resource region into a single flow-storage relationship, which conceals intra-regional variation in this relationship. Finer detail would show that a reservoir of given capacity on River X would add more to the control of flow, because of the natural pattern of variability of flow, than a reservoir of equal capacity on River Y within the same region. Further variation on this theme is encountered when the complementarity or competitiveness of uses is taken into account and systemic interaction of demand is added to systemic interaction of supply, both converted from physical into monetary units. The full accounting of such interaction and the selection of a development program in light of an optimizing guide are the objective of operations analysis of river basin programs.

smaller, we take advantage of the fact that the costs of the first increments of flow are low for two reasons: (1) they come "early" in the movement along the flow-storage curve (which displays diminishing marginal physical productivity of flow), and (2) they utilize the lowest costs per unit of storage that we postulate for each region. By reversing the sequence so that the first increments to storage come from high-cost reservoirs, declining marginal physical productivity and declining unit costs of storage have opposing effects. The decline in marginal physical productivity is, however, the stronger force, so that the general movement of the marginal cost curve is still upward,[7] but at a markedly lower rate of ascent.[8]

The general pattern that is revealed by comparing marginal costs of "largest-first" with "smallest-first" sequences, is illustrated by the accompanying graphs. Smallest-first marginal costs are below largest-first marginal costs for the earliest stages of development, rise above in the middle stages, and fall below in the final stages. Cumulated capital costs of smallest-first exceed cumulated capital costs of largest-first once a given amount of reservoir capacity has been installed, and remain above until full capacity has been reached.

In none of these comparisons has the question of time as a separate dimension been considered. Time appears in several manifestations: big reservoirs take longer to fill than little reservoirs on the same river; the complementary activities of farm preparation take time; much of the projected demand will not appear until some time in the future, yet work must begin now in order to get ready. Real costs of construction may rise, fall, or remain constant. Land values are likely to change.

[7] These conclusions rest upon the data available to this study and the generalized cost of storage schedule that has been drawn from the data. Should further investigation reveal a different relationship between unit costs of capacity and size of reservoir (or between unit costs of storage and any other characteristic of storage sites that result in an upward sloping supply curve of storage capacity), the effect of changing the sequence of reservoirs might be different. Marginal costs of flow could be constant or declining.

[8] Another consideration is the fact that a "largest-first" sequence may imply relatively large capital outlays in the immediate future and smaller capital outlays in the more remote future. If interest rates are constant over the entire period of investment the present value of capital costs would, therefore, be higher under a largest-first sequence than under a "smallest-first" sequence. If interest rates in the more remote future are expected to decline below near-term levels, the difference between the two sequences in present value of capital costs would be even greater.

It should also be noted that a largest-first sequence does not necessarily imply that capital costs will be higher in earlier years than in later years of the investment period. It all depends on the volume of new storage that must be added in each year. On the assumption that a constant volume of storage is added each year, annual costs of the smallest-first sequence will be higher than costs of the largest-first sequence, since costs per cubic meter of capacity are higher for small than for large reservoirs.

In general, the stream of costs and benefits over time will be different for large and small projects. Under certain circumstances the choice of smallest-first (or a combination of small and large) is more efficient than a sequence in which each succeeding reservoir costs more per unit of capacity. Small reservoirs may be more desirable than large at certain stages of development, even if costs per unit of capacity are higher, because they avoid or reduce the costs of excess capacity or because of capital rationing.

If the experience of the United States is typical,[9] we can conclude that most countries follow a sequence of smallest-first; which means that the economic limits of water resource development are extended farther than if the reverse policy had been adopted from the beginning. The cost of the extension of the economic limit is a greater cumulative capital outlay for intermediate levels of development. These relationships are indicated by points A, B, and C on Figures 1 and 2. Marginal and cumulative capital costs of regulation to $0A$ are less by following the smallest-first sequence. Regulation to $0B$ costs less by following the largest-first sequence. At point C, the smallest-first sequence displays lower marginal but higher cumulative capital costs than the largest-first sequence.

Figures 3 and 4 are based upon the unit cost and flow-storage functions that were used in Chapter XII. Atacama and Santiago were selected for illustrative purposes without special justification. Shown are the curves for cumulative capital costs and marginal annual costs per million cubic meters of flow. The values are taken from Appendix Tables A-20, A-23, A-33, and A-34 and are plotted as step functions. These curves, based as they are on hypothetical rather than actual values, indicate the importance of having the underlying information. For Santiago, an increase in minimum flow to, say, 2,850 million cubic meters per year can be acquired for a cumulated capital outlay of $E^{0}90$ million by following the largest-first sequence, and for $E^{0}190$ million by following the opposite sequence. The advantages are reversed, however, for the first 500 million cubic meters of additional minimum flow.

In Atacama, the advantage of a smallest-first sequence persists over a relatively longer interval of regulation than in Santiago. Marginal costs of the smallest-first sequence rise rapidly, however, and could inhibit development more than a largest-first sequence. Only a very restrictive and prolonged capital constraint coupled with relatively high marginal benefits would justify a smallest-first sequence.

---

[9] U.S. Geological Survey, *Reservoirs in the United States*, Water-Supply Paper 1360-A (Washington: U.S. Government Printing Office, 1956), pp. 9-10.

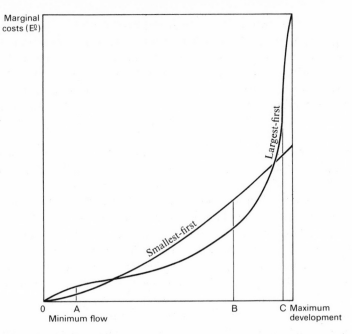

Figure 1. Marginal costs of flow of alternative sequences of reservoirs.

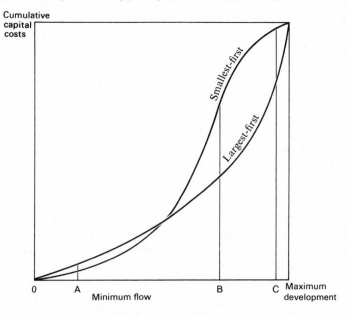

Figure 2. Cumulative capital costs of alternative sequences of reservoirs.

Because the marginal and cumulative costs of regulation *ex ante* are dependent upon the policy that has been followed *ex post*, storage supply curves are not as determinate as may have been implied in Chapter XII. However, within a given planning horizon and on the basis of a given historical record, most indeterminacy resting upon choice of sequence can be removed.[10]

If the information which determined the marginal cost constraints faithfully reflects actual differences in the marginal productivity of irrigated land in different provinces (other inputs being given), the optimum sequence of investment would be reasonably well correlated with the gaps that now prevail between present levels of regulation and projected levels of regulation in each water resource region. One can hardly attach such credibility to the figures we have fabricated. Presumably the tax assessment schedule reflects agricultural productivity, but the evidence appears to be contradictory. Because of the mild climate and long growing season,[11] one would imagine that yields of a well-watered hectare of land in northern coastal regions (such as Tarapacá and Antofagasta) would be the highest in Chile; yet, on the average, irrigated lands around Santiago have the highest assessed values. Should the relative physical productivity of irrigated land be different from the relative value for tax purposes, the differences may reflect several factors, among which is cost of transportation to the central part of the country. Under these circumstances, any significant lowering of transportation costs would alter the relative merits of a given geographic sequence of water resource investments.[12]

Several other factors must also be taken into account. One is the crop mix, which today may reflect, on the one hand, security of water supply, and, on the other, the fact that the overwhelming mass of Chileans exist on subsistence incomes, the purchasing power of which is protected by selective price controls. Price controls, in turn, have generated other controls, the total effect of which cannot always be explained by economic logic.[13]

---

[10] Indeterminacy associated with the probability of guessing what the future will bring still remains. Note also that in computing the amount of storage (and change in regulated flow) permitted by an upper limit on marginal cost, the method of interpolating linearly between zero regulation and the first interval makes more sense if a smallest-first rather than largest-first policy had been followed, whereas interpolations made within "later" intervals contain less error if a largest-first policy had been followed.

[11] The oases of Pica and Mantilla, inland in the province of Tarapacá, have agricultural land that is assessed at the highest of all values in Chile. Coastal areas of the Norte Grande, at lower elevations, have much lower valuations.

[12] Differences in land values reflecting prospective shifts from agricultural to urban uses could, of course, persist after transportation costs were reduced.

[13] A possible instance of the unforeseen effects of government policies is the October 1965 shortage of sulfur, which is used as an antifungicide in the vineyards. Chile apparently has no shortage of sulfuric raw materials but, it is alleged, has controlled price so effectively that production fails to meet demand.

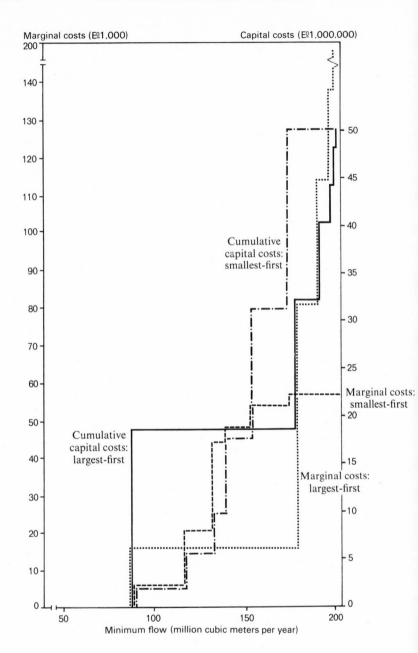

Figure 3. Atacama: cumulative capital and annual marginal costs.

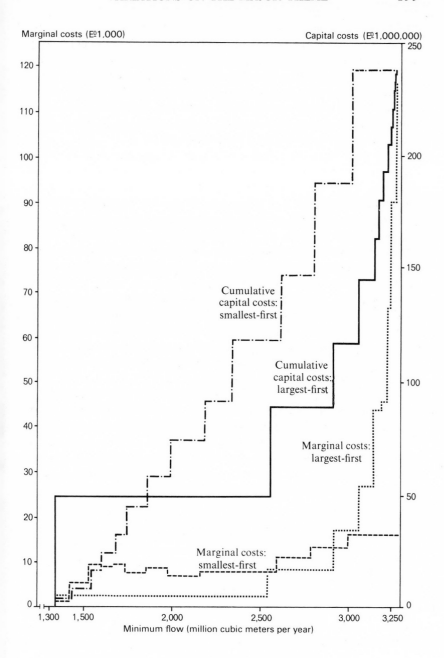

Figure 4. Santiago: cumulative capital and annual marginal costs.

As an example, one might cite the governmental plans for agricultural production in the next five-year period.[14] These plans call for an increase in wheat cultivation from 878,000 hectares in 1965 to 967,000 hectares in 1970, but no increase in the area devoted to vineyards. Since the gross product per hectare is six times higher in vineyards than wheat (see Table 14), since land is a major constraint, and since vineyards do not require unusually large amounts of water, the proposed changes in cropping areas probably cannot be justified by economic criteria.

A serious error in the schedule of marginal cost constraints could have been introduced by the present security (or insecurity) of water supply. Only knowledge of production functions for various cropping patterns can eliminate the possibility of error. If the natural variability of flow in a given region is such that relatively large amounts of storage are needed to regulate irrigation flows, agriculture in that region will have adopted an extensive, minimum-risk pattern of cultivation rather than an intensive, high-risk pattern. Present land values would reflect this circumstance and yield a corresponding schedule of marginal cost constraints. By uncritically adopting such constraints as the basis of policy, one fails to explore the possibility that a large-scale change in the character of the agricultural economy might warrant much greater development of water resources. On the other hand, short of desalination and transbasin movements, potentials are limited no matter how optimistically they are viewed.

Whether one has grossly overstated or understated irrigation possibilities in any one region, or in all regions together, has relatively little importance for the country as a whole. The limited supply of land is the major constraining factor in total agricultural output. If the costs of water have been misstated, "required" future output per hectare may be only 2.0 times present output instead of 2.2; or it may be 2.4 or 2.5 times the present. But these variations are relatively small compared with the big jump in productivity that is obviously needed if agricultural objectives are set against land resources.

OTHER PROJECTED RATES OF GROWTH

Virtually all of the analysis up to this point has been based upon the medium rate of population growth and the high rate of growth of GNP. It was previously concluded that the differences between this projection and that based upon the medium rate of population growth and low growth rate of GNP did not warrant detailed study. This conclusion rested upon the fact that because of its limited amount, irrigable land

[14] Unpublished data supplied by Klaus Gerber, ODEPLAN.

would be put to maximum use at either projection, and the other variations in water requirements were relatively small.

The effect of broadening the range of possibilities, by associating low rates of population growth with low-income projections and high rates of population growth with high-income projections, would not materially change the results, mainly because the range between high and low rates of population growth and high and low rates of change in income growth were narrowly separated in the first place. In light of the poor state of basic data, an elaboration of the implications of extreme possibilities does not seem worthwhile. Should the matter be pursued further at a later date, it is likely that the effects of adjusting to a wider range of possibilities would be most important for gross industrial uses of water, accommodation to the threat of pollution, and the level of nutrition attainable per capita. A lower rate of population growth than has been postulated would materially alter certain implications of our projections. The strain on resources to meet the pressure of numbers would be reduced; a smaller increase in productivity per hectare could provide a larger increase in per capita food and fiber; capital costs of urbanization would be reduced. It should be noted that, measured by arable land per capita, Chile is already a relatively densely populated country.[15] At the medium rate of population growth, by 1985 Chile would have about 0.35 hectares of arable land per capita. This can be compared with the 1962 figures of 0.67 hectares per capita for Denmark, 0.25 for Germany, 0.73 for France, 0.41 for Italy, and 0.56 for the European average.

One might also consider the effect on water resource plans of extending the time horizon from 1985 to, say, the year 2000. To make plans covering a span of thirty-five years is nothing strange to ENDESA, although other governmental agencies have not customarily looked so far ahead. For a date so far in the future commitment of physical facilities today would presumably be kept to a minimum. What ought not be minimized, however, are the data collection effort and the steady elaboration of essential investigations.

[15] See Appendix B, "Productivity of Agriculture in Chile in Comparison with Selected Countries," especially Table B-1.

XVI

CONCLUSIONS AND OBSERVATIONS

The main conclusion to be drawn from the previous fifteen chapters will hardly startle anyone: "efficient" or "rational" choices regarding water use cannot be made without adequate facts and figures, and Chile is short on both.

We can, if we wish, draw substantive inferences regarding the place of water in the Chilean economy, the prospective investments required to assure a specified water supply, the distribution of economic activity consonant with a designated expenditure in water resources, and the implicit impact of water shortage on the productivity of related inputs. Succumbing briefly to the lure of figures we have confected, one can point out that implied capital costs of flow regulation and waste treatment (at 1964 prices) range between E°1,900 million and E°1,400 million (roughly US$600 million to $400 million) depending upon whether the model is unrestrained Case I or Case I restrained by marginal costs with agriculture in residual position. One can also point out that even with such expenditures, the shortage of water in the seven northern provinces of Chile will restrict agriculture, or industry, or both, to levels below those projected before taking water supplies into account. And one can point out that the difference in required investment between complete control over water resources and a lesser degree of control as set by a marginal cost limit is on the order of E°500 million ($150 million), and that the cumulated capital costs of maintaining water quality is on the order of E°900 million ($280 million).

The possible range of choices in the face of a growing shortage of both land and water is so great that a few additional comments are in order.

One accommodation is to keep all irrigable land under cultivation in the hope that each year will be wet enough for a successful crop. The needed increase in productivity will be more difficult to achieve if land is brought (or kept) under cultivation with water that is available only during relatively wet years, or if water is shared as widely as possible rather than allocated with greater security to a smaller total area. Unless water supplies are reasonably certain, the necessary complementary inputs for a doubling of output will not be provided. The mere possession of irrigable land will not be adequate justification for a claim to water, since there will be more irrigable land than water where water is in short supply.

If Chile is to come as close as possible to meeting its production goals, water will have to be rationed in the seven northern provinces in accordance with a marginal-product-of-water criterion. This implies either sensitive administrative controls or separate markets for water and land in which participants are impelled to maximize net product. Neither of these conditions can now be found. To the degree that institutional changes are not adopted, to that degree will the increase in productivity probably fall short of what is needed. While we are likely to emphasize efficiency of water use in an agricultural context, the special problems of mining, manufacturing, and steam electric power in the northern provinces cannot be ignored. As already noted, our projections, emphasizing losses rather than intake as they do, imply a high degree of engineering efficiency in nonagricultural uses, and a level of efficiency in agriculture comparable to what is projected for California in 1980. The question at hand is whether or not the legal-economic framework will induce the degree of efficiency that is implied in the projected requirements.

The likelihood that the marginal costs of water will vary substantially between water-short and water-surplus regions of the country, granting a wide margin of error in the specific values that have been computed, is a clear signal for someone to undertake detailed studies of regional economic plans that embrace costs of transportation and preferences for domicile as well as costs of water. Substantial savings of capital can be enjoyed by encouraging a greater growth of municipal and industrial water use in the southern part of the Central Valley than is projected, with a corresponding reduction in the northern part of the Central Valley and provinces farther to the north. This conclusion is especially valid if oxygen content is to be maintained by high-level waste treatment and waste dilution flows. The desirability of encouraging a different pattern of urban concentration from what has been projected will be most intimately related to the question of water quality.

If it turns out that land capable of being irrigated in the Norte Grande exists in larger quantity than the implausibly small amounts now shown for Antofagasta and Tarapacá, augmentation of the region's water supply by importation or desalination becomes a provocative speculation, especially if such lands can be found at relatively low elevation where the growing season extends throughout the year. If Chilean desert soils are like some desert soils elsewhere, their rich endowment of minerals will make them among the most productive of the country and may warrant expenditures on water supply that now seem absurd. The possibility of a series of transbasin diversions from south to north ought not be discarded without serious study in light of the rapid advances that have been made in large-scale, earth-moving technology.

Our findings not only suggest what are likely to be the trouble spots in the more distant future but provide a clue for near-term policy as well. The deficiency in reliable information and the unsystematic financial arrangements followed for municipal and irrigation water supplies indicate that aggregate welfare has been enhanced only by accident, if at all, by public expenditures in water resources. There is little doubt that income has been transferred from the public at large to the beneficiaries of public water resource projects, except, perhaps, in the case of hydroelectric power.[1] While income transfers are neither desirable nor undesirable as such, in the case of municipal and irrigation water supplies they have not been contemplated by the laws under which the services have been supplied.[2] In view of probable increases in the marginal costs of water, the matter of income transfers will become more pressing. Who is going to pay? Will it be the taxpayer, the water user, a foreign entity, or some combination? The present system, whereby payments are only remotely related to benefits within the framework of a law that assumes otherwise is apt to yield unsatisfactory results when measured against an economic efficiency criterion.

It is likely that use of Chile's scarce capital resources and professional skills would be improved if in the next year or two a massive effort were devoted to the acquisition, upgrading, and systematic analysis of data relating to land and water resources, the institution of new programs for data collection, and the analysis of projects already constructed.

There is no question but that a public works program is an integral part of economic development; but it is equally essential that decisions regarding new construction be based upon adequate knowledge. At present there are serious deficiencies in the state of knowledge regarding such basic questions as the quantity of irrigable and dry arable land, water use coefficients, stream runoff, soil qualities, reservoir sites, evaporation rates, water quality characteristics, other technical characteristics of agriculture, and optimum land use patterns.

[1] No study was made of ENDESA's operations. It seems likely that power consumers pay their way, and that income transfers are not significant.

[2] No data are at hand on the incidence of Chile's tax system. It is likely that the system is regressive. If so, the effect of the income transfers has been to make the poor poorer and rich richer, a result that might even be encountered if the tax system were progressive. (See *El Sistema Tributario Chileno* [Santiago: Oficina de Estudios Tributarios, 1960], Chap. 5.)

Plans for rapid expansion of irrigated agriculture are not supported by the record of the past thirty years, in which a total of 116,000 hectares was brought under irrigation. At the same time it is equally unrealistic to separate the required increase in agricultural productivity from the need to improve the regularity of water supply. This means that priority should go to the projects that serve the best land for which present supplies of water are so erratic that farmers have been reluctant to make the necessary complementary investments. Methods of fixing priorities of new construction, and the procedures that are followed in cost estimating, contracting, and repayment are subject to ever-changing stresses that require continuous re-examination—re-examination that is not only imperative but also a drain upon the limited supply of professional skills. The speed with which new projects are undertaken should be controlled by the capacity of the professional staff to do a workmanlike job of project evaluation.

The urgency with which output per hectare must be increased can hardly be overemphasized, since no other way of feeding Chile's population offers more promise. Present plans of the Chilean government[3] call for the following increases in output per hectare during the period 1965–70:

Product	Per Cent
wheat	22
rice	20
corn	28–40
grains	24
beans	11
oil seeds	11–24
sunflower seeds	25
rape	0–15
sugar beets	0
potatoes	10
vegetables	3–4
garlic	8–24
onions	10–20
fruits	0
grapes	10
livestock and poultry	4
milk	21
wool	3
total livestock and products	8
agriculture, except livestock	17–18

[3] Information supplied by Klaus Gerber, ODEPLAN.

The expected rate of increase in productivity per hectare, averaged for the agricultural and livestock sectors on the basis of the relative values of production in 1959–60, is 14 per cent for the quinquennium 1965–70. If this rate of improvement is achieved and if it is maintained for each of the next three quinquennia, total agricultural and livestock output per hectare will grow about 70 per cent during the twenty-year period 1965–85, leaving a shortage by 1985 of about 25 per cent relative to projected requirements. Unless productivity goals are raised we can expect the demand for food and fibers to exert pressure on Chile's balance of payments indefinitely into the future, with corresponding adverse effects on the rest of the economy.[4]

It had been hoped that this study would advance our understanding of the role of water resources in economic development as well as supply an evaluation of the existing state of information in light of what is needed if economical (i.e., cost-minimizing—output-maximizing) decisions regarding water resources are to be made. Several conclusions can be drawn: (1) Most of the unsuccessful public projects that have been built in the past owe their failure to the lack of reliable data on flows, soils, land capabilities, and water requirements. (2) The government has not undertaken a systematic program of data collection on ground water, water quality, and water use by agriculture, industry, and municipalities. (3) During the past fifteen years or so a number of studies dealing with Chilean water resources have unanimously identified the same deficiencies.

One ought to be aware of the possible irrelevance of economic analysis to policies that actually are adopted. It is clear that Chile's poor state of economic health cannot be blamed on lack of water or lack of land since both are used now at relatively low levels of efficiency. Moreover, without knowing why so little attention has been paid to reports already written, analyses already made, and prescriptions already offered, a limit is quickly reached to what can be added to our knowledge of the way in which natural resources relate to economic development. It follows, therefore, that an understanding of the role of water resources in economic development rests upon knowledge of motivation, habits of thought, the

---

[4] See Appendix B, "Productivity of Agriculture in Chile in Comparison with Selected Countries."

Sr. Alvaro Marfan J. (in a letter of January 30, 1967) has called attention to the fact that the Chilean government plans to encourage substitution of high-valued for low-valued crops, thereby inducing an increase in productivity per hectare beyond that indicated by the increase in output per hectare of each crop. Should the rearrangement of cropping patterns be successful, the projected required increase in productivity could be met, either directly or by way of foreign trade, assuming that products were traded at price ratios approximately equal to the Chilean ratios.

distribution of economic and political power, and the factors inducing or inhibiting their change.[5]

An "economic analysis" of Chilean water resources is relevant only within a context in which the analyst and Chilean policy makers are in agreement on the importance of the goal of economic efficiency and the constraints within which attainment of the goal will be sought. There is no reason to believe in the existence of such consensus and, in fact, one can cite examples to prove its absence. Irrelevance may explain the oblivion to which previous studies were consigned.

Within the broad context of economic development inefficient use of water is not likely to be of greater consequence than waste of land, labor, and equipment. Attention to water is merited for other reasons. First, most of the development in the future will be dependent upon government financing, subject to government budgetary forces rather than to the more decentralized controls of private markets. (This contrast is weakened by the many controls over private markets exercised by the government.) Second, the efficient use of water can have an important catalytic effect on the prickly matter of agrarian reform and land ownership. The public utility characteristics of water supply offer a legitimacy in the exercise of power over private property that is reasonably well accepted and which can serve as an instrument of land reform. Third, limitations imposed by the geographic distribution of land and water resources reduce the indeterminacy which the regional planner faces in accounting for various interregional possibilities within the context of a given set of national outputs. By pursuing further the question of cost constraints and settling the question of water quality, indeterminacy might be further reduced. While technological innovations may widen the range of alternative regional distributions of activity at some time in the future, the risk of being wrong is no greater than is assumed in any other sector of planning. Fourth and last, the scope of data that must be acquired and the web of decisions that are interwoven in the process of efficiently developing and using water resources draw upon many diverse disciplines of the social and physical sciences and establish their relevance to each other with a clarity not matched by many other undertakings.

UNFINISHED BUSINESS

The termination of this study should be the beginning of another. There is much unfinished business. Paramount are the inadequacies of data that have already been identified. To summarize these inadequacies would be

[5] My interest in pursuing these lines of thought led to Everett H. Hagen, *On the Theory of Social Change* (Homewood, Ill.: Dorsey, 1962). Hagen's book is required reading for anyone interested in economic development.

tedious. They encompass all aspects of hydrologic, engineering, and economic measurements that are relevant to the effective planning of water resource use.

In addition to the need for systematic acquisition of basic data, the most valuable contribution that could be made to an understanding of the demand for water would be a model of the agricultural sector that revealed the crop mix, quantity of output, regional distribution of output, and marginal revenue product of water under specified conditions. From the point of view of supply, the most valuable contribution would be a schedule of reservoir sites for each basin systematically related to increments of control over flow and with information on costs of storage and delivery to points of use. Costs of desalinating sea water, transbasin movement, and exploitation of ground water as well as costs of reducing waste as an alternative to increased flow regulation also ought to be developed. It is likely that brackish waters are available in some places and that their desalination may be economically feasible in the not too distant future.

The question of water quality has scarcely been touched by Chilean authorities but will become a matter of urgency in the foreseeable future. In the area around Santiago, pollution will be urban in origin. Farther north, downstream flows may become too mineralized for further use if irrigation is extended to the limit of water supplies. Under these circumstances the requirement for water may have to include waste dilution flows, in which case the relevant model would involve a demand consisting of upstream losses plus the greater of waste dilution flows or downstream intake. Even urban uses can contribute to the build-up of salinity, and the possibility of damage by detergents will also be a matter of concern as Santiago grows and the level of income increases. Related to the unknowns of water quality problems is the fate of coastal and fresh-water fisheries and the necessary precautions that must be taken to preserve the ocean beaches and lakes for recreational uses. Also related to water quality is the question of costs of treatment. Are Chilean costs one-half the level of costs in the United States, as this study has assumed, or are they equal to or more than U.S. costs?

The reader will appreciate that nothing has been said of water rights and administrative organization, although no program of water resource planning could ignore them. Little has been said of the problems of benefit-cost analysis and the recovery of governmental expenditures, especially in a context of persistent and relatively severe (but not hyper) inflation. Related to these questions is the matter of multiple versus single-purpose projects and the techniques of analysis, construction, and administration that must be adopted in order to be certain that net benefits are maximized and costs equitably distributed.

APPENDICES

A. Supporting Tables—Projections, 1985

B. Productivity of Agriculture in Chile in Comparison with Selected Countries

C. Current Irrigation Capacity of Rivers in the Central Zone of Chile

APPENDIX A
Supporting Tables—Projections, 1985[1]

Table A-1
MANUFACTURING: WATER INTAKE, 1985, MEDIUM B

(Million m³/yr)

Province	Food	Pulp	Paper	Chemicals	Petro-chemicals	Petroleum refining	Steel	All others	Total
Tarapacá	0.6	–	–	2.7	–	–	–	–	3.3
Antofagasta	0.6	–	–	10.8	–	–	–	–	11.4
Atacama	–	–	–	–	–	–	–	–	–
Coquimbo	1.2	–	–	2.7	–	–	–	1.8	5.7
Aconcagua	1.2	–	–	–	–	–	–	1.8	3.0
Valparaíso	13.0	1.1	1.2	21.6	39.4	104.7	–	30.5	211.5
Santiago	21.3	4.3	12.9	85.2	–	125.7	10.1	114.9	374.4
O'Higgins	3.0	–	–	1.4	–	–	–	–	4.4
Colchagua	0.6	–	–	–	–	–	–	1.8	2.4
Curicó	0.6	–	–	–	–	–	–	–	0.6

Talca	2.4	1.0	1.1	2.7	–	–	–	1.8	9.0
Maule	–	32.0	–	–	–	–	–	–	32.0
Linares	0.6	–	–	–	–	–	–	–	0.6
Ñuble	0.6	–	–	–	–	–	–	–	0.6
Concepción	3.5	19.2	14.7	6.8	105.1	83.8	191.4	19.7	444.2
Arauco	–	32.0	–	–	–	–	–	–	32.0
Bío-Bío	1.2	121.4	26.5	–	–	–	–	–	149.1
Malleco	1.1	–	–	–	–	–	–	–	1.1
Cautín	1.2	–	–	–	–	–	–	1.8	3.0
Valdivia	2.4	2.1	2.3	–	–	–	–	3.6	10.4
Osorno	2.4	–	–	–	–	–	–	–	2.4
Llanquihue	1.2	–	–	–	–	–	–	–	1.2
Chiloé	–	–	–	–	–	–	–	–	–
Aysén	–	–	–	–	–	–	–	–	–
Magallanes	0.6	–	–	–	33.4	–	–	–	34.0
Total country	59.3	213.1	58.7	133.9	177.9	314.2	201.5	177.7	1,336.3

[1] Details may not add due to rounding.

APPENDIX A

Table A-2
FOOD AND BEVERAGES, 1985, MEDIUM B

(*Thousands m³/yr*)

Province	Percentages		Total intake	Total loss	Intake of down-stream plants	Loss of up-stream plants	Total
	Down-stream	Up-stream					
Tarapacá	88	12	600	36	528	4	532
Antofagasta	58	42	600	36	348	15	363
Atacama	–	–	–	–	–	–	–
Coquimbo	50	50	1,200	72	600	36	636
Aconcagua	3	97	1,200	72	36	70	106
Valparaíso	70	30	13,000	780	9,100	234	9,334
Santiago	2	98	21,300	1,278	426	1,252	1,678
O'Higgins	–	100	3,000	180	–	180	180
Colchagua	4	96	600	36	24	35	59
Curicó	1	99	600	36	6	36	42
Talca	–	100	2,400	144	–	144	144
Maule	–	–	–	–	–	–	–
Linares	–	100	600	36	–	36	36
Ñuble	1	99	600	36	6	36	42
Concepción	94	6	3,500	210	3,290	13	3,303
Arauco	–	–	–	–	–	–	–
Bío-Bío	–	100	1,200	72	–	72	72
Malleco	–	100	1,100	66	–	66	66
Cautín	2	98	1,200	72	24	71	95
Valdivia	58	42	2,400	144	1,392	60	1,452
Osorno	–	100	2,400	144	–	144	144
Llanquihue	70	30	1,200	72	840	22	862
Aysén	–	–	–	–	–	–	–
Magallanes	100	–	600	36	600	–	600
Total country			59,300	3,558	17,220	2,526	19,746

Table A-3
PULP AND PAPER, 1985, MEDIUM B

(Thousand m³/yr)

Province	Percentages		Total intake	Total loss	Intake of down-stream plants	Loss of up-stream plants	Total
	Down-stream	Up-stream					
Tarapacá							
Antofagasta							
Atacama							
Coquimbo							
Aconcagua							
Valparaíso	100		2,300	207	2,300		2,300
Santiago		100	17,200	1,548		1,548	1,548
O'Higgins							
Colchagua							
Curicó							
Talca		100	2,100	189		189	189
Maule	100		32,000	2,880	32,000		32,000
Linares							
Ñuble							
Concepción	100		33,900	3,051	33,900		33,900
Arauco	100		32,000	2,880	32,000		32,000
Bío-Bío		100	147,900	13,311		13,311	13,311
Malleco							
Cautín							
Valdivia	100		4,400	396	4,400		4,400
Osorno							
Llanquihue							
Chiloé							
Aysén							
Magallanes							
Total country			271,800	24,462	104,600	15,048	119,648

Table A-4
CHEMICALS, 1985, MEDIUM B

(*Thousand m³/yr*)

Province	Percentages		Total intake	Total loss	Intake of down-stream plants	Loss of up-stream plants	Total
	Down-stream	Up-stream					
Tarapacá	100		2,700	189	2,700		2,700
Antofagasta	100		10,800	756	10,800		10,800
Atacama							
Coquimbo	100		2,700	189	2,700		2,700
Aconcagua							
Valparaíso	100		21,600	1,512	21,600		21,600
Santiago		100	85,200	5,964		5,964	5,964
O'Higgins		100	1,400	98		98	98
Colchagua							
Curicó							
Talca		100	2,700	189		189	189
Maule							
Linares							
Ñuble							
Concepción	100		6,800	476	6,800		6,800
Arauco							
Bío-Bío							
Malleco							
Cautín							
Valdivia							
Osorno							
Llanquihue							
Chiloé							
Aysén							
Magallanes							
Total country			133,900	9,373	44,600	6,251	50,851

Table A-5
PETROLEUM REFINING, 1985, MEDIUM B

(*Thousand m³/yr*)

Province	Percentages		Total intake	Total loss	Intake of down-stream plants	Loss of up-stream plants	Total
	Down-stream	Up-stream					
Tarapacá							
Antofagasta							
Atacama							
Coquimbo							
Aconcagua							
Valparaíso	100		104,700	4,188	107,400		107,400
Santiago		100	125,700	5,028		5,028	5,028
O'Higgins							
Colchagua							
Curicó							
Talca							
Maule							
Linares							
Ñuble							
Concepción	100		83,800	3,352	83,800		83,800
Arauco							
Bío-Bío							
Malleco							
Cautín							
Valdivia							
Osorno							
Llanquihue							
Chiloé							
Aysén							
Magallanes							
Total country			314,200	12,568	191,200	5,028	196,228

Table A-6
PETROCHEMICALS, 1985, MEDIUM B

(Thousand m³/yr)

Province	Percentages		Total intake	Total loss	Intake of down-stream plants	Loss of up-stream plants	Total
	Down-stream	Up-stream					
Tarapacá							
Antofagasta							
Atacama							
Coquimbo							
Aconcagua							
Valparaíso	100		39,400	788	39,400		39,400
Santiago							
O'Higgins							
Colchagua							
Curicó							
Talca							
Maule							
Linares							
Ñuble							
Concepción	100		105,100	2,102	105,100		105,100
Arauco							
Bío-Bío							
Malleco							
Cautín							
Valdivia							
Osorno							
Llanquihue							
Chiloé							
Aysén							
Magallanes	100		33,400	668	33,400		33,400
Total country			177,900	3,558	177,900		177,900

Table A-7
STEEL, 1985, MEDIUM B

(Thousand m³/yr)

Province	Percentages		Total intake	Total loss	Intake of down- stream plants	Loss of up- stream plants	Total
	Down- stream	Up- stream					
Tarapacá							
Antofagasta							
Atacama							
Coquimbo							
Aconcagua							
Valparaíso							
Santiago		100	10,100	303		303	303
O'Higgins							
Colchagua							
Curicó							
Talca							
Maule							
Linares							
Ñuble							
Concepción	100		191,400	5,742	191,400		191,400
Arauco							
Bío-Bío							
Malleco							
Cautín							
Valdivia							
Osorno							
Llanquihue							
Chiloé							
Aysén							
Magallanes							
Total country			201,500	6,045	191,400	303	191,703

APPENDIX A

Table A-8
ALL OTHER INDUSTRIES, 1985, MEDIUM B

(Thousand m³/yr)

Province	Percentages		Total intake	Total loss	Intake of down- stream plants	Loss of up- stream plants	Total
	Down- stream	Up- stream					
Tarapacá							
Antofagasta							
Atacama							
Coquimbo	100		1,800	126	1,800		1,800
Aconcagua		100	1,800	126		126	126
Valparaíso	100		30,500	2,135	30,500		30,500
Santiago		100	114,900	8,043		8,043	8,043
Colchagua		100	1,800	126		126	126
Curicó							
Talca		100	1,800	126		126	126
Maule							
Linares							
Ñuble							
Concepción	100		19,700	1,379	19,700		19,700
Arauco							
Bío-Bío							
Malleco							
Cautín		100	1,800	126		126	126
Valdivia	100		3,600	252	3,600		3,600
Osorno							
Llanquihue							
Chiloé							
Aysén							
Magallanes							
Total country			177,700	12,439	55,600	8,547	64,147

Table A-9

MANUFACTURING—LOSS I: 1985, MEDIUM B

(Thousand m³/yr)

Province	Food and beverages	Pulp and paper	Inorganic chemicals	Petroleum refining	Petro-chemicals	Steel	All others	Total
Tarapacá	532	–	2,700	–	–	–	–	3,232
Antofagasta	363	–	10,800	–	–	–	–	11,163
Atacama	–	–	–	–	–	–	–	–
Coquimbo	636	–	2,700	–	–	–	1,800	5,136
Aconcagua-Valparaíso	9,440	2,300	21,600	107,400	39,400	–	30,626	210,766
Santiago	1,678	1,548	5,964	5,028	–	303	8,043	22,564
O'Higgins-Colchagua	239	–	98	–	–	–	126	463
Curicó-Linares	222	32,189	189	–	–	–	126	32,726
Ñuble	42	–	–	–	–	–	–	42
Concepción-Cautín	3,536	79,211	6,800	83,800	105,100	191,400	19,826	489,673
Valdivia-Llanquihue	2,458	4,400	–	–	–	–	3,600	10,458
Chiloé	–	–	–	–	–	–	–	–
Aysén	–	–	–	–	–	–	–	–
Magallanes	600	–	–	–	33,400	–	–	34,000
Total	19,746	119,648	50,851	196,228	177,900	191,703	64,147	820,223

Table A-10

MANUFACTURING—LOSS II: 1985, MEDIUM B

(Thousand m³/yr)

Province	Food and beverages	Pulp and paper	Inorganic chemicals	Petroleum refining	Petro-chemicals	Steel	All others	Total
Tarapacá	36	–	189	–	–	–	–	225
Antofagasta	36	–	756	–	–	–	–	792
Atacama	–	–	–	–	–	–	–	–
Coquimbo	72	–	189	–	–	–	126	387
Aconcagua-Valparaíso	852	207	1,512	4,188	788	–	2,261	9,808
Santiago	1,278	1,548	5,964	5,028	–	303	8,043	22,164
O'Higgins-Colchagua	216	–	98	–	–	–	126	440
Curicó-Linares	216	3,069	189	–	–	–	126	3,600
Ñuble	36	–	–	–	–	–	–	36
Concepción-Cautín	420	19,242	476	3,352	2,102	5,742	1,505	32,839
Valdivia-Llanquihue	360	396	–	–	–	–	252	1,008
Chiloé	–	–	–	–	–	–	–	–
Aysén	–	–	–	–	–	–	–	–
Magallanes	36	–	–	–	668	–	–	704
Total	3,558	24,462	9,373	12,568	3,558	6,045	12,439	72,003

APPENDIX A

221

Table A-11
INDUSTRIAL P.E.'s PRODUCED[a]

Province	Food	Pulp and paper	Chemicals	Petroleum refining	Total
Tarapacá	.012	–	.011	–	.023
Antofagasta	.012	–	.043	–	.055
Atacama	–	–	–	–	–
Coquimbo	.024	–	.011	–	.035
Aconcagua	.024	–	–	–	.024
Valparaíso	.260	.015	.244	.088	.607
Santiago	.426	.114	.341	.052	.933
O'Higgins	.060	–	.006	–	.066
Colchagua	.012	–	–	–	.012
Curicó	.012	–	–	–	.012
Talca	.048	.014	.011	–	.073
Maule	–	.211	–	–	.211
Linares	.012	–	–	–	.012
Ñuble	.012	–	–	–	.012
Concepción	.070	.224	.448	.035	.777
Arauco	–	.211	–	–	.211
Bío-Bío	.024	.976	–	–	1.000
Malleco	.022	–	–	–	.022
Cautín	.024	–	–	–	.024
Valdivia	.048	.029	–	–	.077
Osorno	.048	–	–	–	.048
Llanquihue	.024	–	–	–	.024
Chiloé	–	–	–	–	–
Aysén	–	–	–	–	–
Magallanes	.012	–	.134	–	.146
Total country	1.186	1.794	1.249	.175	4.404

[a] P.E. = Population equivalent in millions.

Table A-12

P.E.'s DISCHARGED UPSTREAM AND DOWNSTREAM, 1985[a]

| Province | Industrial | | | | Municipal discharge | |
| | Upstream | | | Down-stream | Up-stream | Down-stream |
	Food	All others	Total			
Tarapacá	.001	–	.001	.022	.027	.200
Antofagasta	.005	–	.005	.050	.187	.258
Atacama	–	–	–	–	.159	.026
Coquimbo	.012	–	.012	.023	.174	.174
Aconcagua	.023	–	.023	.001	.121	.052
Valparaíso	.078	–	.078	.529	.316	.736
Santiago	.417	.507	.924	.009	4.814	.098
O'Higgins	.060	.006	.066	–	.293	–
Colchagua	.012	–	.012	–	.104	.003
Curicó	.012	–	.012	–	.097	.001
Talca	.048	.025	.073	–	.195	–
Maule	–	–	–	.211	.046	.020
Linares	.012	–	.012	–	.130	–
Ñuble	.012	–	.012	–	.236	.002
Concepción	.004	–	.004	.773	.059	.917
Arauco	–	–	–	.211	.040	.025
Bío-Bío	.024	.976	1.000	–	.141	–
Malleco	.022	–	.022	–	.152	–
Cautín	.024	–	.024	–	.276	.006
Valdivia	.020	–	.020	.057	.105	.145
Osorno	.048	–	.048	–	.141	–
Llanquihue	.007	–	.007	.017	.049	.114
Chiloé	–	–	–	–	.007	.037
Aysén	–	–	–	–	–	.043
Magallanes	–	–	–	.146	–	.119
Total country	.841	1.514	2.355	2.049	7.869	2.977

[a] P.E. = Population equivalent in millions.

Table A-13
INDUSTRIAL WASTE DILUTION, 1985, MEDIUM A,
4 mg/l of Dissolved Oxygen

(*Million m³/yr*)

Province	Treatment level			
	0	35	70	90
Tarapacá	3.2	2.1	1.0	0.4
Antofagasta	9.5	6.2	2.9	1.1
Atacama	–	–	–	–
Coquimbo	28.6	18.7	8.6	3.4
Aconcagua-Valparaíso	241.6	157.6	72.4	28.8
Santiago	1,996.5	1,302.0	598.3	238.4
O'Higgins-Colchagua	181.2	118.2	54.3	21.6
Curicó-Linares	216.1	141.0	64.8	25.8
Ñuble	31.8	20.7	9.5	3.8
Concepción-Cautín	2,533.8	1,652.3	759.3	302.5
Valdivia-Llanquihue	178.0	116.1	53.4	21.3
Total of above provinces	5,420.5	3,534.8	1,624.4	647.2
Chiloé	–	–	–	–
Aysén	–	–	–	–
Magallanes	–	–	–	–
Total	5,420.5	3,534.8	1,624.4	647.2

Table A-14

CASES I, II, III, UPSTREAM LOSSES, 1985, MEDIUM B

(Thousand m³/yr)

Province	Municipal	Manufacturing	Total (1+2)	Agriculture	Total (3+4)	Mining	Steam electricity	Rural domestic	Non-agricultural losses (3+6+7+8)	Total losses (5+6+7+8)
	(1)	(2)	(3)	(4)	(5)	(6)	(7)	(8)	(9)	(10)
Tarapacá	393	4	397	121,048	121,445	–	–	341	738	121,786
Antofagasta	3,347	15	3,362	59,234	62,596	9,167	3,243	361	16,133	75,367
Atacama	3,671	–	3,671	337,021	340,692	16,466	34	1,844	22,015	359,036
Coquimbo	2,940	36	2,976	1,288,186	1,291,162	1,944	32	4,603	9,555	1,297,741
Aconcagua-Valparaíso	10,009	430	10,439	1,589,445	1,599,884	–	–	4,294	14,733	1,604,178
Santiago	170,840	22,138	192,978	3,903,608	4,096,586	2,894	329	14,037	210,238	4,113,846
O'Higgins-Colchagua	8,016	439	8,455	4,499,596	4,508,051	5,341	–	8,412	22,208	4,521,804
Curicó-Linares	11,078	720	11,798	7,211,381	7,223,179	–	8	12,310	24,116	7,235,497
Ñuble	3,421	36	3,457	2,321,759	2,325,216	–	–	7,453	10,910	2,332,669
Concepción-Cautín	13,508	13,659	27,167	7,050,630	7,077,797	–	–	22,485	49,652	7,100,282
Valdivia-Llanquihue	7,661	226	7,887	–	7,887	–	–	–	7,887	7,887
Chiloé	97	–	97	–	97	–	–	–	97	97
Aysén	–	–	–	–	–	–	–	–	–	–
Magallanes	–	–	–	–	–	–	–	–	–	–
Total	234,981	37,703	272,684	28,381,908	28,654,592	35,812	3,646	76,140	388,282	28,770,190

Table A-15

CASE I, DOWNSTREAM REQUIREMENTS, 1985, MEDIUM B

(Thousand m³/yr)

Province	Mining	Steam power[a]	Rural domestic[b]	Manufacturing	Total (1+2+3+4)	Municipal intake	Municipal discharge	Agriculture intake	Agricultural intake minus municipal requirements discharge	Total intake downstream (5+6+9)
	(1)	(2)	(3)	(4)	(5)	(6)	(7)	(8)	(9)	(10)
Tarapacá	206	3	342	221	772	14,440	11,552	185,686	174,134	189,346
Antofagasta	2,585	915	—	777	4,277	23,106	18,485	—	—	27,383
Atacama	8,483	17	251	—	8,751	2,988	2,390	70,517	68,127	79,866
Coquimbo	1,191	20	1,080	351	2,642	13,799	11,039	463,225	452,186	468,627
Aconcagua-Valparaíso	13,074	544	586	9,378	23,582	91,736	73,389	332,520	259,131	374,449
Santiago	—	—	286	26	312	17,433	13,946	122,240	108,294	126,039
O'Higgins-Colchagua	—	—	42	1	43	435	348	34,701	34,353	34,831
Curicó-Linares	—	—	786	2,880	3,666	1,890	1,512	706,338	704,826	710,382
Ñuble	—	—	—	—	—	173	138	—	—	173
Concepción-Cautín	—	53	937	19,180	20,170	111,374	89,099	448,560	359,461	491,005
Valdivia-Llanquihue	—	3	11,622	782	12,407	35,257	28,206	28,739	533	48,197
Chiloé	—	—	1,712	—	1,712	2,760	2,208	4,652	2,444	6,916
Aysén	53	—	1,241	—	1,294	5,545	4,436	8,338	3,902	10,741
Magallanes	—	8	748	704	1,460	19,163	15,330	22,827	7,497	28,120
Total	25,592	1,563	19,633	34,300	81,088	340,099	272,078	2,428,343	2,174,888	2,596,075

[a] Distribution between downstream and upstream is the same as for mining. From Aconcagua-Valparaíso to Ñuble all losses are classified "upstream." South of Ñuble they are considered downstream.

[b] Distribution between downstream and upstream based on distribution of irrigated land. South of Cautín all losses were considered as downstream.

Table A-16
CASE III, DOWNSTREAM INTAKES, 1985, MEDIUM B

(Thousand m³/yr)

Province	Agriculture	Manufacturing	Rural domestic	Municipal	Mining	Steam electricity	Total
Tarapacá	185,686	3,228	342	14,440	1,390	637	205,723
Antofagasta	—	11,148	—	23,106	17,236	217,560	269,050
Atacama	70,517	—	251	2,988	56,551	4,115	134,422
Coquimbo	463,225	5,100	1,080	13,799	7,941	4,693	495,838
Aconcagua-Valparaíso	332,520	210,336	586	91,736	87,160	129,622	851,960
Santiago	122,240	426	286	17,433	—	—	140,385
O'Higgins-Colchagua	34,701	24	42	435	—	—	35,202
Curicó-Linares	706,338	32,006	786	1,890	—	—	741,020
Ñuble	—	6	—	173	—	—	179
Concepción-Cautín	448,560	476,014	937	111,374	—	12,752	1,049,637
Valdivia-Llanquihue	28,739	10,232	11,622	35,257	—	769	86,619
Chiloé	4,652	—	1,712	2,760	—	1	9,125
Aysén	8,338	—	1,241	5,545	350	1	15,475
Magallanes	22,827	34,000	748	19,163	—	1,882	78,620
Total	2,428,343	782,520	19,633	340,099	170,628	372,032	4,113,255

Table A-17

UPSTREAM-DOWNSTREAM SUMMARY REQUIREMENTS, 1985, MEDIUM B

(Thousand m³/yr)

Province	Upstream losses	Downstream: losses, municipal intake, excess of agricultural intake over municipal discharge	Total: Case I (1+2)	Mining losses	Mining intake	Total: Case II (3−4+5)	Total: Downstream intake	Total: Case III (1+7)
	(1)	(2)	(3)	(4)	(5)	(6)	(7)	(8)
Tarapacá	121,786	189,346	311,132	206	1,390	312,316	205,723	327,509
Antofagasta	75,367	27,383	102,750	11,752	78,345	169,343	269,050	344,417
Atacama	359,036	79,866	438,902	29,949	166,326	580,279	134,422	493,458
Coquimbo	1,297,741	468,627	1,766,368	3,135	20,898	1,784,131	495,838	1,793,579
Aconcagua-Valparaíso	1,604,178	374,449	1,978,627	13,074	87,160	2,052,713	851,960	2,456,138
Santiago	4,113,846	126,039	4,239,885	2,894	19,294	4,256,285	140,385	4,254,231
O'Higgins-Colchagua	4,521,804	34,831	4,556,635	5,341	35,607	4,586,901	35,202	4,557,006
Curicó-Linares	7,235,497	710,382	7,945,879	—	—	7,945,879	741,020	7,976,517
Ñuble	2,332,669	173	2,332,842	—	—	2,332,842	179	2,332,848
Concepción-Cautín	7,100,282	491,005	7,591,287	—	—	7,591,287	1,049,637	8,149,919
Valdivia-Llanquihue	7,887	48,197	56,084	—	—	56,084	86,619	94,506
Chiloé	97	6,916	7,013	—	—	7,013	9,125	9,222
Aysén	—	10,741	10,741	53	350	11,038	15,475	15,475
Magallanes	—	28,120	28,120	—	—	28,120	78,620	78,620
Total	28,770,190	2,596,075	31,366,265	61,404	409,370	31,714,231	4,113,255	32,883,445

Table A-18
TARAPACÁ: COSTS OF FLOW

Storage (million m³)	Net minimum flow (million m³/yr)	Cumulative capital costs of storage (E⁰1,000)ᵃ	Cumulative annual costs of storage (E⁰1)	Annual marginal cost per million m³/yr of minimum flow (E⁰1)	Marginal costs in $/acre-ft of minimum flow
–	41.0	–	–	–	–
0.5	46.0	100	8,170	1,634	0.63
1.0	50.9	200	16,340	1,634	0.63
2.0	55.8	400	32,680	3,333	1.28
5.0	63.5	1,000	81,700	6,366	2.43
8.0	67.2	1,600	130,720	13,249	5.10
10.0	69.5	2,000	163,400	14,209	5.47
15.0	72.5	3,000	245,100	27,233	10.05
20.0	75.0	4,000	326,800	32,680	12.96
25.0	77.0	5,000	408,500	40,850	15.75
30.0	78.5	6,000	490,200	54,466	20.93
35.0	79.5	7,000	571,900	81,700	31.49
40.0	80.4	8,000	653,600	90,778	35.00
44.7	81.2	8,940	730,400	96,000	37.00

ᵃ Escudo values are in 1964 prices.

Table A-19
ANTOFAGASTA: COSTS OF FLOW

Storage (million m³)	Net minimum flow (million m³/yr)	Cumulative capital costs of storage (E°1,000)ª	Cumulative annual costs of storage (E°1)	Annual marginal costs per million m³/yr of minimum flow (E°1)
–	81.0	–	–	–
2	91.8	400	32,680	3,026
3	95.0	600	49,020	5,106
4	97.3	800	65,360	7,104
5	98.9	1,000	81,700	10,213
6	100.9	1,200	98,040	16,340
7	101.7	1,400	114,380	20,425
8	102.5	1,600	130,720	20,425
8.8	103.1	1,760	143,792	21,787

ª Escudo values are in 1964 prices.

Table A-20
ATACAMA: COSTS OF FLOW

Storage (million m³)	Net minimum flow (million m³/yr)	Cumulative capital costs of storage (E°1)ª	Cumulative annual costs of storage (E°1)	Annual marginal costs per million m³/yr of minimum flow (E°1)
–	81.3	–	–	–
190	177.6	19,000	1,552,300	16,119
280	191.4	32,500	2,655,250	79,924
320	197.2	40,500	3,308,850	112,690
340	199.6	44,500	3,635,650	136,167
360	201.0	48,500	3,962,450	233,429
370	201.2	50,500	4,125,850	817,000

ª Escudo values are in 1964 prices.

Table A-21
COQUIMBO: COSTS OF FLOW

Storage (million m³)	Net minimum flow (million m³/yr)	Cumulative capital costs of storage (E°1,000)ª	Cumulative annual costs of storage (E°1)	Annual marginal costs per million m³/yr of minimum flow (E°1)
–	199.0	–	–	–
770	665.0	38,500	3,145,450	6,838
1,270	741.6	63,500	5,187,950	26,664
1,570	767.6	87,500	7,148,750	70,028
1,770	783.6	103,500	8,455,950	81,700
1,920	791.3	118,500	9,681,450	169,766
2,020	795.8	128,500	10,498,450	181,556
2,110	797.8	142,000	11,601,400	551,475
2,190	797.8			
2,270	797.8			
2,310	797.8			
2,350	797.8			
2,390	797.8			
2,430	797.8			
2,470	797.8			
2,490	797.8			
2,500	797.8			
2,510	797.8			
2,520	797.8			

ª Escudo values are in 1964 prices.

Table A-22
ACONCAGUA-VALPARAÍSO: COSTS OF FLOW

Storage (*million m³*)	Net minimum flow (*million m³/yr*)	Cumulative capital costs of storage ($E°1,000$)[a]	Cumulative annual costs of storage ($E°1$)	Annual marginal costs per million m³/yr of minimum flow ($E°1$)
–	373.0	–	–	–
780	1,057.7	39,000	3,186,300	4,654
1,280	1,183.4	64,000	5,228,800	16,249
1,580	1,226.4	88,000	7,189,600	45,600
1,780	1,248.4	104,000	8,496,800	59,418
1,940	1,265.4	120,000	9,804,000	76,894
2,040	1,275.4	130,000	10,621,000	81,700
2,130	1,282.4	143,500	11,723,950	157,564
2,220	1,288.4	157,000	12,826,900	183,825
2,300	1,293.1	169,000	13,807,300	208,596
2,340	1,295.4	177,000	14,460,900	284,174
2,380	1,297.7	185,000	15,114,500	284,174
2,420	1,300.0	193,000	15,768,100	284,174
2,460	1,302.3	201,000	16,421,700	284,174
2,500	1,304.6	209,000	17,075,300	284,174
2,550	1,306.3	219,000	17,892,300	480,588

[a] Escudo values are in 1964 prices.

Table A-23
SANTIAGO: COSTS OF FLOW

Storage (million m³)	Net minimum flow (million m³/yr)	Cumulative capital costs of storage (E°1,000)ᵃ	Cumulative annual costs of storage (E°1)	Annual marginal costs per million m³/yr of minimum flow (E°1)
–	1,222.0	–	–	–
1,000	2,541.4	50,000	4,085,000	3,091
1,800	2,908.5	.90,000	7,353,000	8,902
2,370	3,037.2	118,500	9,681,450	18,092
2,710	3,118.6	145,700	11,903,690	27,300
2,880	3,150.1	162,700	13,292,590	44,092
3,050	3,181.6	179,700	14,681,490	44,092
3,140	3,205.6	193,200	15,784,440	45,956
3,220	3,220.3	205,200	16,764,840	66,694
3,260	3,227.6	213,200	17,418,440	89,534
3,300	3,234.9	221,200	18,072,040	89,534
3,340	3,242.2	229,200	18,725,640	89,534
3,380	3,249.5	237,200	19,379,240	89,534
3,385	3,250.2	238,200	19,460,940	116,714

ᵃ Escudo values are in 1964 prices.

Table A-24
O'HIGGINS-COLCHAGUA: COSTS OF FLOW

Storage (million m³)	Net minimum flow (million m³/yr)	Cumulative capital costs of storage (E°1,000)ᵃ	Cumulative annual costs of storage (E°1)	Annual marginal costs per million m³/yr of minimum flow (E°1)
–	1,604.0	–	–	–
3,320	5,914.6	166,000	13,562,200	3,144
4,320	6,288.9	216,000	17,647,200	10,914
4,940	6,466.6	265,600	21,699,520	22,804
5,260	6,552.2	297,600	24,313,920	30,542
5,560	6,628.7	327,600	26,764,920	32,039
5,870	6,700.1	374,100	30,563,970	53,208
6,070	6,748.1	414,100	33,831,970	68,083
6,175	6,771.8	435,100	35,547,670	72,392

ᵃ Escudo values are in 1964 prices.

Table A-25
CURICÓ-LINARES: COSTS OF FLOW

Storage (million m³)	Net minimum flow (million m³/yr)	Cumulative capital costs of storage (E°1,000)ᵃ	Cumulative annual costs of storage (E°1)	Annual marginal costs per million m³/yr of minimum flow (E°1)
–	3,264	–	–	–
15,000	18,300	750,000	61,275,000	4,075
24,600	21,008	1,230,000	100,491,000	14,482
26,600	21,552	1,390,000	113,563,000	24,029
28,600	21,996	1,550,000	126,635,000	38,000
29,600	22,168	1,630,000	133,171,000	38,000
30,400	22,290	1,710,000	139,707,000	53,574
31,200	22,412	1,790,000	146,243,000	53,574
31,700	22,479	1,865,000	152,370,500	91,867
32,200	22,515	1,940,000	158,498,000	166,962
32,400	22,526	1,980,000	161,766,000	305,421
32,600	22,537	2,020,000	165,034,000	305,421
32,800	22,538	2,060,000	168,302,000	4,668,571

ᵃ Escudo values are in 1964 prices.

Table A-26
ÑUBLE: COSTS OF FLOW

Storage (*million m³*)	Net minimum flow (*million m³/yr*)	Cumulative capital costs of storage (*E°1,000*) [a]	Cumulative annual costs of storage (*E°1*)	Annual marginal costs per million m³/yr of minimum flow (*E°1*)
–	1,009.0	–	–	–
5,000	5,374.3	250,000	20,425,000	4,679
8,400	6,101.0	420,000	34,314,000	19,112
9,100	6,224.2	476,000	38,889,200	37,136
9,600	6,312.2	516,000	42,157,200	37,136
10,100	6,400.2	556,000	45,425,200	37,136
10,400	6,441.2	586,000	47,876,200	59,780
10,700	6,467.2	616,000	50,327,200	94,269
10,900	6,489.2	646,000	52,778,200	111,409
11,000	6,500.2	661,000	54,003,700	111,409
11,100	6,511.2	681,000	55,637,700	148,545
11,200	6,520.2	701,000	57,271,700	181,556
11,250	6,524.2	711,000	58,088,700	204,250

[a] Escudo values are in 1964 prices.

Table A-27
CONCEPCIÓN-CAUTÍN: COSTS OF FLOW

Storage (*million m³*)	Net minimum flow (*million m³/yr*)	Cumulative capital costs of storage ($E°1,000$)[a]	Cumulative annual costs of storage ($E°1$)	Annual marginal costs per million m³/yr of minimum flow ($E°1$)
–	10,940.0	–	–	–
10,000	36,857.1	500,000	40,850,000	1,575
20,000	46,414.2	1,000,000	81,700,000	4,274
30,000	53,071.3	1,500,000	122,550,000	6,136
34,000	55,314.2	1,700,000	138,890,000	7,285
36,800	56,958.2	1,924,000	157,190,800	11,132
38,800	57,818.2	2,084,000	170,261,800	15,200
40,800	58,678.2	2,244,000	183,334,800	15,200
42,100	59,345.7	2,374,000	193,955,800	15,912
43,100	59,820.7	2,474,000	202,125,800	17,200
43,600	60,104.0	2,549,000	208,253,300	21,629
44,100	60,287.3	2,624,000	214,380,800	33,429
44,500	60,423.9	2,684,000	219,282,800	35,886
44,800	60,543.9	2,744,000	224,184,800	40,850
45,100	60,653.9	2,804,000	229,086,800	44,563
45,361	60,732.2	2,856,200	233,351,540	54,467

[a] Escudo values are in 1964 prices.

Table A-28
VALDIVIA-LLANQUIHUE: COSTS OF FLOW

Storage (*million m³*)	Net minimum flow (*million m³/yr*)	Cumulative capital costs of storage (*E°1,000*)ᵃ	Cumulative annual costs of storage (*E°1*)	Annual marginal costs per million m³/yr of minimum flow (*E°1*)
–	22,088.0	–	–	–
10,900	49,075.4	545,000	44,526,500	1,650
20,900	58,761.1	1,045,000	85,376,500	4,218
30,900	65,546.8	1,545,000	126,226,500	6,020
34,100	67,395.6	1,801,000	147,141,700	11,313
37,100	68,847.6	2,041,000	166,749,700	13,504
38,200	69,425.6	2,151,000	175,736,700	15,548
39,200	69,805.6	2,251,000	183,906,700	17,021
39,800	70,089.6	2,341,000	191,259,700	25,891
40,400	70,323.6	2,431,000	198,612,700	31,423
40,900	70,510.3	2,531,000	206,782,700	43,760
41,228	70,615.5	2,596,600	212,142,220	50,946

ᵃ Escudo values are in 1964 prices.

Table A-29

AGRICULTURAL PRODUCTION: CASE I, MARGINAL CONSTRAINT, AGRICULTURE RESIDUARY

Province	Hectares irrigated [a]	Output per hectare (qqm W.E.) [b]	Output (qqm W.E.)	Added dry (hectares)	Output per hectare (qqm W.E.)	Added dry output (qqm W.E.)	Total output [c] (qqm W.E.)
Tarapacá	1,786	50	89,300	–	–	–	89,300
Antofagasta	1,965	50	98,250	–	–	–	98,250
Atacama	5,640	50	282,000	21,648	.5	10,824	292,824
Coquimbo	41,100	30	1,233,000	71,923	2.0	143,846	1,396,846
Aconcagua-Valparaíso	68,750	22.5	1,546,875	59,891	4.6	275,499	1,822,374
Santiago	192,000	22.5	4,320,000	91,852	4.6	422,519	4,742,519
Subtotal	311,241		7,569,425	245,314		857,688	8,422,113 [d]
O'Higgins-Colchagua Curicó-Linares Ñuble Concepción-Cautín Valdivia-Llanquihue	NO CHANGE						

[a] Some rounding of larger amounts.
[b] Metric quintals of wheat equivalent.
[c] Original projected output from irrigated land: 14,706,133 qqm W.E.
        Reduction: 6,284,020 qqm W.E.

[d] Total output for each province are these amounts plus the amounts originally projected from dry land.

Table A-30

TREATMENT COSTS OF MILLION POPULATION EQUIVALENTS DISCHARGED INTO
RIVERS WITHOUT COLLECTION COSTS, 1985, MEDIUM B

(1964 Escudos)

Province	Municipal			Total		
	35 P.E.	70 P.E.	90 P.E.	35 P.E.	70 P.E.	90 P.E.
Tarapacá	52,650	95,580	128,790	54,890	99,640	134,250
Antofagasta	364,650	661,980	891,990	375,850	682,280	919,290
Atacama	310,050	562,860	758,430	310,050	562,860	758,430
Coquimbo	339,300	615,960	829,980	366,180	664,680	895,500
Aconcagua-Valparaíso	852,150	1,546,980	2,084,490	1,078,390	1,957,040	2,635,950
Santiago	9,387,300	17,041,560	22,962,780	11,457,060	20,793,000	28,007,820
O'Higgins-Colchagua	774,150	1,405,380	1,893,690	948,870	1,722,060	2,319,570
Curicó-Linares	912,600	1,656,720	2,232,360	1,129,880	2,050,540	2,761,980
Ñuble	460,200	835,440	1,125,720	487,080	884,160	1,191,240
Concepción-Cautín	1,302,600	2,364,720	3,186,360	3,654,600	6,627,720	8,919,360
Valdivia-Llanquihue	575,250	1,044,300	1,407,150	743,250	1,348,800	1,816,650
Chiloé	13,650	24,780	33,390	13,650	24,780	33,390
Total	15,344,550	27,856,260	37,535,130	20,619,750	37,417,560	50,393,430

Table A-31

TREATMENT COSTS OF MILLION POPULATION EQUIVALENTS DISCHARGED INTO RIVERS, AT 35%, 70%, AND 90% BOD REMOVAL, 1985, MEDIUM B

(1964 Escudos)

Province	Manufacturing			Municipal[a]			Total			
	35%	70%	90%	35%	70%	90%	35%	70%	90%	90% Collection
Tarapacá	2,240	4,060	5,460	108,810	151,740	184,950	111,050	155,800	190,410	56,160
Antofagasta	11,200	20,300	27,300	753,610	1,050,940	1,280,950	764,810	1,071,240	1,308,250	388,960
Atacama	—	—	—	640,770	893,580	1,089,150	640,770	893,580	1,089,150	330,720
Coquimbo	26,880	48,720	65,520	701,220	977,880	1,191,900	728,100	1,026,600	1,257,420	361,920
Aconcagua-Valparaíso	226,240	410,060	551,460	1,761,110	2,455,940	2,993,450	1,987,350	2,866,000	3,544,910	908,960
Santiago	2,069,760	3,751,440	5,045,040	19,400,420	27,054,680	32,975,900	21,470,180	30,806,120	38,020,940	10,013,120
O'Higgins-Colchagua	174,720	316,680	425,880	1,599,910	2,231,140	2,719,450	1,774,630	2,547,820	3,145,330	825,760
Curicó-Linares	217,280	393,820	529,620	1,886,040	2,630,160	3,205,800	2,103,320	3,023,980	3,735,420	973,440
Ñuble	26,880	48,720	65,520	951,080	1,326,320	1,616,600	977,960	1,375,040	1,682,120	490,880
Concepción-Cautín	2,352,000	4,263,000	5,733,000	2,692,040	3,754,160	4,575,800	5,044,040	8,017,160	10,308,800	1,389,440
Valdivia-Llanquihue	168,000	304,500	409,500	1,188,850	1,657,900	2,020,750	1,356,850	1,963,400	2,430,250	613,600
Chiloé	—	—	—	28,210	39,340	47,950	28,210	39,340	47,950	14,560
Total	5,275,200	9,561,300	12,858,300	31,712,070	44,223,780	53,902,650	36,987,270	53,785,080	66,760,950	16,367,520

[a] Includes collection costs.

Table A-32

ADDITIONAL COSTS OF STORAGE FOR QUALITY MAINTENANCE, 4 mg/l, 1985, MEDIUM B

Province	Minimum flow at constrained marginal cost (agricultural residuary)	Total upstream losses	Available for waste dilution and downstream use	Extra flow requirement for waste dilution (million m³/yr)			Annual cost of additional flow for waste dilution (Eº1,000)ª		
				35%	70%	90%	35%	70%	90%
Tarapacá	56	41	15	43	12	—	b	109	0
Antofagasta	88	60	28	370	155	45	b	b	138 c
Atacama	113	101	12	318	139	48	b	b	774
Coquimbo	601	585	16	370	161	55	b	3,909	376
Aconcagua-Valparaíso	1,093	978	115	1,000	398	89	b	b	1,446
Santiago	2,920	2,902	18	11,878	5,449	2,160	b	b	11,900 c
O'Higgins-Colchagua	4,557	4,522	35	950	418	145	2,987	1,314	456
Curicó-Linares	7,946	7,235	711	460	—		1,875	0	0
Ñuble	2,333	2,333	—	514	236	94	2,405	1,104	440
Concepción-Cautín	10,940	7,100	3,840	—	—	—	0	0	0
Valdivia-Llanquihue	22,088	8	22,080	—	—	—	Min. flow dilutes at zero treatment		
Chiloé	7	—	—	—	—	—	Min. flow dilutes at zero treatment		
Aysén	11	—	—	—	—	—	Min. flow dilutes at zero treatment		
Magallanes	28	—	—	—	—	—	Min. flow dilutes at zero treatment		

ª Computed by multiplying required flow by marginal cost.
b Required flow is beyond capacity of region.
c Beyond capacity; cost of going to full regulation.

Table A-33
ATACAMA: SMALLEST RESERVOIRS FIRST
(*1964 Escudos*)

Storage	Net minimum flow (*mil. m³/yr*)	Cumulative capital costs (*E°1,000*)	Cumulative annual costs (*E°1*)	Annual marginal costs per million m³/yr of net minimum flow (*E°1*)
–	88.0	–	–	–
10	116.2	2,000	163,400	5,794
30	131.6	6,000	490,200	21,221
50	139.0	10,000	817,000	44,162
90	152.8	18,000	1,470,600	47,362
180	173.6	31,500	2,573,550	53,026
370	201.2	50,500	4,125,850	56,243

Table A-34
SANTIAGO: SMALLEST RESERVOIRS FIRST
(*1964 Escudos*)

Storage	Net minimum flow (*mil. m³/yr*)	Cumulative capital costs (*E°1,000*)	Cumulative annual costs (*E°1*)	Annual marginal costs per million m³/yr of net minimum flow (*E°1*)
–	1,340.3	–	–	–
5	1,419.7	1,000	81,700	1,029
45	1,537.0	9,000	735,300	5,572
85	1,604.3	17,000	1,388,900	9,712
125	1,671.6	25,000	2,042,500	9,712
165	1,733.9	33,000	2,696,100	10,491
245	1,853.6	45,000	3,676,500	8,190
335	1,977.6	58,500	4,779,450	8,895
505	2,169.1	75,500	6,168,350	7,253
675	2,330.6	92,500	7,557,250	8,600
1,015	2,587.0	119,700	9,779,490	8,667
1,585	2,780.7	148,200	12,107,940	12,021
2,385	3,007.8	188,200	15,375,940	14,390
3,385	3,250.2	238,200	19,460,940	16,852

APPENDIX B

PRODUCTIVITY OF AGRICULTURE IN CHILE IN COMPARISON WITH SELECTED COUNTRIES[1]

The conclusion reached in Chapter XIII is that without an output per hectare amounting to about 2.2 times present output Chile cannot meet its output goals in 1985. Is such an increase in productivity credible? A satisfactory answer to this question ultimately rests upon experimental activity carried out on the land. In the absence of information so derived, one must rely on inference drawn from comparisons of past and present yields in Chile and in several other countries. These comparisons suffer several weaknesses: They do not distinguish between irrigated land and dry land and they do not account for qualitative differences in the product. Furthermore, the comparisons display serious gaps stemming from deficiencies in information. There is a complete absence of information, for example, on land dedicated to fruit.

Over-all "productivity of land" comparisons between two countries are a reflection of differences in physical output per unit of land and crop mix. Where the comparisons involve crop mix, the Chilean distribution of hectarage among crops was used (excluding, because information is lacking, natural pasture, artificial pasture, vegetables and fruits). Productivity in value terms reflects prices. Comparisons were made using Chilean prices and European prices as weights. The differences between the results of the two sets of prices turned out to be negligible.

An estimate of arable land[2] per capita for Chile and selected other countries is given in Table B-1. Chile's arable land endowment per capita

---

[1] Based on a study made in 1965 by Manuel Agosín.

[2] See *Production Yearbook, 1963* (Rome: Food and Agriculture Organization of the United Nations, 1964), p. 406, for definition of arable land. The amount shown in the *Yearbook* for Chile is 5,514,000 hectares. In this study the figure given by the Instituto de Investigaciones de Recursos Naturales, based upon the air photogrammetric survey, has been used. The FAO figure yields 0.70 hectares per capita for Chile.

Table B-1
ARABLE LAND PER CAPITA IN SELECTED COUNTRIES, 1962

Country	Arable land (1,000 ha.)	Population (1,000)	Arable land (ha. per cap.)
Chile	4,893 [a]	8,001	.61
Belgium	1,695	9,221	.18
Denmark	3,141	4,654	.67
Germany	14,179	56,947	.25
France	34,522	46,998	.73
Italy	20,652	50,170	.41
Greece	8,902	8,451	1.05
Spain	35,091	30,817	1.14
European average	243,000	432,500	.56
Argentina	143,151	21,418	6.68
Brazil	126,728	75,271	1.68
Japan	7,020	94,930	.07
U.S.A.	441,366	186,591	2.37

[a] Instituto de Investigaciones de Recursos Naturales, Proyecto Aerofotogramétrico, Chile/OEA/BID.
Source: FAO, Production Yearbook, 1963 (Rome, 1964).

is roughly comparable to Denmark's—a little less when based on the air photogrammetric survey; a little more if based on the figure reported to FAO. It is substantially below the amounts indicated for Argentina, Brazil, or the United States. Chile's future agricultural policies presumably will be directed toward an intensive technique of land use, comparable to that used in European countries, rather than an extensive technique such as is found in countries where per capita land resources are notably higher.

Outputs per hectare for Denmark, France, and Italy were selected for comparison with Chile's output in order to gain some appreciation of conceivable levels of output Chile might attain. It was assumed that differences in land quality and climate did not introduce significant errors since Denmark represents a relatively cool and humid region, comparable to the southern part of Chile's Central Valley, and France and Italy represent regions of Mediterranean climate comparable to the northern part of the Central Valley.

The results for eighteen crops for which productivity measures could be computed are given in Tables B-1 and B-2. In order to eliminate some of the vagaries associated with annual variations in weather, estimates were made of average output and best and worst yields experienced by each of the four countries. Chile's average output per hectare is below that of Denmark for every crop except onions; it is below that of France

Table B-2
AVERAGE YIELDS OF SELECTED CROPS, 1948/49-1952/53 to 1962/63
(*100 kg. per hectare*)

Crop	Chile	Denmark	France	Italy
Wheat	13.3	39.4	23.5	17.9
Rye	8.7	26.4	12.7	14.5
Barley	16.4	35.6	23.8	12.1
Oats	11.0	32.9	18.0	12.6
Corn	18.9	–	25.4	27.6
Rice	27.2	–	39.3	51.2
Sugar beets	308.0	337.0	315.0	310.0
Potatoes	91.0	189.0	152.0	89.0
Onions	269.0	203.0	157.0	133.0
Dry beans	9.3	–	9.5	4.0
Dry peas	6.5	–	18.4	6.9
Chick peas	4.9	–	–	5.5
Lentils	5.8	–	7.7	6.0
Grapes	49.0	–	57.0	51.0
Linseed	7.4	10.0	6.0	6.8
Rapeseed	10.9	17.0	14.2	12.0
Sunflower seed	13.3	–	14.5	14.0
Tobacco	22.4	–	19.1	13.8

Source: FAO, *Production Yearbooks.*

for every crop except onions, linseed, and tobacco; and is below that of Italy for every crop except barley, potatoes, onions, dry beans, linseed, and tobacco. The picture is not materially altered when we make the comparisons on the basis of best yields or worst yields.

One possible explanation of the differences in yields could be the differences in market prices among the countries, on the ground that unduly low prices in Chile (alleged by some to be the case) might have discouraged the expenditure of funds on fertilizer and other inputs. No data are available on the relative cost among countries of various output-increasing outlays, but a comparison can be made of 1962 product prices as reported for the four countries. In 1962 the estimated purchasing power parity was one escudo for one U.S. dollar. The figures in Table B-4 indicate that for every product except onions, tobacco, and wheat, Chilean prices were higher than the prices in Denmark, France, and Italy.

A set of prices, when weighted by hectarage in Chile devoted to the various crops and multiplied by the yields of the respective countries, indicates average value productivities per hectare for a uniform set of

Table B-3
BEST AND WORST YIELDS (1948/49-1952/53 to 1962/63)

(100 kg. per hectare)

	Best yields				Worst yields			
Crop	Chile	Den-mark	France	Italy	Chile	Den-mark	France	Italy
Wheat	15.6	42.7	30.7	20.9	11.9	34.4	18.3	15.2
Rye	10.3	29.4	14.6	16.6	6.3	23.7	11.4	12.7
Barley	18.6	39.8	28.1	13.6	11.7	31.1	16.1	10.3
Oats	12.9	37.1	20.2	14.5	8.7	27.8	14.4	10.5
Corn	21.4	–	34.0	32.9	13.8	–	13.8	18.4
Rice	31.1	–	48.3	56.8	20.0	–	26.7	47.4
Sugar beets	329.0	410.0	445.0	387.0	192.0	270.0	198.0	273.0
Potatoes	107.0	223.0	175.0	104.0	84.0	153.0	125.0	70.0
Onions	323.0	261.0	179.0	172.0	248.0	101.0	136.0	84.0
Dry beans	10.6	–	10.3	5.1	6.8	–	7.5	2.9
Dry peas	7.9	–	24.3	8.2	4.7	–	15.2	5.4
Chick peas	5.8	–	–	5.9	3.8	–	–	4.8
Lentils	7.3	–	10.4	6.8	4.4	–	5.5	4.7
Grapes	53.0	–	81.0	62.0	46.0	–	35.0	39.0
Linseed	8.2	10.7	9.4	8.4	6.1	10.0	3.3	5.6
Rapeseed	12.4	24.5	17.8	15.1	9.6	8.5	11.6	9.5
Sunflower seed	15.9	–	17.2	19.4	10.2	–	10.6	12.8
Tobacco	24.6	–	21.5	15.6	19.7	–	15.7	5.4

Source: FAO, *Production Yearbooks.*

prices and crop mixes. These comparisons are shown in Table B-5. The crops that are common to Chile and Denmark are not the same as those compared for Chile and France or for Chile and Italy, since data on prices and land use were not uniformly available in all countries for all crops. The net result of including crop mix and prices in the measure of land productivity indicates that output per hectare in Denmark is about 2.5 times that of Chile; in France, 1.5 times; and in Italy, 1.1 times. Use of European rather than Chilean prices made virtually no difference in the comparisons. Productivity based upon a relatively large sample, using Chilean prices as weights, revealed little difference from the results obtained from the smaller groups of products for which price data in each country existed.

Additional information leading to the inference that Chilean agricultural productivity is capable of substantial improvement is given in Table B-6.

Table B-4
SELECTED AGRICULTURAL PRICES
(*1962 prices per 100 kg.*)

Crop	Chile [a] (E⁰)	Denmark (US$)	France (US$)	Italy (US$)
Wheat	9.01	7.1 [b]	10.2	10.9
Rye	8.10	8.0	7.2	[c]
Barley	8.46	6.6	7.8	6.3
Oats	8.04	6.7	7.1	[c]
Corn	9.98	–	5.8 [b]	7.0
Rice	9.74	–	[c]	9.8
Sugar beets	1.69	1.5	1.5	1.5
Potatoes	8.75	6.1	5.2	6.3
Onions	4.86	[c]	9.8	6.4
Dry beans	22.61	–	17.9 [b]	17.4
Dry peas	12.91	[c]	[c]	[c]
Chick peas	17.78	–	–	[c]
Lentils	27.63	–	[c]	[c]
Grapes	16.55 [d]	–	[c]	[c]
Linseed	18.73	[c]	[c]	[c]
Rapeseed	14.40	12.3 [b]	12.3	12.3 [b]
Sunflower seed	14.01	–	[c]	[c]
Tobacco	26.09	–	[c]	61.0

[a] From "Sinopsis de la Agricultura Chilena, 1961-1963," Ministerio de Agricultura, Santiago, August 1964.
[b] European port price.
[c] Not available.
[d] "All fruits" price; price of grapes not available.
Source: FAO, *Production Yearbooks*, Rome.

Average annual growth rates in productivity per hectare were estimated for the period 1952-53 to 1962-63 for Denmark, France, Italy, United States, Japan, and Chile.[3] Whereas the five other countries found productivity per hectare rising annually by amounts ranging between 1.4 per cent and 4.0 per cent per annum, Chile's increase in productivity amounted to 0.2 per cent. If the same rates were to be continued into the future, between 1965 and 1985 productivity per hectare would rise by 70 per cent in France and 78 per cent in Italy, compared with 4 per cent in Chile.

A comparison was made of the productivity of farms in various size classes in the province of O'Higgins with the most productive in each size

[3] Computed as the ratio of index of output divided by the index of area of cultivated land. No adjustments were made for the possibility that a given amount of land was used for two or more crops or for inclusion of livestock products such as milk.

Table B-5
PRODUCTIVITY PER HECTARE IN
CHILE, DENMARK, FRANCE, AND ITALY
Based on average yields

(1962 prices; index, Chile = 100)

	Reduced samples				Large samples	
	In Chilean prices		In foreign prices		In Chilean prices	
Country	E^o	*Index*	*US$*	*Index*	E^o	*Index*
Chile	171.5	100	131.5	100	176.0	100
Denmark	433.1	253	333.3	253	433.8	246
Chile	179.2	100	163.9	100	220.9	100
France	281.5	157	255.6	156	322.4	146
Chile	191.7	100	187.3	100	220.0	100
Italy	215.9	113	217.2	116	243.0	110

Table B-6
RATES OF INCREASE IN PRODUCTIVITY PER HECTARE
IN SELECTED COUNTRIES, 1952/53-1962/63

Country	Average annual increase rate of 1952/53-1962/63 *(per cent)*	Estimated 1962/63 productivity index *(1952/53 = 100)*
Denmark	1.4	114
France	2.7	130
Italy	3.0	133
United States	3.4	140
Japan	4.0	148
Chile	0.2	102

class and the most productive regardless of size class.[4] This study, conducted by Morales, revealed that the highest output per hectare in each size class, after adjusting for differences in soil productivity, ranged from 1.6 times to 2.2 times the average output per hectare, and that if all yields were equal to the highest yields being obtained in 1959, total output would

[4] Hector Morales, *Productividad presente y potencial en 96 predios de la Provincia de O'Higgins y en relación con el tamaño de las propiedades* (Santiago: Universidad de Chile, Escuela de Agronomía, 1964).

be 92 per cent higher than actually achieved. If yields rose to the average productivity of all farms whose outputs per hectare exceeded the average of the total sample, productivity would rise by 35 per cent.

Studies of comparative yields of farms both inside and outside of Chile indicate, therefore, a reasonable presumption in favor of readily attainable increases in output per hectare. A doubling of average output per hectare would leave Chile somewhat below the present level attained by Denmark and somewhat above the level of France and Italy. If changes in crop mix are taken into account, through which more land is devoted to crops with a high market value per unit of crop, and account is taken of possible improvements in fruits, poultry, and livestock—none of which were included in the international measures of productivity—there is no reason to consider a potential doubling of output, within a very short period of time, beyond the physical or economic capability of the country. In light of the present Chilean government's awareness of the importance of agriculture, the success or failure of its program will be an important augury of what can be expected of economic development within the country.

APPENDIX C

CURRENT IRRIGATION CAPACITY OF RIVERS IN THE CENTRAL ZONE OF CHILE[1]

The purpose of the present study is to analyze current practices in respect of the use of water resources for irrigation in Chile. There are marked discrepancies among the various data that have been published on the country's total irrigated area; and even greater discrepancies emerge when the problem of the use of water for irrigation is studied. Patently, a disproportionate amount of the land under irrigation is taken up by natural pastures: according to some statisticians, as much as 400,000 hectares. From the national standpoint, therefore, it is clearly well worth while to look into the matter, since more efficient utilization of the land in question could boost agricultural production without the need for heavy investment in new irrigation works.

The existence of so large an underutilized area may be imputed to various causes, but the following are among those most commonly adduced: water shortages in given years, or during given months of the irrigation season; application of unduly high irrigation rates, with the result that the water does not reach the whole of the land covered by the canal system; indifference on the part of farmers to the possibility of increasing their output; deficiencies of the land tenure system; lack of the capital required to bring larger areas under cultivation, etc. The truth probably is that all these factors, and others not listed here, affect the problem under discussion in varying degrees, and only integrated research on each of these individual determinants and on their reciprocal interaction could furnish the data on which appropriate solutions might be based.

[1] Translation of a report prepared by the Research Unit of the Irrigation Department, Ministry of Public Works, Santiago, Chile, after reviewing the manuscript of *The Water Resources of Chile*. (Ricardo Edwards Gana, Ing., *Capacidad de Riego Actual de los Ríos de la Zona Central de Chile*, January 1967, mimeo.)

The present study aims at analyzing the first two causes mentioned—those relating to the availability and utilization of water resources—which, in the opinion of the Irrigation Department, are of decisive importance.

AREA COVERED BY THE SURVEY

The part of the country selected for analysis is the whole of the area lying between and including the provinces of Santiago and Ñuble, and comprises the basins of the rivers Maipo, Rapel, Mataquito, Maule, and Itata. This is a reasonably representative sample, for, according to the studies carried out by the Institute for Research on Natural Resources (Instituto de Investigaciones de Recursos Naturales), it includes irrigated land totalling 948,000 hectares, plus an additional 378,000 hectares under occasional irrigation. The following are the figures given by the same Institute for Chile as a whole: 1,212,000 and 700,000 hectares under permanent and occasional irrigation, respectively.

In establishing the taxable value of rural properties, the Inland Revenue Department worked on the assumption that some of the land classified as under occasional irrigation could in fact be defined as irrigated, the proportions varying from one part of the country to another. Application of the percentages fixed for the area covered by the present survey gives 1,088,000 hectares as the amount of land under irrigation. The sample therefore corresponds to about 80 per cent of the total irrigated area in Chile.

HYDROLOGICAL DATA

The following are the sources from which water is obtained during the irrigation season in the area studies: (a) discharges of rivers rising in the Cordillera of the Andes, at the points where they flow down into the Central Valley; and (b) discharges in the middle reaches of rivers and natural streams rising in the Central Valley itself or in the lower foothills of the Cordillera. The water resources included under (a) are usually known, as stream-gauging stations exist which keep sufficiently long-term and carefully checked records. Those mentioned under (b), on the other hand, are very difficult to ascertain, as the flow shows wide variations along the course of the stream, both because water is drawn off by the irrigation canals, and because the stream is fed on its way from two possible sources: (i) effluent seepage of ground water, attributable in its turn either to infiltration of the winter rains in the Central Valley, or to direct percolation from the river beds; and (ii) return flows of irrigation water, through surface run-off, infiltration or effluent seepage due to overwatering, and/or infiltration from irrigation canals and ditches.

The effects of effluent seepage of ground water resulting from winter rainfall are particularly marked in spring, when water-table levels are high. As the dry season advances, this source gradually decreases in importance until in February and March it virtually fails altogether, as is testified by the very low summer flow of streamlets running through dry-soil farmlands.

Return flows of irrigation water are the basic source of the summer flow in natural streams and rivers traversing the Central Valley.

The hydrological pattern of the area under study may be defined as follows. Rivers that flow down from the Cordillera of the Andes into the Central Valley are tapped by irrigation canals during spring and summer. A considerable proportion of the water distributed by these canals, which are generally old, unsatisfactorily laid out, and unlined, is lost en route, and returns to the river itself or feeds natural brooks and streams. Next, the water that does reach the farm that is to be irrigated is so liberally and often so wastefully used that the percentage efficiently utilized by the irrigation crop is only small. The rest runs off into the natural channels, and as a rule is used again by the same estate or by farms lying farther downstream. The topography of the Central Valley, with its average gradient of 1 per cent, enables the water to be used several times over, only a small residual flow finally running off into the sea.

Hence the inference is that the only water resource of any significance for irrigation purposes is constituted by the discharge of rivers rising in the Cordillera at the point where they flow into the Central Valley. In other words, the following hypothesis may be established: If no water were drawn off from the rivers rising in the Cordillera, their summer flow would remain constant all along the Central Valley, while natural brooks and streams with no catchment area in the Andes would dry up.

This hypothesis which, if not absolutely accurate, is a close approximation to actual fact where most of the river basins are concerned, greatly simplifies the problem of estimating the maximum areas that could be irrigated on the basis of existing resources, with varying degrees of security.

IRRIGATION RATES

Generally speaking, the irrigation rates applied in Chile are very high. For the purposes of the present survey, irrigation rates corresponding to strict crop requirements will be adopted, and a study will thus be made of the area that could be served if the water were carefully utilized, and if, at the same time, better distribution and watering practices were introduced.

The average annual rate adopted is 10,000 cubic meters per hectare at the farm boundary, which represents a coefficient of irrigation efficiency at the farm level of approximately 0.60, since evapotranspirational consumption may be estimated at an annual figure of about 6,000 cubic meters per hectare. The foregoing rate must be taken in conjunction with distribution losses, which, even if the existing canal networks were improved, could not be reduced to less than 13 per cent of the flow tapped at the intake point. Thus, the annual irrigation rate measured at the intake point works out at 11,500 cubic meters per hectare.

Of course, out of the 11,500 cubic meters per hectare tapped from the river, only 6,000 cubic meters are actually consumed through evapotranspiration, and the remaining 5,500 cubic meters are lost. But to reduce these losses still further would seem to be a very difficult task. Part of the lost water drains off into the natural streams, and part of it is wasted altogether, through direct evaporation from water surfaces, transpiration from weeds, or capillary suspension in parts of the soil not reached by plant roots. In aggregate terms, it may be estimated that 50 per cent of the water is lost for good, and the other half drains off into natural streams. Careful irrigation, at a lower rate, will reduce influent seepage towards the water table, the level of which will tend to sink, particularly during the latter months of the irrigation season. The result is that drainage into natural streams will take place at lower levels, making it more difficult to use the water in question for irrigation. Return flows in the part of the Central Valley that lies to the east of the railway running from north to south may possibly drain off into areas where they can be turned to account for irrigation; but in the western section of the Valley they will drain into the lower reaches of the river, where they cannot be harnessed for this purpose. They will serve, however, to provide a minimum seaward flow which will help to prevent salinization and pollution.

To sum up, it may be assumed that of the 11,500 cubic meters per hectare tapped from the river, consumption accounts for 6,000 cubic meters, while 2,750 cubic meters are wasted altogether, 1,375 can be recovered for irrigation purposes, and another 1,375 can be recovered but not used for irrigation. Consequently, for drawing up a water supply balance a net rate of 10,125 cubic meters per hectare will be adopted.

Monthly variations in water requirements are determined as shown in the following table, in line with studies carried out by the Irrigation Department.

It will be noted that at the beginning and end of the irrigation season the irrigation rate for the provinces of Santiago, O'Higgins, and Colchagua is higher, because in this part of the country the influence of rainfall is less important. The mid-season rates, on the other hand, are higher in the provinces of Curicó, Talca, Linares, Maule, and Ñuble, because midsummer temperatures are practically the same throughout the whole of the

MONTHLY VARIATIONS IN WATER REQUIREMENTS
(Cubic meters per hectare per annum)

Month	Provinces of Santiago, O'Higgins, and Colchagua [a]	Provinces of Curicó, Talca, Linares, Maule, and Ñuble [b]
September	625	380
October	1,080	1,125
November	1,480	1,700
December	1,735	1,875
January	1,735	1,875
February	1,570	1,585
March	1,190	1,030
April	710	555
Total	10,125	10,125

[a] This seasonal variation pattern was taken from studies of the Maipo River Basin carried out by the Irrigation Department on the basis of inquiries among consumers.
[b] This seasonal variation pattern is the one used for the Colbún Project study.

Central Valley and the summer daylight hours are longer in the southern part of the area under study.

RATE OF DEPENDABILITY OF IRRIGATION

The variations in precipitation that take place from one year to another cause river runoffs to fluctuate widely, so that the available supply of irrigation water cannot be constant in the absence of sufficient flow regulation facilities. Since the number of hectares that can be irrigated differs every year, the concept of dependability of irrigation must be introduced. The rate of dependability may be defined as the percentage of years in which the land receives the necessary amount of irrigation water. The rate that can be considered satisfactory varies in direct ratio to the degree in which intensive methods of farming are used. It need not be very high in the case of extensive farming, based, for example, on cereal crops and natural pastures. When water is not to be had, the land can be left unirrigated with no worse consequences than the necessity of slaughtering some of the livestock, which usually consists of poor-quality animals or fat stock that stays only a few months on the farm. As progress is made in the direction of intensive farming, with its dairy plants and selected breeds of cattle, the rate of dependability must improve, and should rise to almost 100 per cent where fruit is grown. The land tenure system is another factor determining the rate of dependability that is required. On large farms, parts of the estate can be left to lie fallow; whereas in the case of small family units, the whole of the land available must be farmed intensively to ensure their economic survival.

The government's policy of land reform and intensification of agricultural production implies that the dependability rates envisaged must be very high—as close as possible to 100 per cent. But the acute water shortages that occur in years of severe drought make such rates impracticable where river flows are not regulated. According to Irrigation Department studies, in river basins without flow regulation facilities the most economic dependability rate is one of about 85 per cent; for if it is lower, productivity will be seriously affected, while if it is higher, the amount of land irrigated will decrease, generally to an appreciable extent. For the purposes of the present study, the term "under permanent irrigation" will be considered applicable to land where the dependability rate is 85 per cent, i.e., where the requisite amount of water is available throughout the irrigation season in 85 out of every 100 years. Certain rivers tend to run so dry in the month of April that there is not enough water to cover irrigation requirements; in these cases, April shortfalls are not taken into account, for although irrigation may be needed, it is not absolutely essential for production. A dependability rate of 85 per cent means that in 15 out of every 100 years the land receives only part of the water it needs during one or more months of the irrigation season. Given the economic possibility of constructing regulation facilities by means of which the rate could be raised to nearly 100 per cent, this would, of course, be the ideal water supply target.

GENERAL METHODOLOGY

The procedure adopted consists in determining the maximum irrigable area in each river basin in a standard "85-per-cent year," by comparing the flows of the various rivers and the irrigation rates selected. An "85-per-cent year" is defined as one in which precipitation or discharge exceeds the amount reached in 85 out of every 100 years. The maximum irrigable area is calculated by estimating the number of hectares that can be irrigated in the different months of the year selected and then adopting the lowest of the figures thus obtained, excluding the month of April. In practice, the number of hectares that can be irrigated in each month varies widely, as the fluctuations in river flows bear no relation to those of irrigation water requirements. Generally speaking, there is plenty of water in the spring, except in the Maipo Basin, and from January onwards the flow gradually dwindles. In most cases the critical month is February or March.

Water resources have been evaluated on the basis of the flows at present available, without reference to the execution of new regulation projects. Only the reservoirs now in operation have been taken into account: i.e.,

Laguna del Planchón, in the Teno River Basin; Laguna del Maule, on the river of the same name; and the Bullileo Reservoir in the basin of the River Longaví. Once the Yeso and Digua reservoirs, in the Maipo and Perquilauquén river basins, respectively, have been brought into service, the number of hectares irrigable will increase.

MAIPO RIVER BASIN

The main streams in this catchment area are the Rivers Mapocho and Maipo, which are interconnected by the San Carlos Canal. The flow statistics used for the Maipo River were those recorded at El Manzano, and for the Mapocho, the sum of the flows at Los Almendros and through the Arrayán gorge at La Montosa. These three figures can be added together, since the rivers are interconnected. It was decided that 1962 should be taken as the standard 85-per-cent year, and estimates were based on the statistical data for September 1962–April 1963.

The method of calculating the maximum irrigable area is shown in the table below.

MAIPO AND MAPOCHO RIVERS

Month	River runoff[a] (millions of cubic meters)	Net water requirements per hectare (cubic meters)	Number of hectares irrigable
September	201.86	625	322,976
October	279.97	1,080	259,231
November	513.22	1,480	346,770
December	562.95	1,735	324,467
January	344.66	1,735	198,651
February	269.11	1,570	*171,408*[b]
March	231.84	1,190	194,824
April	–	710	–
Total		10,125	

[a] No figure is available for April, but, as explained above, this month was not taken into account in the calculation of the irrigable area.

[b] Here and in later river basin tables, the figure italicized is the lowest for any month in the irrigation season (excluding April).

Thus, the maximum irrigable area works out at 171,408 hectares. It should be noted that the Maipo River is not only used for irrigation but also supplies the city of Santiago with piped water at a flow rate of about 6 cubic meters per second, with the consequent reduction of its irrigation potential. But according to Irrigation Department studies, the discharge of sewage water is approximately 50 per cent of the flow drawn off for piped water. Moreover, Santiago's piped water supply is supplemented from other sources not taken into account in the statistics for the rivers Maipo and Mapocho, also at a flow rate of something like 6 cubic meters per second. Consequently, from the supply noted in the foregoing table the flow of 6 cubic meters per second tapped from the Maipo for piped water must be subtracted, and the 50 per cent of 12 cubic meters per second represented by sewage water usable for irrigation must then be added to the remainder. As these two operations cancel each other out, the statistical data were adopted without adjustment.

The estimated area of 171,408 hectares must be augmented by a small amount of land for which irrigation water can be obtained from the following Andean streams: Colina, Lampa, Clarillo, Paine, and Puangue.

Accordingly, in the case of the Maipo River Basin the figure adopted for the maximum area irrigable at a dependability rate of 85 per cent will be 175,000 hectares. It will, of course, be higher when the Yeso Reservoir is brought into service.

The amount of land under irrigation in the province of Santiago, which coincides with the area irrigated by the water resources of the Maipo Basin, is 237,327.8 hectares, according to the Organization of American States–International Development Bank–Chile Project.

RAPEL RIVER BASIN

The water resources of the Rapel River Basin are constituted by the rivers Cachapoal, Claro de Rengo, and Tinguiririca. The statistics used were those recorded for the Cachapoal at Coya, the Claro at Las Nieves, and the Tinguiririca at Bajos los Briones plus the Claro at El Valle. The average for 1955–62 was taken to represent the standard 85-per-cent year.

The estimates of maximum irrigable areas are shown in the group of tables presented as follows:

CACHAPOAL RIVER

Month	River runoff (*millions of cubic meters*)	Water requirements per hectare (*cubic meters*)	Number of hectares irrigable
September	79.83	625	127,728
October	133.65	1,080	123,750
November	253.76	1,480	171,459
December	264.89	1,735	152,674
January	200.34	1,735	115,470
February	167.62	1,570	106,764
March	118.92	1,190	*99,933*
April	80.09	710	112,803
		Total 10,125	

CLARO DE RENGO RIVER

Month	River runoff (millions of cubic meters)	Water requirements per hectare (cubic meters)	Number of hectares irrigable
September	10.32	625	16,512
October	21.37	1,080	19,787
November	26.70	1,480	18,040
December	23.03	1,735	13,274
January	12.91	1,735	7,441
February	8.81	1,570	5,611
March	6.40	1,190	*5,378*
April	4.04	710	5,690
		Total 10,125	

TINGUIRIRICA RIVER

Month	River runoff (millions of cubic meters)	Water requirements per hectare (cubic meters)	Number of hectares irrigable
September	93.83	625	129,421
October	152.67	1,080	141,361
November	223.17	1,480	150,791
December	200.68	1,735	115,320
January	145.44	1,735	83,827
February	115.40	1,570	73,503
March	73.12	1,190	*61,445*
April	44.06	710	62,056
		Total 10,125	

Lowest monthly figures:

	Hectares
Cachapoal River	99,933
Claro de Rengo River	5,378
Tinguiririca River	61,445
Total for Rapel River Basin	166,756

If March shortages are excluded, the February figures give the maximum irrigable areas, as follows:

	Hectares
Cachapoal River	106,764
Claro de Rengo River	5,611
Tinguiririca River	73,503
Total	185,878

To the foregoing figures must be added the area that other smaller streams—such as the Codegua, Cadena, Tipaume, Antivero, and Chimbarongo—can be used to irrigate. In round figures, the maximum irrigable area may be estimated at 170,000 hectares if March is taken as the critical month, and at 190,000 hectares if February is selected.

According to the OAS/IDB/Chile project, the area under irrigation in the provinces of O'Higgins and Colchagua, which coincides almost exactly with the area irrigated by the water resources of the Rapel River Basin, is 265,781.1 hectares.

MATAQUITO RIVER BASIN

The rivers Teno and Lontué account for the water resources of this catchment area. Data for the Teno below Juntas are available, together with the sum of the statistics for the rivers Palos and Colorado, which join to form the River Lontué. For the Teno, 1956 was taken as the standard 85-per-cent year, and for the Lontué, 1957.

The flow of the Teno is partly regulated by the Laguna del Planchón reservoir, but the statistics are recorded at a point on the river where this regulatory effect is already taken into account.

The irrigation capacity of these rivers is calculated as shown below.

TENO RIVER

Month	River runoff (*millions of cubic meters*)	Water requirements per hectare (*cubic meters*)	Number of hectares irrigable
September	108.86	380	286,474
October	166.06	1,125	147,609
November	230.69	1,700	135,700
December	206.24	1,875	109,995
January	117.85	1,875	62,853
February	79.83	1,585	*50,366*
March	56.25	1,030	54,612
April	23.33	555	42,036
		Total 10,125	

LONTUÉ RIVER

Month	River runoff (*millions of cubic meters*)	Water requirements per hectare (*cubic meters*)	Number of hectares irrigable
September	110.68	380	291,263
October	176.77	1,125	157,129
November	314.93	1,700	185,253
December	282.57	1,875	150,704
January	148.92	1,875	79,424
February	84.67	1,585	*53,420*
March	75.53	1,030	73,330
April	61.69	555	111,153
		Total 10,125	

Lowest monthly figures:

	Hectares
Teno River	50,366
Lontué River	53,420
Total for Mataquito River Basin	103,786

The only other natural stream flowing down from the Cordillera into this drainage area is the Huaiquillo, whose irrigation capacity is very small. A rounded aggregate figure of 105,000 hectares will be adopted.

According to the OAS/IDB/Chile Project, the area under irrigation in the Mataquito River Basin, which comprises the province of Curicó and the department of Molina in the province of Talca, is 105,050.9 hectares.

THE MAULE RIVER BASIN

The water resources of this catchment area are constituted by the following rivers: Claro, Lircay, Maule, Ancoa, Achibueno, Longaví, and Perquilauquén. Statistics are recorded for the Claro at Camarico, for the Lircay at Puente Las Rastras, for the Maule at Armerillo, for the Ancoa at El Morro, for the Achibueno at Los Peñascos, for the Longaví at la Quiriquina and for the Perquilauquén at San Manuel. The standard 85-per-cent year adopted was 1957, except in respect of the River Perquilauquén, for which the year 1946 was selected. In the special case of the River Maule, whose flow is partly regulated by the Laguna del Maule Reservoir, the statistical data were not directly adopted, but, instead, the river runoff available at a dependability rate of 85 per cent was used for the calculation, as being a much more representative figure. The Ancoa statistics include the tributary flow of the Melado Canal, which is fed by the river of the same name, an affluent of the Maule rising in the Cordillera. As the figure for the regulated runoff of the Maule does not take into account the Melado Canal flow, it is not incorrect to adopt the Ancoa statistics without adjustment. The flow of the River Longaví is partly regulated by the Bullileo Reservoir, but the data are recorded at a point where this regulatory effect is already taken into consideration.

The areas for which irrigation water can be obtained from each of these sources are estimated as shown in the group of tables below.

CLARO RIVER

Month	River runoff (millions of cubic meters)	Water requirements per hectare (cubic meters)	Number of hectares irrigable
September [a]	–	380	–
October	39.37	1,125	34,996
November	42.77	1,700	25,159
December	26.25	1,875	14,000
January	10.98	1,875	5,856
February	7.26	1,585	4,610
March [a]	–	1,030	–
April [a]	–	555	–
		Total	10,125

[a] No data are available for September, March, and April. If these months were taken into account, the maximum irrigable area might be smaller.

LIRCAY RIVER

Month	River runoff (millions of cubic meters)	Water requirements per hectare (cubic meters)	Number of hectares irrigable
September	15.55	380	40,921
October	33.48	1,125	29,760
November	6.25	1,700	3,674
December	1.02	1,875	544
January [a]	–	1,875	–
February	1.45	1,585	915
March	3.36	1,030	3,456
April	2.23	555	4,018
		Total	10,125

[a] No figure is available for January. If this month were taken into account, the irrigable area might be smaller.

MAULE RIVER

At a dependability rate of 85 per cent, the Maule River, regulated by the Laguna del Maule Reservoir, has a usable runoff of 2,306.33 million cubic meters *per annum*. Given an irrigation rate of 10,125 cubic meters per hectare, the number of hectares irrigable works out at 233,516.

ANCOA RIVER (plus Melado Canal)

Month	River runoff (*millions of cubic meters*)	Water requirements per hectare (*cubic meters*)	Number of hectares irrigable
September	62.47	380	164,395
October	40.44	1,125	35,947
November	63.24	1,700	37,200
December	75.80	1,875	40,427
January	45.53	1,875	*24,283*
February	38.95	1,585	24,574
March	36.96	1,030	35,883
April	29.55	555	53,243
		Total 10,125	

ACHIBUENO RIVER

Month	River runoff (*millions of cubic meters*)	Water requirements per hectare (*cubic meters*)	Number of hectares irrigable
September	111.97	380	294,658
October	107.14	1,125	95,236
November	122.08	1,700	71,812
December	95.89	1,875	51,141
January	40.98	1,875	21,856
February	9.43	1,585	*5,950*
March	10.18	1,030	9,883
April	62.21	555	112,090
		Total 10,125	

LONGAVÍ RIVER

Month	River runoff (millions of cubic meters)	Water requirements per hectare (cubic meters)	Number of hectares irrigable
September	128.04	380	336,947
October	115.71	1,125	102,853
November	120.79	1,700	71,053
December	102.31	1,875	54,565
January	58.39	1,875	31,141
February	49.11	1,585	30,984
March	29.46	1,030	*28,602*
April [a]	–	555	–
		Total 10,125	

[a] No figure is available for April, but this does not affect the size of the irrigable area.

PERQUILAUQUÉN RIVER

Month	River runoff (millions of cubic meters)	Water requirements per hectare (cubic meters)	Number of hectares irrigable
September	137.38	380	361,526
October	82.23	1,125	73,093
November	80.35	1,700	47,265
December	41.78	1,875	22,283
January	12.05	1,875	6,427
February	7.02	1,585	*4,429*
March	6.96	1,030	6,757
April	7.78	555	14,018
		Total 10,125	

Lowest monthly figures:

	Hectares
Claro River	4,610
Lircay River	544
Maule River	233,516
Ancoa River	24,283
Achibueno River	5,950
Longaví River	28,602
Perquilauquén River	4,429
Total for Maule River Basin	301,934

If the shortages occurring in the month of March were disregarded, the areas that could be irrigated by each river would be as follows:

	Hectares
Claro River	4,610
Lircay River	544
Maule River	233,516
Ancoa River	24,283
Achibueno River	5,950
Longaví River	30,984
Perquilauquén River	4,429
Total	304,316

To the foregoing figure must be added the area irrigated by a branch of the Melado Canal not taken into account in the River Ancoa statistics; a small area irrigable by the Andean water resources of the River Putagán; and the areas irrigated by the Maule River upstream from the gauging station, and by the Tutuvén Reservoir. The aggregate figures that may be adopted are 310,000 hectares if March is taken as the critical month, and 313,000 hectares if the March shortages are not taken into consideration.

According to the OAS/IDB/Chile Project, in this same sector, comprising the province of Talca (with the exclusion of the department of Molina) and the provinces of Linares and Maule, the total area under irrigation amounts to 303,831.2 hectares.

It must be noted that the Maule Norte Canal network has just been inaugurated, and will bring another 40,000 hectares under irrigation, utilizing the resources of the River Maule regulated by the Laguna del Maule Reservoir.

THE ITATA RIVER BASIN

The rivers Ñuble, Cato, Chillán and Diguillín supply this drainage area with water resources. The data used were those recorded for the Ñuble at San Fabián, for the Cato at Puento Cato and for the Chillán at Esperanza, while in the case of the River Diguillín the sum of the statistics for the Diguillín at San Lorenzo and the Renegado at Invernada was taken.

The gauging stations on the River Diguillín lie far upstream, and between them and the first canal intake points there is a sizable drainage area in the Cordillera. Studies carried out by the Irrigation Department suggest that the flow contributed by this middle basin may be estimated at 3 cubic meters per second throughout the irrigation season.

For the Ñuble River, the standard 85-per-cent year adopted was 1956, while for the other rivers in this catchment area the 1960–61 average was taken.

The irrigation capacity of each of these rivers is calculated as shown in the tables presented below:

ÑUBLE RIVER

Month	River runoff (*millions of cubic meters*)	Water requirements per hectare (*cubic meters*)	Number of hectares irrigable
September	228.10	380	600,263
October	401.76	1,125	357,120
November	404.35	1,700	237,853
December	214.27	1,875	114,277
January	96.42	1,875	51,424
February	60.48	1,585	*38,158*
March	56.25	1,030	54,612
April	46.66	555	84,072
		Total 10,125	

CATO RIVER

Month	River runoff (*millions of cubic meters*)	Water requirements per hectare (*cubic meters*)	Number of hectares irrigable
September	207.36	380	545,684
October	139.28	1,125	123,804
November	111.46	1,700	65,565
December	29.46	1,875	15,712
January	19.28	1,875	10,283
February	7.74	1,585	*4,883*
March	9.64	1,030	9,359
April	248.83	555	448,342
		Total 10,125	

CHILLÁN RIVER

Month	River runoff (*millions of cubic meters*)	Water requirements per hectare (*cubic meters*)	Number of hectares irrigable
September	72.96	380	192,000
October	68.30	1,125	60,711
November	31.36	1,700	18,447
December	21.16	1,875	11,285
January	19.82	1,875	10,571
February	15.48	1,585	*9,766*
March	14.73	1,030	14,301
April	10.37	555	18,685
		Total 10,125	

DIGUILLÍN RIVER (plus 3 cubic meters per second)

Month	River runoff (*millions of cubic meters*)	Water requirements per hectare (*cubic meters*)	Number of hectares irrigable
September	107.05	380	281,711
October	103.92	1,125	92,373
November	59.88	1,700	35,224
December	32.95	1,875	17,572
January	23.37	1,875	12,464
February	16.69	1,585	*10,530*
March	19.02	1,030	18,466
April	16.07	555	28,955
		Total 10,125	

Lowest monthly figures:

	Hectares
Ñuble River	38,158
Cato River	4,883
Chillán River	9,766
Diguillín River	10,530
Total for Itata River Basin	63,337

A round figure of 65,000 hectares may be adopted, to make allowance for a few smaller rivulets and streams.

According to the OAS/IDB/Chile Project, the area under irrigation in the province of Ñuble, which approximately corresponds to the area served by the Itata River Basin, amounts to 176,237.1 hectares.

ANALYSIS OF FINDINGS

The foregoing analysis can be summarized in tabulated form, as shown below.

	Area Irrigable at a Dependability Rate of 85 Per Cent		
River basin	Excluding April shortages	Excluding March and April shortages	Area under irrigation according to OAS/IDB/Chile Project
Maipo	175,000	175,000	237,327.8
Rapel	170,000	190,000	265,781.1
Mataquito	105,000	105,000	105,050.9
Maule	310,000	313,000	303,831.2
Itata	65,000	65,000	176,237.1
Total	825,000	848,000	1,088,228.1

An over-all study of the finding reveals that the area considered to be under irrigation is 236,228.1 hectares in excess of the area that can be served at a dependability rate of 85 per cent, given a rate of irrigation that implies careful and intelligent use of water resources. Since the discrepancy between the two figures means that the rate of dependability for the area regarded as under irrigation is a good deal lower than 85 per cent, recourse must be had to extensive farming. In practice, water consumers served at a low rate of dependability divide the area under irrigation into two sections. Part of the farm is irrigated at the standard 85-per-cent rate of dependability, and is used for growing crops; while the remainder is farmed by extensive methods, is irrigated when there is water to be had, and is taken up mainly by natural pastures.

According to an unpublished CORFO study quoted by Nathaniel Wollman in his report on the water resources of Chile [herein], the country's total irrigated area amounts to 1,389,584 hectares, of which 402,637 hectares—i.e., 29 per cent—are used for natural pastures. If the same percentage is applied to the 1,088,228.1 hectares comprised in the area under study here, the amount of land under natural pastures would seem to be 315,586.1 hectares, leaving 772,642 hectares sown to crops or artificial pastures.

It is interesting to note the similarity between this latter figure and the 825,000 hectares estimated to be irrigable at a dependability rate of 85 per cent. The inference appears to be that there is a tendency to grow permanent crops on that part of the irrigated area which is served at a satisfactory rate of dependability, and to turn the rest over to natural pastures.

The difference between the 825,000 hectares that can be irrigated at an 85-per-cent dependability rate in the area under study and the 772,642 hectares actually under cultivation works out at 52,358 hectares. This amount of land, which represents 6.8 per cent of the present cultivated area, could be brought under cultivation without additional regulation of the natural streams. Clearly, however, the methodology applied in this preliminary study is subject to a margin of error in the evaluation of the area under crops, of irrigation rates, of the utilizable proportion of return flows, etc., which may make a 5-per-cent difference to the final figures. What can be asserted without risk of serious error is that on the basis of the existing water resources the cultivated area under irrigation could be increased by 50,000–100,000 hectares in the various river basins covered by the present survey. Only by means of a more detailed study could the figure be established precisely.

In the table presented above, an aggregate figure is given for the area that could be considered irrigable if water shortages occurring in March were not taken into account. The object of this calculation is to analyze the potential importance of looking for crops with a shorter growth cycle, that would not require irrigation after the month of February. It will be seen that the irrigable area could thus be increased by 23,000 hectares.

There was no point in basing a similar analysis on the exclusion of February shortages, since apart from cereals and a few vegetables, all the crops grown in the Central Zone of Chile need water during February.

A breakdown of the water shortage problem by the various catchment areas studied reveals that it is acute in the basins of the Rivers Maipo, Rapel, and Itata, whereas in the basin of the River Mataquito, there is a satisfactory balance between the water supply and the area under irrigation, and in the Maule Basin a small surplus would seem to exist, thanks to the resources obtainable from the River Maule itself since the construction of the Laguna del Maule Reservoir. This surplus represents exactly the amount that will be absorbed by the newly inaugurated Maule Norte Canal, which is to bring an additional 40,000 hectares under irrigation.

The present study also shows that up to a point the application of unduly high irrigation rates is not seriously detrimental to the over-all water economy, since the peculiar topographical formation of the Central Valley enables the water to be used several times over. This means that aggregate efficiency at the level of the drainage area is reasonably high.

The possibility of expanding the area under irrigated crops by a maximum of 100,000 hectares, of which 40,000 will be incorporated by virtue of the Maule Norte Canal Project, calls for study from the economic standpoint. A campaign to promote more efficient irrigation along the whole of the Central Valley implies the establishment of extension services, improvement of canal networks, investment at the farm level in grading the terrain and installing control facilities to reduce distribution losses, and, in general, a radical reform of existing irrigation systems.

Official measures to promote the more efficient use of water are justifiable on the score of the better yields that could be obtained if each crop were given the amount of water it really needs; if even distribution of the irrigation water were ensured, so as to safeguard low-lying parts of the cropland against waterlogging; and, generally speaking, if care were taken to prevent washing-out of the soil by overwatering. But it is doubtful whether sizable areas of currently underutilized land could be brought under irrigation through state action.

CONCLUSIONS

The findings of the present study can be summed up as follows:

1. Existing water resources in the provinces lying between and including Santiago and Ñuble are sufficient for permanent irrigation of a maximum area of 825,000 hectares, given a rational and beneficial rate of irrigation and integrated use of return flows.

2. The area at present under irrigation in the same part of the country is considered to be 1,088,000 hectares, while the area under cultivation may be estimated at 773,000 hectares.

3. The fact that large tracts of irrigated land are being used for natural pastures is attributable to the unreliability of irrigation facilities, which prevents economic utilization of the land for better purposes.

4. Without increasing basic water resources, the area under irrigated crops could be expanded by 50,000–100,000 hectares. The Maule Norte Canal network is at present bringing an additional 40,000 hectares under irrigation on the basis of the currently available resources.

5. The only means of substantially increasing the area under irrigated crops is the construction of facilities to regulate the flow of natural streams.

SELECTED BIBLIOGRAPHY

Basso S., Eduardo. *Inventario de Recursos Hidrológicos Superficiales de Chile*. Santiago: Ministerio de Obras Públicas, Dirección de Planeamiento, 1963.

Bell, Ralph M. *Irrigation and Methods of Irrigation*. Report No. 879 to the Government of Chile. Rome: Food and Agriculture Organization of the United Nations, 1958.

Chavez S., Jorge. *Informe Preliminar*. Santiago: Corporación de Fomento de la Producción, October 7, 1963. (Mimeographed.)

Chile, Ministerio de Agricultura. *La Agricultura Chilena en el Quinquenio 1951-1955*. Santiago, 1967.

———. *La Agricultura Chilena en el Quinquenio 1956-1960*. Santiago, 1963.

Chile, Ministerio de Obras Públicas, Dirección de Planeamiento. *Antecedentes para el Planeamiento Provincial de Obras Públicas*, Vol. I, *Generales e Inversiones*. Santiago, October 1963.

Chile, Ministerio de Obras Públicas, Dirección de Reigo. *Capacidad de Riego Actual de los Ríos de la Zona Central de Chile*. Santiago, January 1967. (Mimeographed.) [Translation included as Appendix C in this volume.]

Chile, Ministerio de Hacienda, Dirección de Presupuesto, Oficina de Estudios Tributarios. *El Sistema Tributario Chileno*. Santiago, 1960.

Comité Interamericano de Desarrollo Agrícola (CIDA). *Estudio Sobre la Tenencia de la Tierra en Chile*. Santiago, 1964. (Mimeographed.)

Corporación de Fomento de la Producción. Programa Nacional de Desarrollo Económico, 1961-1970. Santiago, 1960.

Food and Agriculture Organization of the United Nations. *Yearbook of Food and Agricultural Statistics: Production*, Vol. VI, Part I. Rome, 1952.

―――― and Comisión Económica para América Latina. "El Papel y la Celulosa en América Latina," E/CN.12/570/Rev. 2. New York: United Nations, May 1965. (Mimeographed.)

Fox, Irving K., and Orris C. Herfindahl. "Attainment of Efficiency in Satisfying Demands for Water Resources," *Proceedings*, American Economic Association, May 1964.

Hagen, Everett H. *On the Theory of Social Change*. Homewood, Ill.: Dorsey, 1962.

Hansen, Norman, with H. Baeza and J. Parker. *Proyecciónes de la Demanda de Agua en Chile y su Repartición Geográfica para los Próximos 20 Años*. Santiago: Ministerio de Obras Públicas, Dirección de Planeamiento, 1962.

Ibáñez, Fernán, Ricardo Harboe, and Juan Antonio Poblete. *Estudio de la Disponibilidad de Recursos Hidráulicos en Chile*. Publication No. 655/B. Santiago: Universidad de Chile, Centro de Planeamiento, 1965.

Joint Mission of the International Bank for Reconstruction and Development and the Food and Agriculture Organization of the United Nations. *The Agricultural Economy of Chile*. Washington, 1952. (Mimeographed.)

National Association of Manufacturers. *Water in Industry*. New York, December 1950.

Pourtauborde, Jean. *El Riego en Chile*. Report No. 1622. Rome: Food and Agriculture Organization of the United Nations, 1962.

Reid, George. *Water Requirements for Pollution Abatement*. Statement before Select Committee on National Water Resources, pursuant to S. Res. 48, 86 Cong., 1 sess., Committee Print No. 29. Washington: U.S. Government Printing Office, 1960.

Sadie, Johannes L. *Población y Mano de Obra de Chile, 1930-1975*. Santiago: Centro Latinoamericano de Demografía, 1964.

Stamp, L. Dudley. *Our Undeveloped World*. London: Faber & Faber, 1953.

U.N. Comisión Económica para América Latina. *Boletin Estadistico de América*. Vol. I, No. 1 (1964); Vol. II, Nos. 1 and 2 (1965); Vol. III, No. 1 (1966). Mexico City and New York.

―――――. *Estudios Sobre la Electricidad en América Latina*. Vols. I, II. Mexico City, 1962, 1964.

―――――. *Los Recursos Hidráulicos de América Latina: I, Chile*. Mexico City, 1960. [Referred to as CEPAL in the text.]

U.N. Economic Commission for Latin America. *A Measurement of Price Levels and the Purchasing Power of Currencies in Latin America, 1960-1962*. E/CN. 12/653. New York, 1963. (Mimeographed.)

U.N. Department of Economic and Social Affairs. *Water for Industrial Use.* New York, 1958.

U.S. Commission on Organization of the Executive Branch of the Government. *Task Force Report on Water Resources and Power.* Vol. II. Washington: Government Printing Office, June 1955.

U.S. Department of Agriculture. *Land and Water Potentials and Future Requirements for Water.* Report to U.S. Senate Select Committee on National Water Resources, Committee Print No. 12. Washington: Government Printing Office, 1960.

U.S. Geological Survey. *Reservoirs in the United States,* Water-Supply Paper 1360-A. Washington: Government Printing Office, 1956.

Universidad de Chile, Instituto de Economía. *La Economía de Chile en el Período 1950-1963.* Santiago, 1963.

Villarroel B., René, and Heinrich Horn F. *Rentabilidad de las Obras de Regadío en Explotación Construidas por el Estado.* Santiago: Ministerio de Obras Públicas, Dirección de Planeamiento, June 1963.

INDEX

Aconcagua Province, 6, 152, 166
Aconcagua River, 6, 98, 118
Aconcagua-Valparaíso region, 147, 148, 155, 156, 161, 173, 178, 179, 180, 186, 187, 190, 192n
Agency for International Development (AID), 60n
Agosín, Manuel 66n, 242n
Agricultural production: need for an interregional model, 26
—demand for products: projections of, 19, 73–76; factor of dietary deficiencies in, 74, 75, 76; hectarage requirements for, 76–77
—imports of products: excess over exports, 30, 32; imports and domestic output, 74n; need for eliminating import of goods producible in Chile, 74, 75n
—output: low growth rate of, 29–30; comparison of with world average, 40–42; hectares devoted to selected crops and output value, 50, 51; estimates of for irrigated and dry land, 75–76, 78, 81, 85–91; estimates of total by *1985*, 92; government plans for increases in, 205–6
—productivity comparisons with Denmark, Italy, and France: output per hectare, 243–48; yields of selected crops (*1948–63*), 244, 245; prices of selected crops (*1962*), 246; rates of increase, 246 *See also* Agriculture; Farms; Irrigation; Land use
Agriculture: diversity of, 6; need for improved methods of cultivation, 76
—arable land: distribution by type of crops, 35–36; projection for Chile by

1985, 201; per capita comparison with selected countries (*1962*), 242–43
—water requirements: measures of for specific provinces, 78–84; effects of changes in land use, 81–83; estimate for livestock watering, 84–85, 140; seasonal distribution of irrigation requirements, 85
—water use for irrigated agriculture: assumptions for projection model, 73; availability of water, 76, 89; extravagance of use, 78 *See also* Agricultural production; Farms; Irrigation; Land use
AID. *See* Agency for International Development
Alliance for Progress, 127
Anaconda Company, 93, 94
Andes, 5, 86, 102, 152
Antofagasta, city, 125
Antofagasta Province, 4, 5, 6, 32, 63, 84, 93, 94, 96, 142, 145, 147, 148, 166, 170n, 171, 172, 173, 177, 182, 187, 190, 197, 203
Aqueducts: for water supply to urban and mining communities, 5
Aquifers: as an alternative to surface storage, 27, 140
Arauco Province, 7
Argentina, 243
Arica, 5–6
Atacama-Linares region, 84
Atacama Province, 4, 5, 6, 93, 94, 96, 142, 147, 170n, 171, 173, 187, 195, 198
Aysén Province, 4, 7, 8
Azapa River, 5

272

Baeza, H., 76n
Baker River, 98
Basso S., Eduardo, 34, 47, 49, 50, 62, 85
Bell, Ralph M,, 45, 46, 47, 49, 53n
Bennet L., Alberto, 102n
Bío-Bío Province, 7
Bío-Bío River, 7, 130
Biochemical-oxygen-demanding (BOD) substances: removal of from wastes, 9, 13, 22, 131, 137, 142, 182, 187
Blaney-Criddle formula: in measures of water use, 46, 47, 62
BOD. *See* Biochemical-oxygen-demanding substances
Bower, Blair T., 3n, 26n
Brazil, 243

California: use of coefficients of in projections for Chile, 46, 82, 145, 203. *See also* Chile-California Program
Canals for irrigation: haphazard development of, 43–44; water losses in, 46, 47, 63; in government projects, 54, 55, 56, 61; cost of single-project building of, 63
CAP. *See* Compañía de Acero del Pacífico
Castagnino, Walter A., 182n
Castro, Patricio, 112n
Cautín Province, 7, 22, 32, 35, 56, 60, 77, 80n, 84, 162, 181
Censo Nacional de Manufacturas, 115
Centro de Investigaciones Económicas, Universidad Católica, 73n, 77n, 78, 80, 84, 94n, 95, 96, 97, 111, 127, 128
Centro de Planeamiento, 60, 157, 164, 172n, 191
CEPAL. *See* Comisión Económica para América Latina
Chavez S., Jorge, 35, 53n, 54, 55, 56, 57, 58, 65
Chemicals industry, 109, 112, 114, 133
Chile-California Program, 60, 65, 102
Chiloé Province, 4, 7, 126
Choapa River, 6
Chuquicamata, 5, 93, 94
CIDA. *See* Comité Interamericano de Desarrollo Agrícola
Colchagua Province, 6
Comisión Económica para América Latina (CEPAL), 1, 2, 32, 33, 46, 49, 52, 62, 63, 78n, 94, 97, 99n, 105, 111–19 *passim*, 125, 126, 127, 130, 154, 159n
Comité Interamericano de Desarrollo Agrícola (CIDA), 37, 39
Compañía de Acero del Pacífico (CAP), 113

Concepción, city, 7, 93, 106, 123
Concepción-Cautín region, 166, 187
Concepción Province, 7, 106
Copiapó River, 6
Copper: mining, smelting, and processing of, 5, 6, 7; Chile's share of world market, 93; output projections to *1985*, 94, 95; water requirements intake projections, 94–95; contamination of water by copper mines, 130
Coquimbo Province, 6, 94, 145, 170n, 173, 187
Corbo, Mario, 111n
CORFO. *See* Corporación de Fomento de la Producción
Corporación de Fomento de la Producción (CORFO), 34, 36, 48, 50, 51n, 54, 56, 58, 76, 79 87, 89, 94, 100, 109, 112, 174n, 266
Cost of water: defined, 9–11, 151; regional grouping of river basins for calculation purposes, 151, 153; costs of surface-flow regulation, 151, 154, 158–61; effect of evaporation losses on marginal costs, 157; method of constructing cost curves, 159–61. *See also* Reservoirs; Storage of water; Stream-flow regulation
Craig-Martin, Paul F., 31n
Croxatto, Carlos, 101n
Curicó-Linares region, 148, 167, 187
Curicó Province, 7, 150

Dams: projects undertaken, 65, 102–3; cost curves for rock-fill and earth-fill dams, 158
Data: need for systematic acquisition of, 2, 11, 17, 43, 47–48, 61, 202, 204, 206, 207–8
Denmark, 201, 243–48 *passim*
Departamento de Conservación de Recursos Agrícolas y Forestales, 45–46
Departamento de Economía Agraria, 74n
Departamento de Explotación of Dirección de Riego, 68
Departamento de Extensión Agrícola, 46
Desalination plants: consideration of, 9, 27, 203, 208
Desert areas, 5, 203
de Vries, Egbert, 31n
Dilution flows. *See* Wastes
Dirección de Estadística y Censos, 67, 106n, 108n, 111
Dirección de Obras Sanitarias del Ministerio de Obras Públicas, 125, 127

Dirección de Planeamiento del Ministerio de Obras Públicas, 1, 105, 126
Dirección de Riego (Irrigation Administration), 34, 52, 55, 56, 58, 66n, 78, 86, 105, 155, 159, 163n, 171
Domínguez, Javier, 49, 62n
Dorfman, Adolfo, 26n
Drainage systems in government projects, 56

Economic Commission for Latin America (UN). See Comisión Económica para América Latina
Economy of Chile: role of water resources in, 1, 7, 202, 206–7; policies for development of, 11, 24–25, 207; balance of payments and inflation difficulties, 24, 28, 29, 31, 72, 75n, 206, 208; metamorphosis from a rural to an urban economy, 28; effect of price controls, 197, 200; impediments to growth of, 204
Edwards Gana, Ricardo, 249n
Electric power: projected water-supply needs for, 19; plans for additions to production of, 96; price of electric power and capital costs, 99–100
—hydroelectric power: administration of installations, 14; projected main source of, 19; government plans for increased capacity, 97–98; competitive use of water for hydro installations and for irrigation, 98; interconnecting systems vs. separate plants for each region, 101; multi-purpose projects, 102–3; effect of hydro requirements on models of water use, 103–4
—thermal power: projected increase of water use in, 96–97
Ellsworth, Paul T., 31n
Elqui River, 6, 60, 156
El Salvador, 95
El Teniente, 93, 94, 130, 146
Empresa Nacional de Electricidad, S. A. (ENDESA), 14, 19, 27, 96–103 passim; 114, 201
Empresa Nacional de Petróleo (ENAP), 112, 118
ENAP. See Empresa Nacional de Petróleo
ENDESA. See Empresa Nacional de Electricidad
Estuarine waters: Chilean non-concern for quality of, 13, 17–18, 130
Evaporation-transpiration losses, 15, 21, 22–23, 78, 104, 122, 123, 127, 142, 148

Fabres, Estanislao, 112n, 114
FAO. See Food and Agriculture Organization
FAO-CEPAL study of pulp and paper, 110, 111–12, 120n
Farms; ownership of land and percentage of arable land in, 37, 39; land use by size of farm units, 37–39; output and farm income, 39–40; rates of water use, 63. See also Agriculture; Land Use
Finne, Grace W., 31n
Fisheries, 17, 130, 181, 208
Food and Agriculture Organization of the United Nations (FAO), 31n, 32, 74, 111, 243
Food and beverages industry, 106–11 passim, 114, 116; computations on waste discharge produced by, 132–33
Fox, Irving K., 102n
France, 201, 243–48 passim
Fruits, vegetables, and vineyards, 6, 36, 39, 40, 62, 200

García, Eduardo, 113n
Gerber, Klaus, 200n, 205n
Germany, 201
GNP. See Gross national product
Government irrigation projects: administration of by Dirección de Riego, 52; hectares under irrigation, 52, 57, 59; laws controlling construction and repayment, 52, 66–68; design areas vs. areas actually irrigated, 54, 56, 58, 59n; political and economic pressures in decision making, 58–59
—appraisals: studies by Chilean and foreign experts, 53–58; Riego's criticism of, 56–57
—criteria for selection of projects: "economic project" defined, 57n; uneconomic projects, 57, 65; priorities established by Riego, 58
—payments for water use: charges to irrigators, 66–70, 72; erosion of arrangements through inflation, 68, 72; costs and payments in sample projects, 70; distribution of shares by size of land holdings, 71, 72; subsidies paid to irrigators, 72
—plans for 1965–73, 60–61
—water costs: total investment for projects in 1962, 57; percentage of capital costs of public works, 61–62; estimates

for water-distributing structures and land preparation, 63–64; design costs vs. irrigated-area costs, 64–65
See also Irrigation
Gran Minería, 93, 94
Gross national product: projections based on, 18–21, 73–77, 109n, 137, 163n, 200
Ground water, 9, 27, 60, 61, 151–52, 208

Hagen, Everett, H., 207n
Hansen, Norman, 76n, 94, 105–6, 125n, 126, 130
Harboe, Ricardo, 60n, 151n, 152, 155, 158, 179n, 191n
Herfindahl, Orris C., 102n, 192n
Hohl, Paul H., 31n
Holsen, John, 73n, 74, 78n, 79
Horn F., Heinrich, 52n, 53n, 56–64 *passim*, 86–92 *passim*, 171
Huasco River, 6

IANSA. *See* Industria Azucarera Nacional
Ibáñez, Fernán, 60n, 151n, 152, 158, 179n
IBRD. *See* International Bank for Reconstruction and Development
IBRD-FAO mission report, 31–32, 43–44
Imperial River, 7
Incas: terracing of mountains for irrigation purposes, 60
Income: and demand for water use, 18; government policy for improved distribution of, 74n; projected increase in per capita income, 75, 76, 111, 112, 113; assumptions on rate of increase, 109; subsistence incomes for majority of Chileans, 197
Industria Azucarera Nacional, S.A. (IANSA), 116
Industrial uses of water. *See* Manufacturing industry
Instituto de Investigaciones de Recursos Naturales, 33, 34, 77n, 89, 242n, 250
Instituto Latinoamericano de Planificación Económica y Social, 1–2, 105n, 107n
International Bank for Reconstruction and Development (IBRD), 31–32, 43–44
Investment in water resources development: requirements approach to benefits of, 12–13; levels of compared with rates for capital goods, 26; relative merits of a given geographic sequence of, 197

Iquique, 5
Irrigation: "irrigated land" and "contingent irrigation" (*riego eventual*) defined, 35n; privately financed works on canals and ditches, 52–53, 58; irrigation capacity of rivers in the Central Zone, 249–68
—hectarage figures: for projections to *1985*, 23–24, 76–77; in projects designed for improvement, 32; for "irrigated" land and land of mixed character, 76; in Riego plans for expansion of irrigation, 78; figures adopted for water-use model, 78–79
—proposals on irrigation practices and farm management: IBRD-FAO mission report of *1952*, 43–45; recommendations in FAO study of *1958*, 45–46
—wastefulness in facilities, 43, 44, 49; limited knowledge of techniques, 55
—water use for: current rates and needs, 46–47; estimated waste, 48, 50; experienced and optimum rates for selected crops, 49, 50
—yield from irrigated land: value of output for selected crops, 51
See also Government irrigation projects; Land use
Irrigation Administration. *See* Dirección de Riego
Italy, 201, 243–48 *passim*
Itata River, 7, 130
Itata River Basin: irrigation capacity of rivers of, 263–66; area under irrigation, 166

Japan, 246, 247
Johnson, Leland L., 5n

Kendall, M. I., 40
Kennecott Copper Corporation, 93, 94
Kneese, Allen V., 56n
Kotok, E. I., 31n

Labor: supply of, 30
Laguna del Maule, 59, 63, 103
Laja River, 98
Lakes of Chile, 7
Land use: discrepancies in measurements of arable and irrigated land, 32–36; photogrammetric surveys of, 33, 34, 35, 56, 60, 76, 77n, 89, 92, 179n, 243; for cultivated and natural pasture, 33, 36,

37, 39, 43, 48, 51, 78–82 *passim*, 249; arable land distribution by type of crop, 35–36; irrigated land distribution by major use, 36; fallow fields, 36, 43; uncertain state of information regarding, 60; land capability classes, 77, 89. *See also* Agriculture; Farms; Irrigation
Larroucau V., Luis, 66*n*, 68*n*
La Serena, 6, 97
Latin America: investment in water resource projects, 1; transfer value of Chilean analysis to other countries of, 3; scarcity of data in, 100–101
Lauca River, 5
Ligua River, 6
Limarí River, 6
Linares Province, 7, 150
Llanquihue Province, 7, 21, 152, 179*n*
Lluta River, 5
Loa River, 6, 95
Lobo, Eugenio, 53*n*

McLeod, W. Norman, 31*n*
Magallanes Province, 4, 7, 8
Maipo-Mapocho Basin, 162
Maipo River, 6, 107, 163
Maipo River Basin: maximum irrigable area of, 255–56; area under irrigation, 266
Malleco Province, 7
Mantilla: value of agricultural land in, 197*n*
Manufacturing industry (*see also individual industries*): demand for products in relation to GNP, 19; products manufactured in Chile, 105, 113; pollution of rivers by, 107; production structure of the factory sector, 107*n*, 108
—industrial output: concentration of among industry classes, 106; distribution of national total among the provinces, 106-7; projections of output, 109–11
—water requirements: water intake of selected industries (*1957*), 117, 120; intake and loss rates as measures of, 119–23
—water use: major water-using and water-polluting industries, 105, 116; planned use for manufacturing as a whole, 113–14; recirculation efforts, 122,123; use of salt water, 124; waste dilution requirements, 137
—water-use coefficients: revision of *1957*

data undertaken, 114–15; adoption of U.S. industry coefficients and exceptions to use of, 116–21 *passim*; value-added method of computation, 116–19; reported-coefficients method, 117; U.S.-Chile differences in recirculation rates, 117, 118–19
Mapocho River, 6, 107, 130
Marfan J., Alvaro, 29*n*, 74*n*, 206*n*
Mataquito River, 7
Mataquito River Basin: irrigation capacity of rivers of, 258–59; area under irrigation, 266
Maule Province, 7, 34, 56
Maule River, 7, 60, 65, 102, 130
Maule River Basin: development plans for, 60; irrigation capacity of rivers of, 259–63; area under irrigation, 266
Meschi, Enzo, 115*n*
Mining: Chile's dependence on copper and nitrates for foreign exchange, 5; necessity of recirculation and streamflow regulation for water use in, 23; principal minerals produced, 93; projections of future output, 94; main export industry, 140. *See also* Copper; Nitrates
Ministerio de Obras Públicas projects, 34, 35, 55
Models of water resources: components of, 9–10; error factors in projections, 10–11; quantity and quality approaches to, 11–14; assumptions adopted for constructing models, 12–13; cost-constrained models, 166–80
—factors in water-requirements models: losses, 21–23; stream regulation, 23–24, 25, 26; expansion of irrigated hectarage, 24; economic policy and planning, 24; water quality, 25–26; investment required for conditions of *1985*, 26
—projections: for agriculture, 17, 18, 23; of population and GNP, 18–21; for non-agricultural needs, 23. *See also specific industries*
—studies needed for multi-purpose models: a systematic model of river basin development, 2; comprehensive models of the agricultural sector and of reservoir sites, 208
Morales, Hector, 247
Municipalities: classes of water use in, 14, 125; percentage distribution of domestic, industrial, and public services water

use, 125; estimate of per capita water use, 127; projected intake and losses, 127–29

—water supply: national responsibility for and rates charged, 125–26; deficiencies in, 126; plans for extending facilities, 127

National Association of Manufacturers (U.S.): water-in-industry studies of, 115

Nelson, Michael, 59, 60n, 78n, 79, 97n, 103n

Nitrates: annual Chilean output and projections to *1985*, 94, 95, 96; water requirements intake projections, 95, 96

Ñuble Province, 7, 187, 188, 190

Nuclear energy: Chilean study on water-supply augmentation by means of, 27

OAS/IDB/Chile Project. *See* Organization of American States–International Development Bank–Chile Project

ODEPLAN. *See* Oficina de Planificación Nacional

Oficina de Planificación Nacional (ODEPLAN), 109, 113

O'Higgins-Colchagua region, 148, 157, 162–63, 187, 188

O'Higgins Province, 5, 6, 93, 94, 246

Organization of American States–International Development Bank-Chile Project (OAS/IDB/Chile Project), 256, 258, 259, 263, 266

Osorno Province, 7, 179n

Paicaví River, 7

Parker, J., 76n

Pastures. *See* Land use

Petorca River, 6

Petroleum industry, 8, 111–19 *passim*; computations on waste discharge, 133

Pica: value of agricultural land in, 197n

Planning. *See* Regional planning; Water resource planning

Poblete, Juan Antonio, 60n, 151n, 152, 158, 179n

Pollution: lack of concern over, 13; information deficiency regarding, 25, 130; "population equivalents" measurement of, 133; urban origins of, 208. *See also* Sewage; Wastes

Population: center of, 6; rate-of-growth figure adopted for projection models,

18–21, 29, 200; estimates of total and urban population for *1985*, 19; demand for agricultural products in relation to, 74, 75

Potrerillos, 95

Pourtauborde, Jean, 32n, 33, 49, 53, 54, 57, 64n

Puerto Montt, 7, 97, 98, 181

Pulp and paper industry, 109, 111–12, 114–19 *passim*; contamination of water by pulp mills, 130; estimate of output measured in "population equivalents," 133

Punta Arenas, 8

Rapel River, 7, 14, 60, 65, 93, 100, 102, 103, 130, 162

Rapel River Basin: estimates of maximum irrigable areas of, 256–58; area under irrigation, 266

Recirculation (reuse) of water, 10, 13, 14–15, 23, 119n, 121, 122, 123, 139, 141, 172

Regional planning: consideration of an interregional agricultural production model, 26; factor of distribution of water costs among various regions, 165; need of studies of regional economic plans, 203

Reid, George, 131–33, 134

Reservoirs: economic life-span of, 62, 161; projects built, under construction, and under study, 64–65, 102-3, 159; evaporation losses in, 155, 157–58; projection of future storage capacity, 158–59

—planning for reservoirs of different capacity: marginal and capital costs comparisons in smallest-first vs. largest-first sequence, 10, 192, 194–99; question of timing of additions, 192, 195; agricultural productivity and transportation costs as factors in sequence of investment, 197

See also Cost of water; Storage of water

Riego. *See* Dirección de Riego

River basins: need for multi-purpose development of, 2; construction of models for, 2-3; points of water use within a basin, 139; regional grouping of basins in cost-of-water calculations, 151; projected transbasin diversion of activities, 162, 163, 200, 204; factor of timing in planning, design, and construction of projects, 192–93

Rivers: pattern of flow, 4; waste-assimilating capacity of, 10–11, 132; range of period of record for computed flows of, 60–61, 152; use of for electric power, 98; variety of natural regimens of, 101, 102, 193. *See also* Stream-flow regulation; Wastes
Ruiz-Tagle P., Miguel, 78

Sadie, Johannes L., 19
Saez, Raúl, 61n, 100–101
Salazar, Renato E., 101n
Salt water: possible use of, 15, 124, 133
Salvador River, 95
Santiago, city, 6, 106, 117, 125, 149, 180n, 208; lack of waste treatment plant in, 13, 130
Santiago Province, 6, 19n, 23–24, 94, 106, 126, 137, 145, 155, 156, 161, 162–80 *passim*, 182, 186, 187, 190, 192n, 195, 197, 199
Seminario Latinoamericano de Energía Eléctrica, 99, 100
Sewage: discharge into water supplies, 18; provisions for sewage systems, 120, 127; resistance of cities to re-use of sewage water, 145; as cause of water-borne diseases, 186. *See also* Pollution; Rivers; Wastes; Water quality
Sewell, copper producing center, 7
Shortage of water: question of diversion of water from water-short to water-surplus regions, 162–63; effects of projected interregional transfer of economic activities on costs of water, 172; estimates on savings from transfers, 178–80. *See also* Storage of water; Water constraints
Stamp, L. Dudley, 40, 41
Steel industry, 111–19 *passim*
Storage of water: influence of stream-flow regulation on, 163–64, 170, 177, 178; implications of yielding to agriculture all flow provided by, 173–75; requirements for higher degrees of security, 190–92; timing of increments to storage capacity, 192-94
—costs: assumptions in computations for projection models, 155–57, 190; surface-flow regulation costs, 158–61; distribution of costs among regions, 165
—requirements to assure stream flows: method of computing, 152–54; seasonal variation in demand, 153, 155–57

See *also* Cost of water; Reservoirs; Shortage of water
Straits of Magellan, 7, 8
Straus, Estevam, 3n
Stream-flow regulation: cost estimates up to projected *1985* demand, 9–10, 22–26, 158–61, 164, 202; disparity between required and available flows, 23, 162; insufficiency of data on virgin flows and return flows, 152; procedures in estimating constant average flow and seasonally regulated flow, 156–57; "maximum regulation" defined, 163n. *See also* Cost of water; Rivers; Storage of water; Water constraints
Sugar refining industry, 114–19 *passim*
Surface flow. *See* Stream-flow regulation

Talca, city, 7
Talca Province, 7
Tarapacá Province, 4, 5, 63, 84, 96, 145, 148, 150, 162, 166, 171, 173, 187, 190, 197, 203
Technological change: a factor in future water supply, 11, 27, 139, 204, 207
Terrain and climate of Chile, 3–6
Tierra del Fuego: source of petroleum and gas, 8, 93
Toltén River, 7, 98

United Nations, 1, 28, 108, 115. *See also* Comisión Económica para América Latina; Food and Agriculture Organization
United States: use of the U.S. data and coefficients taken from, 78, 96, 99, 105, 111–21 *passim*, 126, 131, 132, 133, 140n, 144n, 149, 181–82, 195, 243; Chile's per hectare productivity compared with U.S. rate, 246, 247
Universidad Católica, 19n, 95. *See also* Centro de Investigaciones Económicas
University of Chile, 60, 151n

Valdivia, city, 181
Valdivia-Llanquihue region, 179, 180, 187
Valdivia Province, 7, 157, 179n
Valparaíso, city, 106, 123
Valparaíso Province, 6, 94, 106
Valparaíso-Santiago region, 180
Villarroel B., René, 52n, 53n, 56–64 *passim*, 66n, 86–92 *passim*, 171
Viña del Mar, 6

Wastes: untreated waste discharged with water used for irrigation, 6; lack of treatment plants in large cities, 130
—approaches to treatment: projection model on costs, 10–11, 25–26, 202; governmental authority over industrial waste, 13; plans for constructing plants, 18
—dilution of effluent, 9–16 *passim*, 22, 25; adaptation of U.S. coefficients in computations, 131–34; required municipal and industrial flows, 136-37
See also Pollution; Rivers; Sewage; Water quality
Water constraints: water allocation among competing users, 165; land values for tax assessment purposes in relation to water costs, 166–67; effects of constraints on marginal cost of water, 166–80; potential changes in flow regulation through marginal cost limitations, 171; error factors in the marginal cost curve, 172n–173n; applications to agricultural output, 173–78; cost-constrained models and economic feasibility, 176–77. *See also* Shortage of water; Stream-flow regulation
Water quality: cost estimates on maintenance of, 10–11, 25–26, 181–86 *passim*, 202; Chile's past unconcern with, 13, 181; regional variations in meeting standards, 187–88; projected capital investment requirement for, 188. *See also* Pollution; Sewage Wastes
Water requirements in toto: defined for purposes of the present study, 138–39; regional aspects of, 139

—measures of flow requirements: "intake," "loss," and "discharge" defined, 139–40; projected total intake, 140; dominance of agricultural over non-agricultural intake, 142; method of computing losses, 142–145; examples of upstream losses plus downstream intakes, 146–48, 162, 163n; losses plus waste dilution as an alternative measure, 148–50, 162, 163n
—projections: geographic distribution of intake requirements, 140–41; incompatibilities between distribution of water resources and projected demands, 145
Water resource planning: policies and goals, 27–28, 29n, 31, 177, 204
Water resource regions, 4–6; "upstream" and "downstream" points of use within river basins, 9, 139, 146
Water supply: defined, 9; comparison with projected requirements, 21; regional differences in adequacy of, 22–23; security levels of, 48, 57, 151, 190-92, 208
Water use: projected uses, 10–13 *passim*; types of, 14; dependence on output of water-related goods and services, 18; assumptions on future efficiency in, 28; possible variations in the technology of, 139
Wheat and meat production, 36, 42, 51, 58, 74
World Health Organization, 127

Zaleski, Maciej, 80, 81n, 86n, 88n, 91